Thinking Through Food

THINKING THROUGH

Food

A Philosophical Introduction

ALEXANDRA PLAKIAS

broadview press

BROADVIEW PRESS – www.broadviewpress.com
Peterborough, Ontario, Canada

Founded in 1985, Broadview Press remains a wholly independent publishing house. Broadview's focus is on academic publishing; our titles are accessible to university and college students as well as scholars and general readers. With over 600 titles in print, Broadview has become a leading international publisher in the humanities, with world-wide distribution. Broadview is committed to environmentally responsible publishing and fair business practices.

The interior of this book is printed on 100% recycled paper.

Ancient
Forest
Friendly™

PERMANENT   100%

© 2019 Alexandra Plakias

Library and Archives Canada Cataloguing in Publication

Plakias, Alexandra, author
        Thinking through food : a philosophical introduction / Alexandra Plakias.

Includes bibliographical references and index.
Issued in print and electronic formats.
ISBN 978-1-55481-431-2 (softcover).—ISBN 978-1-77048-691-1 (PDF).—ISBN 978-1-4604-0647-2 (HTML)

        1. Food—Philosophy. 2. Food—Moral and ethical aspects. 3. Food—Social aspects. 4. Food consumption—Philosophy. 5. Food consumption—Moral and ethical aspects. 6. Food industry and trade—Moral and ethical aspects. 7. Diet—Moral and ethical aspects. 8. Diet—Social aspects. I. Title.

B105.F66P53 2018   641.3001   C2018-906454-4
                                                         C2018-906455-2

Broadview Press handles its own distribution in North America:
PO Box 1243, Peterborough, Ontario K9J 7H5, Canada
555 Riverwalk Parkway, Tonawanda, NY 14150, USA
Tel: (705) 743-8990; Fax: (705) 743-8353
email: customerservice@broadviewpress.com

Distribution is handled by Eurospan Group in the UK, Europe, Central Asia, Middle East, Africa, India, Southeast Asia, Central America, South America, and the Caribbean. Distribution is handled by Footprint Books in Australia and New Zealand.

Broadview Press acknowledges the financial support of the Government of Canada for our publishing activities.

Edited by Tania Therien
Book design by Michel Vrana

PRINTED IN CANADA

RECYCLED
Paper made from
recycled material
FSC   FSC® C103567
www.fsc.org

For my mother,
Carolyn Schultz

CONTENTS

CHAPTER FIVE: AGRICULTURE AND THE ENVIRONMENT

CHAPTER SIX: FOOD AND TECHNOLOGY

CHAPTER SEVEN: FOOD, HEALTH, AND FREEDOM

CHAPTER EIGHT: FOOD JUSTICE

CONCLUSION: THE FUTURE OF FOOD?

REFERENCES

INDEX

ACKNOWLEDGMENTS

This book grew out of the Food and Philosophy course I've taught at Hamilton College since 2014. I am grateful to my students; their enthusiasm and curiosity are the reasons this book exists.

Thanks also to participants at the 2017 and 2018 University of Vermont Food Ethics Conference for helpful discussion of many of the topics presented here, especially Chapter Four.

In the fall of 2017, my colleague, Julie Starr, and I organized a reading and speaker series on food justice, which was enormously helpful in thinking about the ideas presented in Chapter Eight of this book. Thanks to those who participated in that series, and to the Hamilton College Humanities Center for supporting it.

Food and family go hand in hand: thanks to my sister Anastasia, founder of Brooklyn Grange farm, for teaching me about the ins and outs of urban agriculture, and for always having an answer to the question, "What should I make for dinner?" And to my parents, for teaching me that reading and talking about food is (almost) as much fun as eating it.

The beginnings of this book coincided with the birth of my son, Theo. I am deeply thankful for his enthusiasm for sleep, which proved essential to the completion of this project. Finally, I am tremendously grateful to my husband Douglas Edwards, whose example inspires me, even as he makes writing a book look far too easy. For all the encouragement, patience, and support, thank you.

INTRODUCTION

The word "diet" comes to us from the ancient Greek term "diatia," meaning "way of life." It seems only fitting to begin this book by pointing out the link between what we eat and how we live, because one of the themes that will recur throughout concerns the way we use food to express our values and identities, both as individuals and communities.

This book is designed to introduce the reader to the philosophical study of food and to philosophy itself. This would be a natural place to give a definition of philosophy, but since there's almost as much disagreement about philosophy as there is about diet, that's not an easy task. Instead, I suggest we think of philosophy not as a subject matter, but as an activity and a way of approaching the world: inquiring into the things we think are most familiar, examining our most basic assumptions, and by doing so, discovering what we really believe and value. If this is our project, food is an ideal way to start: we've spent our whole lives familiarizing ourselves with food. We'll spend the next 182 pages looking at it in an unfamiliar light.

Without food, there would be no philosophy. Before the advent of cooking, digestion required a lot more energy; our brain size was limited because the number of calories we could extract from our food was limited.[1] Once we began cooking our food, our brains expanded. We acquired language. We spent less time eating and more time talking. We developed agriculture and culture. We put down roots and formed communities, and political systems, and views about political systems. Philosophy begins with food and with the human diet.

This book focuses mainly on philosophy in the analytic tradition. This is partly out of necessity: the history of philosophy is nearly as long as the history of food itself, so it would be impossible to do justice to (or even mention) the many issues, authors, and arguments that have taken place at the intersection of the two. Inevitably, there are important issues and questions that this book doesn't address. The areas that are discussed in what follows represent some of the most central questions in philosophy,

---

1   See Wrangham (2009).

but also some of the most pressing and controversial practical questions involving food production and consumption.

The chapters in this book are organized around central areas of philosophy as well as questions in the philosophy of food. While some of the chapters refer to issues and arguments discussed in others, they don't need to be read in order, so readers should feel free to approach the topics in whichever order they like. The first three chapters are organized around areas of philosophical inquiry: metaphysics is the study of the fundamental nature of reality; epistemology is the study of justification and knowledge; aesthetics is the study of beauty and art. Each chapter examines food through these topics: what *is* food, and how do we know about it? Is food beautiful, or just functional? Is it art?

The following three chapters look at the ethics of our food choices. Chapter Four asks whether it is morally permissible to eat animals; Chapter Five looks at the impact of our food choices on the environment; Chapter Six examines the role of technology in food production, with particular attention to the debate over genetically modified foods.

The final chapters of the book look at food and its relationship to issues of social justice, both local and global. Chapter Seven looks at food and health, and asks what role (if any) government should play in regulating the marketing and sale of food. Chapter Eight focuses on questions of food justice: how should we address inequalities in access to food, whether globally or in our own communities? Given that the production of food inevitably carries costs, how should we distribute these?

The book concludes with a discussion of various food movements and labels: veganism and vegetarianism, local and organic food movements, new and emerging technologies such as lab-grown meat, a return to traditional food sources such as insects. This might seem like an odd choice—why wait until the end of the book to talk about such fundamental categories? My hope is that by delaying discussion of these labels, the reader will be able to approach them with a better understanding of the complexity of the issues involved. The label "vegetarian" tells us something about a diet—that it doesn't include meat—but as we'll see, categories like that only take us part of the way to an appreciation of the ethical, social, and aesthetic values involved in our dietary choices. Because our goal here is to challenge the familiar, we'll wait to invoke these familiar categories until the end of the book, by which point I hope the reader will be able to see these diets in a new light.

Chapter One

THE
METAPHYSICS
OF
FOOD

INTRODUCTION

Philosophers have always been interested in the fundamental nature of things. The ancient Greek philosophers debated whether the world was made up of one thing, or many; whether the fundamental form of matter was fire, or water; whether the world was unchanging, or constantly changing. We experience a world apparently populated by many different things: trucks and tigers and trees and emotions and electrons. But are all of these things equally real? Do they all belong to the same category of being—physical objects—or are there differences in kind between thoughts and trucks? The attempt to answer questions like these belongs to the category of philosophy known as *metaphysics*. There are a number of interesting metaphysical questions we can ask about food, beginning with an apparently simple one: what *is* food? This chapter will start with that question, and we'll see why appearance is deceiving: defining food is no easy task. After looking at the problem of definition, we'll move on to a discussion of one of food's properties: flavors. What kinds of things are flavors? Are they real? Are they physical, or mental? And how do those two sets of questions relate to one another?

In answering these questions, we'll also examine a common belief about questions of taste: that they are essentially unresolvable, because they turn on subjective experiences. The distinction between subjective and objective properties, facts, and claims is an important one, and exploring it will take us through the first two chapters of this book. In this chapter, we'll look at the sorts of categories and concepts through which we understand and experience food, asking whether food's properties (such as flavors and tastes, but also the property of being food itself!) are objective—that is, out there in the world independently of us—or subjective. In the next chapter, we'll look at the implications of these questions for our knowledge of and debates about food.

1. WHAT IS FOOD?

When philosophers ask questions of the form, "What is X?" we're not asking how the term is defined in the dictionary, nor are we asking for a list of things that fall under the term. Rather, we're interested in whether there is some essence that all instances of that thing share—and if so, what that essence consists of. This section will investigate different approaches to defining "food," and look at what the failures of various attempts to define the term can tell us about food itself and the role it plays in our lives.

On the one hand, we seem to know food when we see it—or at least, when we eat it. Food is what sustains us throughout our lives; it's the physical substance we require to survive. This points to a promising avenue towards a definition of food: since food plays a particular role in our physical lives, it is tempting to define it in terms of its biological properties—namely, as something that gives us *nutrition*. Call this the "nutritional definition of food."

If we look up "food" in the dictionary, the nutritional definition is in fact what we find: "Any nutritious substance that people or animals eat or drink or that plants absorb in order to maintain life and growth,"[1] and "the general term for all matter that is taken into the body for nourishment."[2] However, philosophers are rarely satisfied with dictionary definitions, and this case illustrates why. Upon examination, the nutritional definition is ambiguous between two readings: on one, food's physical properties—containing nutrients—make it the kind of thing it is; on the other, it's the role that food plays—as something we consume for sustenance—that defines it. This disambiguation parallels two philosophical approaches to classification: the idea that categories like food pick out *natural kinds*, and the idea that they pick out *functional kinds*. We'll look at each of these interpretations in turn, and I will suggest that each falls short of capturing our complex relationship to food. To truly understand food and the kind of thing it is, we must approach it not as a physical or biological phenomenon, but as a social phenomenon.

---

1   "Food" (n.d.).
2   Neufeldt & Guralnik (1997, p. 525).

1.1 Food as a Natural Kind?

Some of the categories in our world seem clearly underwritten by an essential property. For example, a water molecule is composed of two hydrogen molecules and an oxygen molecule. A liquid that has any other molecular structure would not be water—even if it shared many of the same qualities as water (was clear, drinkable, flavorless ...).[3] In this case, the molecular structure H_2O is essential to water: it's what all instances of water share; what makes them members of the category, water. Water is therefore a *natural kind*: the category "water" corresponds to a distinction that is determined by the physical properties of the thing in question. Another example of a natural kind is gold. There are a number of substances that have the appearance of gold, or feel cold and hard to the touch. But not all of these will be *gold*: to be gold is to have the atomic number 79. Other substances can share many of gold's properties, but only gold has this particular property—anything having that atomic number will count as gold; nothing that lacks it will.[4]

Food might seem like a good candidate for a natural kind, since nutrition is a biological and chemical process. Food's ability to nourish us depends on its chemical properties; water, fats, carbohydrates, and protein are the main chemical building blocks of nutrition. With this in mind, we might define food as the collection of substances that are capable of providing nourishment. While there is no single chemical or molecular structure uniting all these substances (as in the case of water or gold), there could nonetheless be a *set* of properties, such that all members of the kind "food" possess some member of that set. Jade is like this: geologists have discovered that, in fact, jade is not one kind of mineral but two: jadeite and nephrite. Still, we talk about jade as a kind, albeit one consisting of two disjunctive underlying essences. To be jade is to be jadeite *or* nephrite. In the case of food, the disjunction might be longer: to be food is to be composed of carbohydrate *or* fat *or* protein ... and so on. But the longer the disjunction, the less appropriate the "natural kind" definition seems to be; it starts to seem that what unites these things is not a shared nature, but a shared role: the role of nourishing us.

1.2 Food as a Functional Kind?

With that in mind, we could define food as a functional kind—as that which performs the function of nourishing us. In this type of definition, food is picked out by its role in the set of physical processes that take place when we ingest and digest; whatever plays the functional role of nourishing substance is defined as food. This has some advantages over the previous approach, namely, that it does not require us

---

3   Putnam (1975).
4   See Kripke (1972), Lecture III, for an in-depth discussion of this example.

to discover or specify all the possible substances that could nourish us, and it allows for new and novel substances to count as food as long as they perform the relevant function. Functional kinds can be natural or man-made (or both): livers, chairs, swimming holes. The objects that make up a functional kind can be quite diverse, and they often resist description in terms of a shared set of features. Chairs are easy enough to identify in practice, but when we try to identify what all chairs have in common, things get tricky, fast: must a chair have legs? If so, how many? Is a beanbag a chair? Do chairs need to have backs, or is a backless chair simply a stool? What does a dentist's chair and an armchair have in common? Ultimately, it seems that what all chairs share is the characteristic of *being something to sit in*. Similarly, we saw above that it's difficult to specify a feature that all foods share, besides the feature of being something to eat. This is not a problem for functional definitions, because they don't require a common or underlying feature (unlike natural kind definitions). But we still need criteria for when some object actually serves the function in question—how successfully must it do so? Is potentially fulfilling it enough, or must it actually do so? As we'll see below, not everything that could serve the function of nourishing us counts as food, and not all of our food functions to nourish us.

1.3 Food as Nutrition: Why Not Eat Pets?

The problem with both of the approaches discussed above is that equating food with nutrition is too simple: we eat—and avoid eating—too many things, for too many reasons, for these definitions to adequately capture the complexity of food. First, we are confronted with the choice of whether to define food as what we actually use for nutritional purposes, or as substances that possibly provide us with nutrition. If we opt for the first definition, we run into trouble because much of what we eat is not consumed for purposes of nutrition. We eat for entertainment, for emotion, and for rituals, both religious and secular—from Passover Seders to popcorn with movies. In these cases, food is consumed for reasons that are explicitly *not* physical nourishment, but have to do with the non-physical, non-biological properties of the foods in question. We could amend our definition by replying that it's not the intended function that matters but the actual function, so that regardless of why we consume food, its defining characteristic is that it does in fact give us nourishment. But this is also too simple, since we sometimes consume food precisely because it lacks nutritional value, as when we eat sugar-free desserts, or drink diet soda (I'm not claiming that diet soda must count as food, just pointing out that on this definition, it won't). For all these reasons, defining food in terms of what we actually consume for purposes of nutrition fails to adequately capture the variety of foods in our lives.

On the other hand, if we choose the latter option above and say that food is anything with the *potential* to nourish us, we include too much. This is related to concerns about defining food in terms of its physical properties, the way we do gold and other natural kinds. There's more to food than the chemical composition of a substance. Human flesh might share many of the nutritional properties of beef, but that doesn't explain why one is food and the other is not. Many animals contain useful calories and nutrients, but we don't typically look at our families or pets and think, "food!"

1.4 Socially Constructed Kinds

These complications arise because food's role goes beyond nourishing us. There are things that are nutritious that we don't eat, and things that we eat that aren't nutritious. Instead, food as a category seems to depend on our attitudes and practices in a way that gold, or water, does not. We can capture this dependency by saying that food is a *socially constructed* kind: rather than a category we discover in nature, it's a category we build and sustain through our beliefs and behaviors. When we talk about food, we're not just describing the biological properties of the thing in question. To label something "food" is to assign it a place in our social practices: food is treated a certain way, ingested at certain times and in certain contexts, and has a certain meaning.

We don't eat certain things *because* they're food; rather, they're food because we eat them. This is evident in legal and regulatory definitions of food. For example, the EU defines food as, "any substance or product, whether processed, partially processed or unprocessed, intended to be, or reasonably expected to be ingested by humans,"[5] and according to the US Food and Drug Administration, "The term 'food' means (1) articles used for food or drink for man or other animals, (2) chewing gum, and (3) articles used for components of any such article."[6]

The difference between natural kinds and socially constructed kinds is a difference between categories in the world that are independent of our practices and beliefs, and categories that depend on us and our beliefs about, and responses to, the world around us. We can understand a socially constructed kind as one where our beliefs about it are necessary for its existence: if some kind k is a socially constructed kind, then beliefs about k are necessary for any ks to exist. The philosopher John Searle gives the example of a cocktail party: part of what it is for me to have a cocktail party is for me to believe that I am having a cocktail party, and for my guests to believe that they are attending a cocktail party.[7] Searle also gives the example of a war: for

---

5   See European Parliament, Council of the European Union (2002, January 28), Chapter 1, Article 2.

6   See Federal Food, Drug, and Cosmetic Act (2018).

7   See Searle (1995, pp. 33–34).

two countries to be at war, they must believe they are at war, and others must also believe this.

To be considered food, part of what is required is that something be treated as such—that we believe it to be food. This explains, in part, why certain animals are food in some cultures and not in others, and why one's parents and one's children are not food in any culture.[8] Food is not just something consumed, but something consumed in specific contexts and for specific reasons. In contemporary Western culture, for example, we distinguish between food and medicine, even when the physical object is ambiguous (for example, a lollipop containing ibuprofen for children, or "gummi vitamins" for adults). Food is also something we treat in certain ways: as a commodity, but also as a social good and as part of a process. We eat food together, at a table, at specific times of day.

1.5 Social Construction and Normativity

One might object that the social construction definition is too narrow and value laden. Food is not always consumed as intentionally and attentively as the foregoing account suggests. We don't always (or even usually) eat food at a table: our meals are consumed in cars, offices, and standing in the kitchen. We do sometimes consume food just for nutrition, with no deeper meaning attached (consider, for example, Soylent, a liquid meal replacement designed by Silicon Valley engineers to allow them to work uninterrupted through mealtimes).

Another worry is that by defining food in terms of beliefs, attitudes, and social practices, the social construction account makes food a distinctively human creation. But don't animals eat food, too, despite lacking the cognitive capacities needed to engage in social construction? Questions about the extent to which animals have beliefs and attitudes are tricky, and it's hard to generalize over a category as broad as "animals." Many animals do seem to take pleasure in their food; Japanese macaques have been observed "washing" sweet potatoes in water (to remove dirt) for decades, but researchers recently noted that some animals choose salt over fresh water, and have surmised that they do so because they prefer the taste. Even if animals lack *our* concept of food, they might still eat food in another sense. Perhaps a social constructivist account is best for the human concept of food, but a functionalist account is more apt at characterizing animals' relationship to food. A useful analogy is the concept of family. Animals have fathers, mothers, sons, and daughters. In animal populations, these relations are genetic and biological. Humans have families too.

---

8   Diamond (1978) reminds us that even in cultures where people do eat their dead, they do it with a kind of ceremony or reverence, making it clear that this is not an act of eating like any other. So even if we do sometimes eat family members, we do not thereby render them *food*.

But in our case, a genetic relationship is not necessary. Instead, there is a constellation of relationships, emotions, obligations, and attitudes that make someone family. Families can be made and unmade. So, while both humans and animals have families, the term "family" picks out very different relationships—and carries very different requirements—in each case. Similarly, food might be a functional concept in the case of animals but a different kind of concept for humans. Since humans are social and cultural in a way that most other animals are not, it wouldn't be surprising if our concepts differed, too.

A related worry is that the idea of food as a socially constructed kind contains implicit normative assumptions about how we *ought* to view food. That is, one might argue that the term "food" refers to a natural kind, but that analyzing it as socially constructed turns it into a normative kind—a classification that incorporates ideas not just about what and how people *do* eat, but how they ought to. This is problematic if we want our definition of food to accommodate the worker who eats a protein bar in the car as well as the family gathered around the table eating Thanksgiving dinner. This is not necessarily an objection to a social construction account, but it is a useful caution: in conducting investigations into the metaphysics of food, we must be careful not to rely on an overly narrow set of assumptions about how one ought to eat. There will certainly be much normative work to do in the chapters that lie ahead, as we investigate the ethics, aesthetics, and politics of our food choices. And it may be that we cannot help but incorporate some normative assumptions into our analyses. But we should be as ecumenical as possible as we investigate what food is—our definition of food should be able to accommodate a plurality of values, lifestyles, and practices. An overly narrow definition, or one that is too dependent on a certain view about what food ought to be, will prevent us from recognizing possibilities for change in what and how we eat.

1.6 Social Construction and Subjectivity

It is tempting to think of socially constructed kinds as less "real" than natural kinds, and, in some sense, this is correct: if no humans had existed, there would still be such a thing as water, and it would still consist of two parts hydrogen and one part oxygen. There would not be such a thing as money. The existence of money depends on beliefs about money, and yet there are many facts about money that do not depend on my beliefs: the amount of money in my bank account is a perfectly real figure, and (unfortunately) it remains unaffected by my beliefs about it.

Another way of putting this point is that food, like other products of social construction, is *subjective*. We call something subjective (the term can be applied to various linguistic and mental entities: facts, claims, truths, beliefs, attitudes, experiences ...) if it depends on, or is constituted by, our mental states—either the mental state of some particular individual, or the mental states of humans taken as a whole. (The fact that I have a headache is subjective in the first sense; the existence of amusement is subjective in the latter sense—it doesn't depend on any particular individual's being amused, but if no human were or ever had experienced amusement, amusement would not exist.) This contrasts with objective facts, which don't depend in any way on our mental states, experiences, or attitudes. It is an objective fact that the earth orbits the sun, since its doing so in no way depends on or is affected by our beliefs about it. The distinction between subjective and objective also applies to objects and their properties, some of which depend on our mental states in a way that others do not.

As we'll see in a moment, an object can have both subjective and objective properties. One of the themes that will emerge from the remainder of this chapter, and the two following chapters, is that food and our judgments about it have both objective and subjective features. In some ways this is unsurprising, since even if the category *food* is socially constructed, the substances included in that category are physical and, in that sense, perfectly objective. The existence of the category of food (and the category of table) might depend on our beliefs, but the fact that an apple sits on the table before me does not. However, when we inquire into the properties of food, and especially tastes and smells, the appearance of objectivity begins to fade: the particular properties of that apple—its redness, its scent, its flavor—are subjective insofar as they depend on our perceptions of them. As a result, these properties of foods are sometimes viewed differently from other, more straightforwardly objective, properties. In the next section, we'll look at a specific type of property: flavor. We'll start by looking at the physiology that underlies our flavor perception, which will help us understand how flavor emerges as a result of our interaction with food. We'll then examine arguments for the subjectivity of flavors, while also looking at some considerations that suggest that there's significant overlap in the way we experience them. Flavor is a particularly interesting case, as we'll see, because it is both constrained by our physiology and widely variable. Eating is a social act, but the experience of flavors is ultimately private and inner, so our ability to communicate and share what we experience is necessarily limited. This in turn will have consequences for our discussion of the epistemology and aesthetics of food in the chapters to come.

2. WHAT IS FLAVOR?

Before we talk about what flavor is, it will be useful to distinguish it from a related term: taste. The two are sometimes used interchangeably, but "taste" is also used to refer to one of the five basic senses (along with sight, sound, touch, and smell)—the one whose corresponding sensory organ is the tongue. Our tongues detect bitter, sweet, sour, and salt. More recently, scientists have included a fifth taste: umami—a kind of savory sensation. Some have even argued for adding fattiness (or "oleogustus," to use their proposed term) to this list.[9] All of these sensations are referred to as tastes, leaving us with a single label for the sense, the act of perception, and the elements perceived.

2.1 Flavor and Taste: Some Background

In addition to using taste to name one of our senses, and to name the "primary" elements of sweet, salty, bitter, and sour, we often talk of the taste of a food in a more specific and comparative sense: a meat tastes like chicken, a drink tastes like bananas. This way of using the term taste is closer to what we will call "flavor." Flavor is more than just taste: it also includes smells and sensations.[10] For example, we might describe a food's flavor as spicy, but spice is actually a kind of tactile sensation rather than a taste—a stimulation of the pain receptors on our tongue (and our skin, and lips, and eyes, as anyone who's cut a hot chili and then accidentally rubbed her face knows) that also detect heat (hence "hot" as a synonym for "spicy"). And many of the discriminations we make between instances of a taste (for example, sweetness) are due to information we take in through our noses rather than our tongues. This can be illustrated by cutting a small piece of an apple and a (raw) potato, and biting into each while holding one's nose; without smell, the experience is strikingly similar. Taste and smell are so closely intertwined that we sometimes confuse them, as when we describe a smell as sour. It's not surprising, then, that the two influence each other: when a caramel smell is added to a sweet solution, for example, people rate it as sweeter than when given the solution by itself.[11] Taste and smell are sometimes described as "chemical senses." One introduction to taste explains: "the sense of taste, also known as gustation, operates by detecting molecules dissolved in liquids and the sense of smell, also known as olfaction, operates by detecting molecules in the air."[12]

The language of "detection" may incline us to think that flavors are physical entities out there in the world—that they are objective, existing independently of us, and we discover, rather than create, them. This inclination is further bolstered by the fact that we can identify the contribution of specific molecules to make a flavor. Such identification is extremely lucrative, and the science of flavor is big—and secretive—business. One of the first commercial flavor factories began in nineteenth-century Germany, where the chemist Wilhelm Hermann discovered that a powder scraped from the inside of pinecones, when combined with acid, formed vanillin,

---

9   Running, Craig, & Mattes (2015).

10 Some scientists argue for the classification of flavor perception as its own sensory system, partly because of the interactions between taste and odor described here.

11 See Auvary & Spence (2008).

12 Logue (2015, pp. 45–46).

an extremely concentrated white powder that had, up until that point, only been obtained by reducing vanilla extracted from the seed pods of orchids. Since vanilla itself was extremely expensive, and vanillin even more so, Hermann's discovery made the powdered form affordable, and the flavor of vanilla became much more commonplace.[13] Nowadays, flavor is a multi-billion dollar business, and factories no longer rely on fortuitous discoveries involving pinecones from the forest; tools such as mass spectrometers and gas chromatography can analyze the chemical constituents of food and identify the flavor compounds, which can then in turn be re-created in the laboratory, essentially "reverse-engineering" the flavor of the food.

The relationship between the chemicals in food and the taste receptors on our tongue send signals to the brain that are then translated into our experience of flavor, but this isn't the only process that determines what we experience. In addition to the presence of molecules in our mouth, the experience of flavor can be affected by verbal descriptions and visual cues: "wild blueberry" rather than simply "blueberry," for example. And we shouldn't overlook the nose, which contains over 300 types of cells that detect odor.[14] Again, when chemicals come into contact with these cells, a signal is sent to the brain, resulting in our experience of odor. And again, how we interpret the experience of smell depends on other contextual cues: the same scent might indicate a deliciously ripe cheese or a dirty diaper.

Contrary to a common misconception, taste cells aren't located just on "buds" along the tongue. The papillae that dot the surface of our tongues (you can see yours by dotting some blue food coloring onto your tongue, if you're curious) do contain taste "pores" (which in turn contain several buds, which in turn contain taste cells) along their sides, and in the trenches between them, but taste cells are also found beneath the surface of the tongue. Nor do different taste buds exclusively perceive different tastes—the old map of the tongue, labeled with regions for sweet, salty, bitter, and sour, is based on a misunderstanding; in fact, all regions of the tongue can detect all tastes, despite some small differences in sensitivity. The taste cells themselves are connected to the chorda tympani nerve, which sends signals to our brain that are in turn translated into the tastes we experience. Different receptors on the tongue relay different tastes to the brain; one way we know this is because we can block certain receptors and thereby "mute" tastes. Gymnemic acid, applied to the tongue, blocks the ability to taste sweetness.[15] One reason why salt makes foods taste sweeter may be that the ions in salt interfere with the receptors that detect bitterness on our tongue. Sensitivity to bitterness actually varies widely between individuals: about 30 per cent of the population is made up of "supertasters." These individuals are more sensitive than others to bitter tastes; they tend to find foods like broccoli, beer, and

---

13   See Schatzker (2016).
14   Logue (2015, p. 53).
15   Logue (2015).

coffee unpleasant. If you know a very picky eater, odds are they're a supertaster (you can order special paper to test this out; if you experience the paper as bitter, chances are, you're a supertaster). About another third of the population are nontasters: they barely detect bitterness at all (ironically, supertasters tend not to be supereaters, while nontasters tend to be quite adventurous!). The rest of us are somewhere in between.

The effect that different substances have on taste receptors is an empirical question. We can describe the interaction between molecules in foods, the receptors on an individual's tongue and in their nasal passages, and the experience they report. But which of these aspects can be identified as *flavor* is a philosophical question. Is the flavor the molecules in a food? Or is it the experience that we have when consuming the food—the sensations a food produces in us? Is the flavor in the banana, or in the eater at the moment of eating? Or is it somewhere in between? Here we find ourselves back at the question with which we began: is flavor objective or subjective?

2.2 *What Is Flavor? The Case of Chloe*

The question of what flavors are is complicated, because while we can explain flavor in terms of physical properties such as the molecular properties of foods and the sensory receptors on our tongue and in our olfactory passages, flavor isn't identical with either of these two things (or with the combination of the two). Indeed, there are reasons to doubt that flavor is identical to any physical property or properties whatsoever. The philosopher Frank Jackson's famous "Mary argument" can help us see why.[16] This fictional Mary, as described by Jackson, is

> a brilliant scientist who is, for whatever reason, forced to investigate the world from a black and white room via a black and white television monitor. She specializes in the neurophysiology of vision and acquires, let us suppose, all the physical information there is to obtain about what goes on when we see ripe tomatoes, or the sky, and use terms like "red," "blue," and so on. She discovers, for example, just which wavelength combinations from the sky stimulate the retina, and exactly how this produces via the central nervous system the contraction of the vocal chords and expulsion of air from the lungs that results in the uttering of the sentence "The sky is blue" ... What will happen when Mary is released from her black and white room or is given a color television monitor? Will she learn anything or not? It seems just obvious that she will learn something about the world and our visual experience of it. But then is it inescapable that her previous knowledge was incomplete? But she had all the physical information. Ergo there is more to have than that.

---

16   Jackson (1982, p. 130).

The argument shows that color facts are not exhausted by the physical information about color; red is not simply a physical property. We can construct a similar example involving taste: imagine Chloe, a scientist who knows all the physical facts about chocolate, but has lived from birth on a tasteless nutritional formula, and has never tasted chocolate or any other flavorful food. Chloe knows all about the flavor compounds in chocolate—she knows what other foods they're in, too—and all about its composition and the process by which it's made. What will happen on the happy day that Chloe finally tastes chocolate?[17] It seems obvious, as Jackson says, that she will learn something new (we will say much more about the role of experience in acquiring knowledge about food, and what this signifies for the objectivity/subjectivity debate, in the next chapter). This shows that flavor is not a physical property: it's not captured by a set of physical facts or descriptions. If it were, Chloe would already *know* everything there is to know about chocolate's flavor; the fact that she learns something upon tasting chocolate means that there is some fact about flavor that is not a physical fact.

2.3 Flavor as a Secondary Quality

If flavor is not purely physical, what kind of property is it and how does it emerge from our interactions with food? The seventeenth-century philosopher Locke distinguished what he called "primary" and "secondary" qualities. For Locke, primary qualities are those that reside in the thing itself: properties like size, shape, solidity, hardness, etc. These qualities are in objects independently of us. Secondary qualities, on the other hand, "are nothing in the objects themselves, but powers to produce various sensations in us."[18] Secondary qualities aren't in the object alone; they emerge out of our interaction with the object. But secondary qualities aren't just in our heads, either: they are powers *in the object* that produce certain responses. Insofar as secondary qualities depend on our experience of an object, they are a kind of subjective property: it's not true that an object is red, or bitter, in itself; rather, its redness and bitterness consists in the response that object produces in us. We can't understand or define these properties without making reference to our own experiences. This is partly because unlike primary qualities such as shape, secondary qualities don't "resemble their causes"—there's nothing in the physical object that resembles the yellowness, or the sourness, of a lemon. To understand sour, or yellow, one must experience them firsthand—a diagram of the molecular structure of citric acid, on its own, won't convey the idea of sourness to us.

---

17 For a similar example, used to different effect, see Meskin & Robson (2015).
18 Locke (1689/1975), Book II, Chapter VIII.

In contemporary terms, Locke's view can be understood as the claim that flavor is a *response-dependent* property: to say that something has a certain flavor is to say that it produces certain responses in subjects under certain conditions. The view is often applied to color: to be red is, on a response-dependence view, to produce certain sensations in viewers under certain lighting and distance conditions. It can also serve as an analysis of properties like funniness: to be funny is to produce mirth in people under the right conditions. In general, analyses of response-dependent properties take the form: *X is P if and only if S would have response R to X under conditions C*, where X is some object (such as a potato chip), P is a property (such as bitterness or saltiness), S is some subject (you, or you and your classmates, or American college students, or human adults ...), R is some response (such as tasting salt, or puckering one's mouth), and C are the relevant conditions (such as not having just eaten a handful of salt, or brushed one's teeth).[19] One challenge for response-dependence theories of properties is to specify which conditions, and which subjects, should count: in the humor case, for example, we might want to specify that we only count responses of those who speak the language in which the joke is told. We might also want to exclude the responses of people who are in suboptimal conditions to be amused (because, say, their dog just died, or they are extremely angry about something). In the case of taste, we might want to exclude responses of those who have recently burned their tongue or brushed their teeth. However, we also know that there are individual differences that make some people more sensitive to bitterness than others. A genetic difference leads some people to experience the taste of cilantro as unpleasantly "soapy," while others enjoy its flavor. Which of the two types of response to cilantro is the one that determines or constitutes its flavor? Which is the correct assessment of broccoli's bitterness? Here there may be no single correct response, but rather a range of acceptable responses, constrained by the physiological features (such as the presence or absence of sense receptors) that enable and determine one's experiences. We will return to this issue in the next two chapters, when we discuss our knowledge about food and flavor, and who counts as an expert on such questions.

CONCLUSION: TASTE, FLAVOR, AND OBJECTIVITY

We often treat taste as a paradigm of subjectivity: some questions are just "a matter of taste," and "there's no disputing taste." "To each according to his taste," we're told; the word "taste" is frequently preceded by the words "my," or "personal." That taste is

---

19   See Johnston (1992) for a discussion of response-dependence; though his analysis is concerned with color properties, much of the discussion applies to flavors and tastes as well.

personal is evidenced by the fact that it varies between individuals. As we saw above, what's bitter in my mouth is mild in another's. Furthermore, there's a certain quality to all our sense experience that is essentially private: a "what it is like" of which we can only have inner experience. I can look at the same painting you are looking at, but I cannot see it through your eyes. In the case of food, the very things we are describing or experiencing—flavors—only emerge as we ingest and consume the food, taking it into ourselves and away from others' experience. In a very literal sense, no two people can taste the same food.

But we shouldn't confuse the subjective aspect of taste with idiosyncrasy or a kind of "anything goes" relativism about taste. Pain is subjective, in that its instantiation depends on someone *being in pain*. But there are lots of similarities in what causes pain in humans, and knowing that you are in pain gives me a good idea of what you feel like. The same is true for taste. After all, while taste is personal, flavor is big business, and companies invest lots of money developing foods that will appeal to millions of people. If no two people experienced food the same way, predicting whether people will like a certain soda or wine or candy would be impossible. But companies do this quite successfully, relying on focus groups of tasters (and, of course, marketing—a topic discussed in Chapter Seven).

If we agree with Locke that flavors are secondary qualities—that the property of flavor exists, not in food alone, but in some response that food evokes in us—are we therefore admitting that flavor is less real? What practical consequence does adopting a response-dependence account of flavor have for our practices surrounding food? The next chapter will look at the implications of subjectivity, and specifically at whether subjectivity affects our ability to acquire knowledge of food and transmit that knowledge to others.

Chapter Two

THE EPISTEMOLOGY OF FOOD

INTRODUCTION

Eating is inherently risky: it involves bringing the outside world into our body, with all its potential contamination and pollution. Managing this risk involves a combination of knowledge and trust: knowledge of what foods are safe, available, and good to eat; and trust in the people who produce and prepare our food, the stores where we buy it, and the producers and processes that manufacture it. This is complicated by the fact that the environment in which we choose and consume food is increasingly far removed from its origins: while some people buy produce and meat at markets where they can talk directly to farmers and producers, most of us buy a significant portion of our food at supermarkets, on the Internet, or from restaurants. This means that we're increasingly reliant on menus, labels, and ingredient lists for information about what we're eating. How do we know what we're eating? How do we know it's safe? How do we know what's healthy and what's tasty? The answers to these questions bring us to the area of philosophy known as *epistemology*: the study of belief, justification, and knowledge.

1. EPISTEMOLOGY AND FOOD

If asked, most of us would say we know what we had for dinner last night. But do we really? If so, how? In this chapter, we'll look at the epistemology of food: what do we know about the things we eat, and how do we know it? Food raises a number of interesting epistemological challenges and puzzles. Indeed, while this chapter investigates the ways that traditional epistemic concepts like knowledge and justification apply to and help us interact with food, we'll also look at the ways that these accounts are complicated by facts about our role as consumers. Contemporary epistemology recognizes that we do not encounter the world abstracted from our social and material conditions. Rather, the kinds of knowledge and justification available to us, and the ways in which our own experiences are accorded epistemic credibility, are influenced by our social situations: the time, place, and circumstances we inhabit as knowers and inquirers. We will begin our investigations by looking at traditional stances on the relationship between knowledge and the senses (since much of our knowledge of food comes to us via sensation), before turning to questions about justification and belief, and finally to the more complicated issues of how we navigate the problem of acquiring knowledge about food in our particular social and economic environments.

Some of our knowledge of food is acquired through our senses; in this way food is like other objects of sensation. But unlike looking at a tree, or hearing traffic, tasting food involves destroying it, so that our experience of food is private and unique: the food I've consumed is necessarily unavailable for anyone else to experience. We also rely heavily on other sources for knowledge of food, an issue we'll take up in Section 2 of this chapter. Again, this is not unique to food; we rely on the testimony of others for all kinds of information—from the mundane (is it raining?) to the momentous (what's the right dose of medication?). But in the case of food, the sources upon which we rely are often very far removed from our experience: they are faceless and even nameless, making their credibility difficult to assess. Few of us understand how or even where our food is grown and manufactured, or the standards and regulations that govern those practices. With that in mind, are we really in a position to accept the labels and packaging on our food as evidence of its contents? If we do view such information as a kind of testimony, is it testimony we can and should accept? If not, are we forced to remain skeptical about the nature of what we're eating? What role does trust play in our food choices—can we, or must we, trust food manufacturers? If so, we seem to leave ourselves vulnerable to deception, but as we'll see, exactly how to characterize the problem with misleading food packaging and marketing raises questions about the difference between lying and other forms of deception such as bullshit (see Section 5 of this chapter). The issues of trust, risk, and deception are discussed in Section 4. The epistemology of food goes beyond our role as consumers, though; we also prepare our food, and this raises questions about how to characterize the kind of knowledge involved in cooking and even eating: is it theoretical knowledge, or a kind of skill, or both? In answering these questions in Section 7, we'll look at accounts of knowledge as a kind of activity, introducing an approach to epistemology known as *virtue epistemology*. The idea of virtue epistemology is that we can model successful intellectual inquiry on moral virtue, appraising beliefs not in isolation, but in terms of the skills and traits from which they issue. By asking about which traits and skills an epistemic agent should possess, we can move away from appraising beliefs in isolation, and look at how they function in social and practical situations. This is one reason that virtue epistemology is well-suited to food, so we'll apply it to problems about how to assess the trustworthiness of information as we go about choosing what to eat.

2. EMPIRICIST VS. RATIONALIST APPROACHES TO KNOWLEDGE

Historically, philosophers have debated whether our primary route to knowledge is through the senses or through reason. Empiricists argue that we acquire knowledge via the senses. Rationalists argue that we gain knowledge of topics such as logic, mathematics, and morality through reflection on concepts alone, unaided by the senses. Explained this way, the distinction is primarily methodological: it's a debate over how we get knowledge. But the two camps also assign very different values to the operations of reasoning and sensation.

Rationalists argue that knowledge gained through reflection and reasoning is superior to, and more stable than, knowledge gained through experience. This is partly because our senses sometimes deceive us, and partly because the world as experienced through sensation is constantly changing, while the world we come to know through reason is unchanging and eternal. Numbers, concepts, truths about logic—these are the things we know through reason alone, and philosophers have treated these truths as the most valuable kind. This assumption goes at least as far back as Plato, who writes that the ideal thinker "employs pure, absolute reason in his attempt to search out the pure, absolute essence of things, and ... removes himself, so far as possible, from eyes and ears, and, in a word, from his whole body, because he feels that its companionship disturbs the soul and hinders it from attaining truth and wisdom."[1] On the rationalist account of knowledge, if we want to know what justice, or beauty, or knowledge is, we don't go out into the world and investigate; instead, we reflect on the concepts themselves, drawing out their applications to possible cases and the relationships between these concepts and associated ones like virtue, or piety, or justification. The senses can only give us acquaintance with particular instances of these concepts, but reflection is not limited by the examples we happen to have access to, so rational reflection is the route to attain certain, timeless knowledge.

---

1   Plato (1997b, 65d–66a). When citing Plato, I'll use "Stephanus numbers" rather than page numbers. These are the numbers found in the margins of the text, and are common to all editions—the name refers to a sixteenth-century translation by Henri Estienne (or Henri "Stephanus," in Latin). Because this numbering system is shared by all editions and translations, it enables the reader to quickly locate a passage in any translation or edition.

Empiricist philosophers argue that knowledge must come from our senses, and that experience is the best and often only available source of knowledge. Locke famously claimed that we enter the world as a "tabula rasa"—a blank slate onto which knowledge must be inscribed via experience. So, contrary to the rationalist's claim that we have access to certain kinds of knowledge via reflection on (innate) concepts, the empiricists argue that we must acquire knowledge from experience. But we can understand empiricist theories of human knowledge as compatible with the claim that we are born with the cognitive (and physiological) architecture necessary to acquire certain concepts and experiences. Food is a good example in making the case for empiricism, since here our reliance on the senses is evident; reflection on the concept of an apple won't tell us whether the apple is good to eat or nourishing. It's only by empirically testing our hypothesis that we confirm: the apple is in fact good to eat. This is arguably the reason we *have* the sense of taste: in fruits and plants, sweetness is a reliable indicator of the presence of calories, and bitterness correlates with the presence of toxins. So, the sense of taste evolves to provide a source of information about the foods we eat—by experiencing tastes, we come to know about the nutritive properties of the associated foods.

This explains the fact that humans are born with an instinctive liking for sweetness and aversion to bitterness. But we're not born knowing anything about particular foods, and because of the diversity of human cuisines, we end up with knowledge of a wide variety of tastes and flavors. There is lots of overlap between the elements of cuisines, though, precisely *because* we enter the world with a physiology that constrains the flavors we can experience (and the foods we can ingest and digest). This shared physiology and psychology explains how we can have both subjective variation in judgments of taste as well as shared standards of evaluation: absent extenuating conditions, all humans experience sugar as sweet, but individual differences in preference, history, and circumstance will lead to different liking for sweetness, with some individuals preferring sweeter and others preferring less sweet foods. The fact that our exposure to foods (both past and present) can affect our judgments also means that our food environment plays a role in determining both our experiences and liking of food.

3. KNOWLEDGE OF TASTE AND SUBJECTIVE EXPERIENCE

We concluded the last chapter by looking at one way in which facts about food are subjective: in virtue of the kind of properties they are, the existence of flavors (and the associated facts about them) depends on how things are for some subject or group of subjects. We also saw, via the example of Chloe, that *knowledge* of flavor and about taste is subjective insofar as it depends crucially on experience. There are truths about taste that we can only know through first-hand experience of them:

what chocolate tastes like, for example. As an old maxim reminds us, *de gustibus non disputandum est*—there's no disputing taste.

If facts about taste are constituted by subjective experience, we might wonder whether they can ever transcend such experience. Is it possible to make sense of claims about a food being good, or tasty, or can we only make sense of claims about a food tasting good *to me*, *to you*, and so on? If subjective experience is part of what determines the flavor of a food, then we might worry that there are no mind-independent facts about taste. And then it seems we have no way of determining which food in fact tastes good, and no way of resolving disagreements about taste. We can only rely on our experiences, and where these experiences conflict, we seem to have no way of deciding the matter. On one interpretation, then, the maxim is telling us that disputes about taste are pointless, since they cannot be resolved via argument.

However, the maxim also uncovers an apparently paradoxical feature of claims about taste: the sense that both parties to a dispute are correct seems to render the dispute impossible. If we understand each party as making a claim about their own experience, then both parties are correct, but this seems to misunderstand what we're trying to say in these cases: if I say a cheese is tasty, and you say it is not, it seems like we're attempting to describe the *cheese*, rather than ourselves—I'm saying it has a property, being tasty, and you're denying it has that property. But if that's the right interpretation, then one of us must be making a mistake, because either the cheese is tasty, or it is not—it can't be both tasty and not tasty. To make sense of the idea that both our judgments are correct, we must understand my claim as the claim that the cheese is tasty *to me*, and yours as the claim that the cheese is tasty *to you*. This way we can both be speaking truly, but there's a cost: it now seems that we're talking about our individual experiences, rather than about the cheese itself. So, we preserve the intuition that we're both correct (about how things are for us), but at the expense of having a shared subject matter (how things are with respect to the cheese).

This is partly an issue about how to interpret the *meaning* of claims about taste, but also a question about what makes such claims true or false. And the two are naturally related: if we don't know what someone's saying, it's hard to assess the truth of their claim. So, understanding what we mean when we say something tastes good is at least partly a matter of knowing what it is for something to taste good. If we can explain the latter issue only in terms of subjective experience—if the only way for a thing to taste good is for it to taste good *to* someone or another, then it makes sense to understand the meaning of "tastes good" as making implicit reference to a subject, because we require a subject to supply the perspective from which we can evaluate the claim.

We could concede that all food judgments are deeply subjective, and that (as we said above) there's no disputing about taste: any judgment is as good as any other. But anyone who's ever had a sip of orange juice right after brushing her teeth knows that not all judgments are equally well-founded. At the other extreme, it seems too strong to say that facts about taste are entirely independent of any and all human experience. There are some facts about which it seems we could be globally in error or ignorance: the origins of the universe, for example. There's nothing contradictory about imagining that in the entire course of human history, no one ever discovers the truth about how the universe began. But there does seem to be something inherently problematic about imagining that, in the entire course of human history, we remain ignorant about whether or not chocolate tastes good.

The popularity (and profitability) of processed foods and chain restaurants also gives us evidence of shared taste. If taste were completely variable, it should be difficult for companies to predict which products will succeed and which will fail. Why is Coca-Cola so much more popular than Dr Pepper? Why are McDonald's fries so universally beloved? How could the engineering and manufacturing of vats of flavoring become a multi-billion-dollar business? The success of these products is evidence, not necessarily of their aesthetic merits (we'll talk more about that in Chapter Three), but of the fact that humans tend to enjoy the same flavors, tastes, and textures: for example, fat, salt, sugar, crispy, gooey. And if our taste experiences are sufficiently similar, we ought to be able to communicate them to and with others.

4. TASTE AND TESTIMONY

Much of our knowledge of the tastes and qualities of food is acquired through the testimony of others. Indeed, testimony plays a number of crucial roles in our knowledge about food, so it's worth spending a bit of time thinking about it and the issues it raises involving trust, faith, credibility, and prejudice.

This brings us to the question of how we acquire knowledge about what is tasty, and safe, to eat. One route is via experience: we find out whether something is good to eat by eating it. But this is risky; if we're wrong about a food's safety, we face a steep penalty. A better strategy is to learn from others: either by observing what others eat and their reactions to it, or by soliciting advice and information from others. Sharing information about food sources is, arguably, one of the drivers of the evolution of communication in animals and humans: bees perform the so-called waggle dance to communicate the location and quality of food sources to one another,[2] or contemporary human diners, who, when looking for food in a new town, typically start with reviews on sites such as Yelp or TripAdvisor. Our reliance on second-hand information demonstrates the relationship between managing risk and trust: trusting others

---

2   A bee returning to the hive after successfully locating food will perform a kind of figure-eight movement to tell hive mates about the quality and quantity of food she's found. The longer the dance, the further away the food source; the angle at which the dance is performed also tells the other bees about the direction of the food source relative to the sun. Interested readers should see Karl von Frisch's (1973) Nobel Lecture, in which he explains and recounts his Nobel-winning discovery of the dance.

about what to eat removes the risk of having to experiment ourselves, but it incurs new risks—who to trust and imitate? This problem becomes more pressing as food production becomes more centralized and further removed from our everyday experience. As we consume more and more processed food, we're increasingly reliant on others to tell us what we're ingesting. In particular, we depend on food labels to tell us what we're eating: not only is our food produced in ways that are invisible to us, but the product itself is not always recognizable as the sum of its ingredients. If I eat an apple, I know what I'm eating; if I eat an apple pie, I have a rough sense that it contains fruit and some sort of dough. If I eat a PowerBar, or a Dorito, the ingredients are more mysterious. Here, I am dependent on a list of ingredients to tell me what I'm eating, and even this may not be informative enough, depending on what we think knowledge requires: does it suffice that I can name the ingredients in my food, or must I understand what those names—for example, maltodextrin, malic acid, sodium acetate, disodium inosinate, and disodium guanylate[3]—mean and refer to?

4.1 Knowledge, Justification, and Testimony

A natural way to begin our discussion of food and epistemology would be with a definition of knowledge. Until half a century ago, this would have been straightforward: the standard philosophical analysis of knowledge, dating all the way back to Plato, is that knowledge is justified true belief. The justification condition is what separates knowledge from a lucky guess. But in 1963, Edmund Gettier published a famous paper, "Is Justified True Belief Knowledge?" which cast doubt on the adequacy of this definition. Gettier introduced a class of examples—now known as "Gettier cases"— in which an individual has a belief that is both true and justified but seems, intuitively, to fail to count as knowledge. For example:

> Suppose that Smith and Jones have applied for a certain job. And suppose that Smith has strong evidence for the following conjunctive proposition: Jones is the man who will get the job, and Jones has ten coins in his pocket.... But imagine, further, that unknown to Smith, he himself, not Jones, will get the job. And, also, unknown to Smith, he himself has ten coins in his pocket.[4]

According to the analysis of knowledge as justified true belief, Smith knows that the man who will get the job has ten coins in his pocket: he believes this, it's true,

---

3   A sampling of the ingredients in Cool Ranch Doritos. Eschliman & Ettlinger (2015) offer an enjoyable visual survey and explanation of the ingredients in common processed foods.

4   Gettier (1963, p. 122).

and he has justification for the belief (namely, that Jones will get the job and Jones has ten coins in his pocket). But most philosophers have agreed that Smith does not know this, and this shows that justified true belief is not enough for knowledge: it seems that there is some additional condition involving the relationship between the justification for the belief and its truth that is missing from the traditional analysis, a condition that would rule out having accidental knowledge like the kind Gettier describes. But identifying this additional condition has been notoriously difficult. We certainly won't do it here, nor will we survey attempts to do so. But despite the difficulties Gettier's cases have created for traditional analyses of knowledge, most philosophers agree that knowledge does require justification. So, claiming that we know what we are eating requires that we have some justification for our beliefs about what we're eating, and that those beliefs be true. How we acquire that justification varies—above, we saw that experience plays an important role, but that we can't rely on it alone—we also have to rely on the testimony of others, whether those others are people, producers, or packages. In the remainder of Section 4, we'll look at some of the epistemic problems and complications raised by this reliance.

4.2 Testimony and Food

If beliefs based on food labeling aren't justified, we don't know what's in our food (even if our beliefs about it happen to be true). If we don't know what's in our food, it seems that we cannot know our food is safe. We would then be faced with a double skepticism: skepticism about whether we know what we are eating, and a kind of practical paralysis about whether and what to eat. Here we can see the practical implications of food epistemology quite clearly: since few of us manage to avoid packaged food altogether, the question of whether we can accept testimony is not just a theoretical one. It might sound odd to talk about a non-sentient piece of packaging as offering "testimony"—but from the perspective of the inquirer wondering what's in her frozen pizza, that's what it is: a second-hand source of information.

When are we justified in forming beliefs based on testimony? As hearers of testimony, do we have an obligation to investigate the reliability of its source, or are we justified in accepting the testimony at face value? This is a central controversy in the epistemology of testimony, and it dates back at least as far as Hume, who argued that testimony is like other forms of inference, and, therefore, we need to justify any beliefs formed via testimony by inquiring into its source.[5] But other philosophers have argued that we must be able to accept some testimony without additional justification, or else it would be impossible ever to learn anything. Children begin their education knowing very little—certainly not enough to assess the reliability

---

5   See Hume (1740/1978, I.III.IV).

of testimony they receive. So, if it were impossible to be justified in beliefs based on testimony without investigating their source, children would never form any justified beliefs (or at least, would form very few). But they must do so, if they're going to grow up knowing anything about the world around them!

Reductionists like Hume argue that we do need some additional reason to accept testimony: like most other forms of belief formation where I infer my belief from some other source, testimonial belief requires me to do some work to investigate the trustworthiness of my source. *Anti-reductionists* deny this, and allow the recipient of testimony to accept it at face value. For the anti-reductionist, testimony is like memory or perception: it gives us direct access to information. Just as we can move directly from *seeing* a red cup on the table to the *belief* that there's a red cup on the table, I can move directly from Clara's report that there's a red cup on the table to believing there's a red cup on the table; in the absence of disqualifying information, I'm entitled to believe my eyes—and my informants.

The anti-reductionist can explain why we are justified in forming beliefs based on labels when we don't have much of a basis for judging the trustworthiness of their source, or when we believe a pepper is organic because the sign over it says "organic"—despite knowing nothing about the origins of the sign. The reductionist doesn't have to deny that such beliefs are justified, but they do have to explain the basis for their justification. Is it the overall reliability of product labeling in general or food labels in general? This would be a relatively *global* reductionism. Or, it might be because we know the specific producer of that food to be reliable—a more local form of reductionism, where I know that this particular source of testimony is trustworthy or reliable. Of course, this raises the additional question of how and when we come to know that a source is reliable. One sometimes comes across news stories revealing that the fish in our sushi isn't what we believe it to be, or that traces of pork are found in beef burgers; do these stories undermine our justification for believing that we know what's in our sushi? If so, do they also undermine our confidence in food packaging and labeling more generally?

4.3 *Testimony, Vulnerability, and Epistemic Justice*

If the industrial food system puts us in an epistemically vulnerable position by forcing us to rely on labels whose origins we don't really understand or are unable to evaluate, one response is to obtain our food from sources we know to be trustworthy. (We'll talk more about trust in the next section, because it plays a significant role in our food choices—after all, putting a foreign object in one's body is itself an act of trust!) And as we'll see in Chapters Six and Seven, our judgments about risk aren't always rational or trustworthy themselves.

This means that when we shop at markets that allow us to interact directly with producers, or when we buy unprocessed or minimally processed food, we're not just paying for food—we're also paying for knowledge about that food. And this creates a problem of epistemic justice: not everyone is given equal access to knowledge about what they're putting into their body. Because dependence on processed and manufactured food means dependence on testimony from unreliable sources, the consumers who eat these foods are forced into a disadvantageous epistemic position. By virtue of being in a position where they rely on large supermarkets and manufacturers for their food, they also rely on these sources for their information. If the information is inferior, then we may feel that the wrong here is not just limited food choice, but limited opportunities to exercise epistemic agency: to fairly evaluate one's food choices in terms of their ingredients and the manufacturing processes involved. This is a kind of epistemic injustice, where a lack of economic resources or social status places one in a disadvantaged epistemic position with respect to evidence or justification. The epistemic wrong may correlate with other forms of injustice, insofar as a lack of fresh food and a lack of information about the nutritional content of one's food correlate with poor health—we'll discuss this point further in Chapter Seven—but it's distinct from it, since the claim here is that it is wrong for socioeconomic disadvantage to affect one's access to important information about what one's consuming.[6]

One might object that we don't really need to know how our food is produced, as long as the processes are safe. Foods are labeled with information about potential allergens, so that people can avoid these; beyond this point, other information is extraneous and possibly even distracting. We'll talk a bit more about this in Chapter Six, when we look at arguments over whether genetically modified (GM) foods should be labeled as such. But the question here isn't just about whether people have a right to information about certain aspects of their food, it's about the extent to which reliance on testimony is itself a kind of cost, and freedom from such reliance a kind of privilege.

4.4 Testimony and Trust

To accept testimony from a source requires trusting that source. Trust, in turn, involves a kind of vulnerability: we put ourselves in the hands of another. This usually implies that we expect the trustee to fulfill their end of the deal, and to be able to do so. Trust is optimistic in this way; in trusting, we incur a risk, because we make ourselves dependent on the trustee's fulfillment of the bargain. So, if we trust others to tell us what we are eating, it implies that we expect certain things, such as honesty and competence.

---

6   See Fricker's (2007) book of the same name. Fricker points out that the kind of injustice I describe here is not necessarily distinctly epistemic, since we can view it as an instance of *distributive* injustice: injustice resulting from unequal or unfair access to important goods, in this case information.

Does trust accurately characterize our relationship to food labeling and nutritional information? On the one hand, we are extremely vulnerable, when we consume food, to misinformation. We depend on others to tell us what's in our food, and how much information we're entitled to is a controversial issue. Even in cases where our food is ostensibly unprocessed—a package of cut-up fruit, for example—the process by which it's produced is likely to be significantly opaque: the fruit salad we buy in a convenience store, for example, contains not just fruit, but also a patented (and secret) coating containing minerals and vitamins that delay its decay.

Certainly, our inability to verify for ourselves what we're eating makes us *vulnerable* in the way that trust requires: we depend on others to tell us what's in our food. But vulnerability isn't sufficient for trust: someone who is being held hostage is vulnerable, but not trusting. Trust requires both depending on another to meet one's needs, and expecting, or at least hoping, that they will do so. It is accompanied by certain expectations: that the trusted party is competent to do what's expected, and that they will keep their end of the bargain. Does trust also involve ascribing a certain motive to the trustee—that they'll keep their end of the bargain because they care about us, for example, or because it's the right thing to do, rather than because it is a sensible business strategy? If we do require certain motives to be in place for trust to be appropriate, then our analysis might apply less well to institutions. The question of whether corporations are like persons is a complex ontological, moral, and legal one. In 2010, the US Supreme Court ruled that corporations should have the same rights to speech as persons. Does this give us a basis for holding them to the same standards of epistemic evaluation as persons? How we answer the question has implications for our analysis of trust, insofar as our epistemic assessment of food manufacturers and their trustworthiness depends on whether we view corporations as the kinds of things that can engage in deception and have motives or intentions.

In most cases, perhaps without even giving the issue much consideration, we do trust that food labels accurately reflect their contents. But is this trust warranted? Perhaps, instead of being rationally justified, our trust is simply inevitable: without trust, we could not eat. In this case, trust is less an intellectual decision than an inescapable condition of eating—we're forced to trust our food if we're ever going to eat something we didn't grow or kill ourselves. We'll return to the question of risk and trust in our discussion of the precautionary principle in Chapter Six. For now, we'll focus on the issues raised by food labeling more generally: in particular, the ways in which such labels—and the foods themselves—can mislead us.

5. LABELS, LIES, AND BULLSHIT

Food deceives in various ways: it seems safe, but isn't; it tastes like something it is not; it promises to contain something it does not. Sometimes deception is enjoyable: the chocolate cake hides caramel at its center; the meatless burger is indistinguishable from its beefy counterpart. Often, it is not. There may be health consequences of deception, as when risky food is passed off as safe, or when ingredients are mislabeled. There may be aesthetic consequences: if you are expecting sugar but taste salt, you will be unpleasantly surprised. And there are moral consequences, too: someone ingesting food they would not choose to eat for moral or religious reasons may feel that their autonomy and body have been violated. From a philosophical perspective, such deceptions raise questions about the transparency of food and food labeling: labels may not list ingredients, or may list them in ways that are misleading (for example, describing sugar as "cane juice" to appeal to health-conscious customers). Strictly speaking, food cannot lie to us and neither can food labels: according to traditional definitions, lying requires a statement made by a speaker to a hearer with the intention to deceive the hearer. Labels don't meet that definition; there's no speaker and no hearer—just a corporation and a consumer. Moreover, one might question whether the label really *intends* to deceive. Take the case of Kellogg's Strawberry Delight Mini-Wheats cereal, which contains no actual strawberries. Does the name deceive the consumer? Possibly. But cereal names aren't chosen with the intention of causing specific beliefs, but specific behaviors, namely, buying the product. One way to accomplish this goal is to choose a name that will deceive the consumer into forming a certain belief (that the cereal has strawberries in it). But there are other ways to accomplish the same goal: perhaps having a fruit in the name makes the customer associate it with health and freshness; perhaps the customer only cares about flavor, and not ingredients. As long as the customer buys the cereal, the specific belief they have does not matter: the intention is to sell the product.

Because their goal isn't to instill any particular belief in consumers, it's inaccurate to say that these labels *lie*. A more useful concept is *bullshit*. Bullshit is different from lying or deception: the bullshitter's intention is not to deceive, but something unrelated to truth or falsehood. Bullshit is indifferent to truth; its goal is something else altogether. It may well be false, but the falsehood is incidental to its real goal, whether that be selling a product, embellishing one's reputation, or seeming intelligent to an audience.[7] Here, we might say that the name of the cereal is bullshit. It's false, but the name wasn't chosen *because* it is false, or because it would cause a false belief. Rather, the name was chosen to sell cereal: it's bullshitting the consumer.

6. KNOWING FOOD: KNOWING THAT OR KNOWING HOW?

So far, this chapter has discussed a few ways in which the activity of eating involves knowledge and justification, and many of these are centrally involved in choosing

---

7   Frankfurt (2005).

what to eat: the knowledge of food's properties, and what that food is, involve reliance on one's senses, one's judgments about taste, and the testimony of others. But what kind of activity is choosing and preparing food, and how is this activity itself a manifestation of knowledge? How do we decide what to eat and how to prepare it? Put most simply: when we ask ourselves what to have for dinner, what form does our deliberation over the answer and our execution of the meal take?

One challenge for an epistemology of food is that we often make judgments of food without being able to articulate the reasons for those judgments, or the knowledge that guides them. We can look at a dish and see that it is done, or taste the dish and know that it needs more acid, but we may not be able to express how we see this, or justify our judgment in terms of other beliefs or observations. Likewise, the reasons we prepare foods according to specific methods aren't always accessible or known to us: we follow culinary traditions without realizing why; the justification for certain practices (both in cooking or eating) may no longer be known, or may never have been known by a particular individual to begin with.

Similar issues arise when we turn to our reasons for choosing and consuming certain foods. We often find ourselves desiring foods without knowing why; our food choices and preferences are formed and influenced in ways that may not be consciously accessible. We may have been influenced by advertising, or by emotional associations with food—for example, we think of certain foods as comforting, or celebratory, or romantic, but we lack reasons to support such associations. We can explain them by appealing to culture, tradition, or media, but these explanations are not justifications.

The epistemic significance of these observations is that we aren't aware of, or able to access, our reasons for our beliefs, preferences, choices, and practices regarding food. This lack of access raises an even deeper worry: perhaps we don't *have* any reasons or justification for these beliefs. If that's true, then our decisions about what foods to eat might be irrational in one of two ways: first, lacking reasons or evidence deprives them of an important epistemic credential, and raises the possibility that they're unduly influenced by inappropriate factors. We don't typically *endorse* advertising as a source of good reasons, so if we find out that our choice of coffee is determined solely by marketing, we should be skeptical of the choice itself. (The "Pepsi challenge" is a long-standing marketing campaign in which self-professed Coca-Cola fans are challenged to say which of the two sodas they like best in a blind taste-test; most consumers end up preferring Pepsi, yet Coca-Cola continues to sell more soda.) The second worry is that, because the decisions are not *based* on reasons, they're not *responsive* to reasons, either. In that case, they won't be altered by appeals to evidence or reason; instead, to change someone's behavior, we should look to features of their environment, appeal to their emotions, and so on. Failures of rationality like this also suggest we're not really autonomous with respect to food choice—a point we'll discuss more in Chapter Seven. The epistemic consequences are that we lack justification for our beliefs about food and that our food choices or preferences are irrational and not under our conscious, reflective control. This in turn leads to a kind of skepticism about knowledge of our choices, and also about whether we're really choosing in the first place—if I am not aware of the reasons for my choice, am *I* really the one making it, or is it being determined for me?

Regardless, the fact remains that we can and do evaluate such choices as more or less rational: we distinguish between cravings and deliberate food choices, for example, and we identify some acts of eating as more intentional and reflective of our values than others. What we need is an epistemology that can help us make sense of such evaluation and how we can carry it out in the absence of traditional epistemological concepts governing the rational evaluation of consciously formed beliefs.

One approach to this task is to view judgments like the above as instances of a kind of *knowledge how* rather than *knowledge that*. In the case of knowledge *that*, knowledge amounts to possessing a belief. In the case of knowledge *how*, it consists in possession of an ability or skill. No one denies that some, even most, knowledge is propositional—that it involves taking the attitude of belief towards true propositions. It may come as no surprise to learn that there's disagreement over how to define the term "proposition," but for our purposes, we can think of it as the kind of thing that can be true or false—a statement or a belief. What's more controversial is whether there is knowledge that consists in something other than knowing the truth of a proposition. *Intellectualism* is the view that all knowledge is propositional knowledge. As a result, the intellectualist maintains that when we exercise skills, like riding a bike or swimming, we're making use of propositions that tell us *how* to do these things: *moving one's arms while kicking is a way to swim, pushing down the pedals is a way to move forward*, and so on.[8] In the case of cooking, the intellectualist would say that a skillful cook has knowledge of a set of propositions telling her how to execute certain procedures. A skilled baker, for example, is one who knows a set of propositions: *if the bread dough is too wet, add more flour; if the dough isn't rising, place it somewhere warm.*

The main argument against intellectualism comes from the twentieth-century philosopher Gilbert Ryle, who argues that intellectualism leads to a problematic regress. If knowledge consists of propositions, then any act we take with respect to, say, breadmaking, involves considering a proposition (say, that more rising time is needed). But considering that proposition is itself an action. How do we know how to perform the action of considering a proposition? Since (according to intellectualism) all knowledge is propositional, knowing how to consider a proposition must itself consist of some proposition that we consider. But how do we know how to consider *that* proposition? It must be in virtue of another proposition ... and so on down the line. Ryle explains:

---

8   See Stanley & Williamson (2001) for an overview of the debate and a contemporary defense of intellectualism.

The crucial objection to the intellectualist legend is this. The consideration of propositions is itself an operation the execution of which can be more or less intelligent, more or less stupid. But if, for any operation to be intelligently executed, a prior theoretical operation had first to be performed and performed intelligently, it would be a logical impossibility for anyone ever to break into the circle.[9]

This isn't a problem for the anti-intellectualist, since they grant that there is a distinct act of considering a proposition, and that this is an instance of knowing-how; the regress stops because at the end of the chain of considering propositions is an act of a different sort, a non-theoretical operation. Knowledge how is an ability: it contrasts with knowledge of propositions in both the thing that is known—in one case, an action; in the other, a statement—and in the attitude we take towards that thing. In the next section, we'll look at the ways that this picture of knowledge opens up new dimensions of epistemic evaluation, and how these apply to our food choices.

7. SKILL, VIRTUE, AND FOOD CHOICE

Perhaps the most famous and influential discussion of skill in Western philosophy comes from Aristotle's moral theory. Aristotle argues that morality consists of a kind of practical wisdom: seeing what a situation calls for and acting accordingly. Morality could not be taught as a set of rules or principles; it is a kind of activity one must engage in to develop the right sorts of responses and dispositions. It is, like other activities, a skill one develops. Interestingly, Aristotle uses the analogy of eating to explain virtue: just as the right diet will not suit everyone, what counts as a courageous action will also differ for different agents in different situations. Virtue consists in being able to see what will count as courageous in any particular case and acting accordingly. Virtue also requires the right kinds of feelings: one must train not only one's behavior, but one's pleasures, desires, and appetites: "to feel them at the right times, with reference to the right objects, towards the right people, with the right aim, and in the right way ... this is characteristic of excellence."[10]

According to *virtue epistemology*, knowledge should be understood, not as the possession of a belief meeting certain conditions, but as the outcome of an exercise of a certain kind of epistemic skill. These skills might include such features as

---

9   Ryle (1949, p. 31).
10   Aristotle (1984a, 1106b18–20). When citing Aristotle, I'll use "Bekker numbers" rather than page numbers. These are the numbers found in the margins of the text, and are common to all editions—the name refers to a nineteenth-century translation by Immanuel Bekker. Because this numbering system is shared by all editions and translations, it enables the reader to quickly locate a passage in any translation or edition.

open-mindedness, intellectual curiosity, sensitivity to evidence, and fairness; they might also include abilities such as memory and perception, imagination, and foresight. What is distinctive about virtue epistemology is the idea that a belief's epistemic status is best analyzed in terms of an agent's exercise of certain capacities in acquiring a belief, rather than in terms of an agent's possession of a set of justifications. In this way, a good belief might be like a good soufflé—successfully arriving at it requires the right ingredients (evidence and information), but also skill in using them.[11]

Because virtue epistemology does not rely on traditional notions of evidence, justification, and belief, it may be a more promising way of understanding how we can evaluate our attitudes and practices involving food: we can focus on epistemically evaluating eaters and their communities, rather than seeking to evaluate individual beliefs based on conscious reasoning and inference. To return to our example above, an epistemically virtuous eater may be one whose intuitions are attuned to the right features of food (for example, its taste rather than its packaging), who is skilled at evaluating the trustworthiness of various sources, and who responds in appropriate ways to food. Of course, how we understand "right" and "appropriate" in these contexts will determine who counts as a virtuous agent, and one critique of virtue epistemology as applied to food is that it requires us to make normative judgments about how we ought to eat. Just as identifying acts that manifest moral virtues involves morally appraising those actions, identifying acts that manifest intellectual virtues requires us to appraise acts of belief as wise, open-minded, responsible, and so on. But in both the moral and epistemic cases, our appraisals aren't guided by simply applying a rule, or looking at which acts "get it right": to possess and manifest the virtue is what it is to get it right. Recognizing virtue is itself a kind of normative inquiry, and requires us to distinguish the agent who accidentally lands on a true belief, or a kind action, from the agent who arrives at these via the exercise of some capacity or skill.

We can also use virtue epistemology to understand and analyze the complications of evaluating testimony about food. Whose testimony is credible as a source of information about what we're eating and what we ought to eat? Should we defer to scientists, or to farmers, or to activists? Does skill belong to the technically trained French chef, or to the home cook who bakes her own bread and preserves her own vegetables?

One challenge for any attempt to answer these questions will be how to navigate and reconcile the many conflicting values we place on food. To say that a virtuous eater chooses food for the right sorts of reasons is one thing; to specify what sorts of reasons those might be is another. Is eating for pleasure appropriate? Is it appropriate all the time, or just in certain circumstances? Should we always choose foods based on health, or should we sometimes ignore health in favor of convenience? Articles about

---

11   For an overview of virtue epistemology, see Zagzebski (1996, Part I).

weight and diet tell us to avoid "emotional eating," but we often eat for celebration, or comfort: is this always a bad thing? Is it ever? Our judgments about food take place in so many different contexts and must weigh many different requirements. This is not to say that no account can be given; indeed, considering the complex nature of eating, virtue epistemology may be well-equipped to explain the difficulty of giving an account of what justifies food choice and preference.

CONCLUSION

The challenge of knowing what to eat is complicated by the fact that we have an immense amount of information about food and nutrition—every day seems to yield another study telling us what to eat, and every day the prescription seems to be different—and yet, at the same time, too little knowledge about what we're actually eating and how it's produced. We depend on others to tell us about our food, but food is a business, and business is not inherently trustworthy. Being a knowledgeable eater is a virtue, but as we'll see in the chapters to come, the demands we have to navigate are incredibly complex, because our food choices have implications for animals, the environment, our health, and even global justice. Faced with this complex set of criteria, we might wish to throw up our hands, but we can't opt out of food. Constructing an adequate epistemology of food is an ongoing project and a practically urgent one. One might think at this point that food is a daunting challenge, but in the next chapter we'll look at its more pleasurable aspects.

Chapter Three

AESTHETICS

INTRODUCTION

Food is both an everyday necessity and an indulgence. It's also a source of pleasure—eating and drinking gives rise to a variety of enjoyable sensations stemming from the senses of taste and smell. But are these pleasures sufficiently complex and enduring to secure food the status of art? This chapter will explore food's status as an object of aesthetic appreciation. As we will see, food's status as aesthetic object is complicated by a number of factors: its intimate involvement with the senses and our bodies, its impermanence, and its quotidian aspects.

We'll begin by looking at the historical relationship between food and philosophy. Philosophers haven't always treated food and the act of eating as subjects fit for serious consideration, partly because of doubts about the role of bodily and sensory experiences in producing knowledge and insight. So rather than focus solely on what philosophers have said about the aesthetics of food, this chapter looks at philosophical views about aesthetic experience and art more generally, and asks whether food deserves to be considered art. Because "art" (like "food") doesn't refer to a natural kind, the things falling under the term change over time, as does the definition itself. So, in asking whether food is considered art, we're also asking about the role food plays in contemporary society and the value we place on it. After looking at the nature of aesthetic experience and at various attempts to define art, we'll talk about the idea of objective standards of beauty, and how we come to know about them. This will allow us to compare the kind of qualities we find in food with those in other forms of art. We'll then talk about the relationship between food and culture: if foods are expressions of identity, do they belong to particular groups? Is it wrong for one culture to adopt and profit off the culture of another? We'll conclude by raising some questions about the way our attitudes towards various cuisines express our cultural values and prejudices.

I. TASTE AND PHILOSOPHY: A TENDENTIOUS RELATIONSHIP?

Philosophy has always had an ambivalent relationship with food and drink. This is partly due to its associations with pleasure and indulgence, and partly due to the senses via which we experience food. On the one hand, eating is an activity that reminds us of our animal nature and our basest bodily functions; on the other hand, food is a way of expressing culture, particularly in the act of cooking and in our national and regional cuisines. In this section, we'll look at three reasons for philosophical skepticism about the value of food: its relationship to the senses, particularly the "lower" senses of taste and smell; the fact that food is associated with physical pleasure; and its link to objectionable aspects of our physical bodies and their operations.

Eating is an act that unites our physical, cultural, and reflective natures. It engages all our senses. Because many philosophers have been dubious about the value of the senses (and especially taste and smell, as we'll see), they have likewise viewed food and eating as, at best, a trivial distraction from serious philosophical questions, and at worst, a corruption of our rational and reflective nature. Even among the senses themselves, taste and smell are given a status below sight, touch, and hearing. Kant refers to them as "the lower senses" and claims that they are "more subjective than objective," as well as more dispensable than the other senses—their role is not to give us knowledge, but to produce pleasure.[1]

Food and drink are also closely linked to sensual pleasures, and distrust of pleasure has a long philosophical history. Though his name would become shorthand for the enjoyment of food and drink, the philosopher Epicurus recommended an austere diet on the grounds that feasting and drinking feel good in the moment, but only create a craving for more—the pursuit of these pleasures can never be truly satisfied. The contentment we gain from a simple diet is a more stable, enduring form of pleasure. Plato thought that some of our aesthetic responses—to painting, poetry, and music—had value, but he dismissed cooking as a kind of "flattery" of the soul, a "shameful" pursuit, because, "it guesses at what's pleasant with no consideration for what's best."[2] The best we can do, according to Plato and the Epicureans, is to manage our desires for sensual pleasures, and not let them rule us. (Not all Greek philosophers felt this way; a group called the Cyrenaics held that one should constantly work to gratify one's immediate desires, partly because they believed that the only things we could be certain of were our immediate perceptions and sensations.)

Another reason for suspicion about the pleasures of food involves the bodily functions associated with eating and drinking, which are closely linked to the emotions of shame and disgust. Human cultures have elaborate rules governing the ingestion, and

---

1   See Korsmeyer (2002, pp. 57–60).
2   Plato (1997a, 465a).

especially the excretion, of food and drink (while ingestion of food is usually a public and communal activity, its excretion, while also governed by rules, is almost always a function performed in private). The development of norms of etiquette to govern the primal acts of eating and drinking reveals a more generally conflicted attitude towards the relationship between culture and our physical nature: we can't escape the demands of our bodies, but these are also reminders that we are, essentially, animals.

However, we will not be so quick to dismiss the aesthetic value of food. Given the range of forms and contexts in which we encounter food—plucking an apple from a tree; eating a celebratory feast alongside family and friends; experiencing an eighteen-course tasting menu cooked by a world-renowned chef—it may offer opportunities for both purely physical pleasure and challenging artistic encounters. In the next section, we will look at the characteristics of aesthetic experience in general, before examining whether some of our experiences of food might qualify as such. This in turn will inform our discussion of whether food can be art, since one important feature of art is its ability to give rise to aesthetic experiences in us.

2. THE NATURE OF AESTHETIC EXPERIENCE

The term "aesthetic" is often associated with our appreciation of and reaction to works of art, though aesthetic experience isn't limited to art: we can have an aesthetic experience of a beautiful sunset or a butterfly (we will talk more about what separates art from aesthetic objects below). Aesthetic experiences have three features: first, they involve the senses, since they're primarily a response to their elicitor's sensory properties (its appearance, sound, smell, feel, taste). Second, they evaluate their object non-instrumentally. To appraise or react to an object aesthetically is to appreciate it for its own sake, not for its financial value, or its ability to signal status or taste. Aesthetic experience is experience of an object as it is in itself, and not as it is fit to help us attain some goal. Finally, aesthetic experience involves a kind of reaction to or evaluation of its object. This needn't be purely pleasurable: some paintings may elicit disgust, some music makes us sad, and some of the scenes in nature may fill us with a kind of fear or awe. But it can't be completely indifferent—we must feel something, good or bad, to call what we have an aesthetic experience.[3]

This last requirement explains the subjectivity of aesthetic judgment: it consists, at least partly, in having some sort of feeling towards an object. But aesthetic judgments are not purely subjective, because in expressing one, I don't just claim that the object gives pleasure *to me*, I make the stronger claim that others ought to share my response. In other words, I'm saying that the object *merits* a certain kind of reaction or appreciation. My judgment aspires to a kind of objectivity insofar as it claims

---

3   See Telfer (1996), Chapter 3, for an extensive discussion.

to be correct and demands the assent of others. This feature distinguishes aesthetic judgments from judgments of liking, or "agreeableness," as Kant terms them: in the aesthetic case, we aim to say something more than simply how an object is for us. We require that others share our response. In the following passage, Kant explains the difference, while also expressing doubt that judgments about taste can ever rise to the level of an aesthetic judgment:

> With regard to the *agreeable* everyone is content that his judgement, which he grounds on a private feeling, and in which he says of an object that it pleases him, be restricted merely to his own person. Hence, he is perfectly happy if, when he says that sparkling wine from the Canaries is agreeable, someone else should improve his expression and remind him that he should say "It is agreeable to me"; and this is so not only in the case of the taste of the tongue, palate, and throat, but also in the case of that which may be agreeable to someone's eyes and ears. For one person the color violet is gentle and lovely, for another dead and lifeless. One person loves the tone of wind instruments, another that of stringed instruments. It would be folly to dispute the judgement of another that is different from our own in such a matter, with the aim of condemning it as incorrect, as if it were logically opposed to our own; thus with regard to the agreeable, the principle, Everyone has his own taste (of the senses) is valid. With the beautiful it is entirely different.[4]

When we say something is agreeable, or pleasant (as the passage is sometimes translated), we are really saying that it pleases *us*. Talk of agreeableness and pleasantness communicates subjective feelings of pleasure. Talk of beauty says more than this—it makes a statement about the kind of reaction that the object merits, not just the one it actually elicits. If I say canary wine is pleasant, you may disagree with me, and we can agree to leave it there. But if I say canary wine is *beautiful*, then I demand your agreement—if you disagree, there is a real issue between us, and we cannot merely leave it at that. As Kant tells us above: "to strive here with the design of reproving as incorrect another man's judgements [of the pleasant] ... as if the judgements were logically opposed, would be folly...." Kant is claiming that there is in fact no contradiction between my judgment that the wine is *pleasant* with another person's judgment that it is not, because the judgments are not really about the wine—they're about our own responses to it. But aesthetic judgment therefore requires a standard by which it can

---

4   See Kant (1790/2000, 5: 212–13). References to Kant will use what are known as "Akademie" numbers. The first number refers to the book itself (so the reader can ignore these), the second number points readers to that particular passage in the book, and is found in the margins of nearly all translations. This enables readers to easily locate a passage regardless of which edition or translation they're consulting.

be correct or incorrect, or at least that some judgments are better and more accurate than others. As Kant reminds us, if anything goes—if any judgment is as good as any other—we are not dealing with aesthetic judgments but mere agreeableness.

The possibility of aesthetic appreciation—whether of food, wine, or any other object—involves both metaphysical and epistemic requirements. Metaphysical, because the object must have properties in virtue of which we judge it beautiful or ugly. Epistemic, because we require standards by which we can say that an aesthetic judgment is correct, or good, or justified; these standards will also help us navigate cases of conflicting aesthetic judgments. Based on our discussion in the previous two chapters, we can identify a few proposals as to how these requirements might be satisfied. Our analysis in Chapter One of flavor as a secondary quality or response-dependent property illustrates how it can both exist or inhere in the object (and therefore objective in this sense) and be manifest in our sensations (and therefore subjective in this sense). But *detecting* these properties and *evaluating* them from an aesthetic perspective are two different activities. If we're going to treat food as art, we need some way to rise above mere subjective liking or disliking and evaluate it as an aesthetic object. To do this requires a kind of epistemology of judgments of taste: what makes a judgment correct, or justified? Are all such judgments equally good, or are some people better judges of aesthetic merits than others? In the next section, we'll look at how we might reconcile the subjective and objective aspirations of aesthetic evaluation generally and food more specifically.

3. HUME AND THE STANDARD OF TASTE

One proposal comes from the eighteenth-century philosopher, Hume, who begins his essay "Of the Standard of Taste," by observing that "it is natural for us to seek a standard of taste; a rule, by which the various sentiments of men may be reconciled; at least, a decision, afforded, confirming one sentiment, and condemning another...."[5] Like Kant, Hume's task is to reconcile both the subjective and objective aspects of aesthetic judgment. In giving his account, he uses the physical sense of taste as a metaphor for the act of discerning aesthetic quality:

> Though it be certain, that beauty and deformity, more than sweet and bitter, are not qualities in objects, but belong entirely to the sentiment, internal or external; it must be allowed, that there are certain qualities in objects, which are fitted by nature to produce those particular feelings. Now as these qualities may be found in a small degree, or may be mixed and confounded with each other, it often happens, that the taste is not affected with such minute

---

5   See Hume (1777/1987, p. 229).

qualities, or is not able to distinguish all the particular flavours, amidst the disorder, in which they are presented. Where the organs are so fine, as to allow nothing to escape them; and at the same time so exact as to perceive every ingredient in the composition: This we call delicacy of taste, whether we employ these terms in the literal or metaphorical sense.[6]

Hume continues the comparison between literal and metaphorical taste: "A good palate is not tried by strong flavours; but by a mixture of small ingredients, where we are still sensible of each part, notwithstanding its minuteness and its confusion with the rest. In like manner, a quick and acute perception of beauty and deformity must be the perfection of our mental taste...."[7]

Hume's challenge is to reconcile two conflicting observations: first, his point above that beauty and deformity "belong entirely to the sentiment," and that "all sentiment is right; because sentiment has a reference to nothing beyond itself, and is always real, wherever a man is conscious of it."[8] But second, Hume notes our firm conviction that some works of art and literature are *better* than others: "Whoever would assert an equality of genius and elegance between OGILBY and MILTON, or BUNYAN and ADDISON, would be thought to defend no less an extravagance, than if he had maintained a mole-hill to be as high as TENERIFFE, or a pond as extensive as the ocean."[9]

How can we reconcile these conflicting observations? Hume's solution is to locate the standard of taste in aesthetic judgments themselves: the judgments of the "true critic." According to Hume, "the joint verdict of such, wherever they are to be found, is the true standard of taste and beauty."[10] The critics do not track an independent fact about beauty; their judgment itself sets the standard that constitutes those facts. So, we can't identify critics by looking for individuals who are reliable guides to beauty—this approach would be circular in light of the fact that the critics' verdicts are what set the standard of beauty itself.

Instead, Hume offers us a list of qualifications the ideal critics must possess: "Strong sense, united to delicate sentiment, improved by practice, perfected by comparison, and cleared of all prejudice, can alone entitle critics to this valuable character."[11] These qualities enable the critics to detect subtle qualities of a work, and to respond to features of it that will endure and appeal over time, without being influenced by trends or self-interest.

---

6   Hume (1777/1987, p. 235).
7   Hume (1777/1987, p. 235).
8   Hume (1777/1987, p. 230).
9   Hume (1777/1987, pp. 230–31).
10 Hume (1777/1987, p. 241).
11 Hume (1777/1987, p. 241).

Hume points to the importance of experience and training for developing sense and delicate taste: a true critic must have encountered a wide variety of objects and must have practice appraising them. The critic must also be free of prejudice, which Hume points to as a source of distortion of our judgments. This prejudice can come from features of the critic himself: if he is envious of the artist, for example. Or it may come from certain opinions or attitudes on the part of the critic that stops her from entering into the point of view of the work. Trends and fashion can also prejudice us: a work might strike us as "old fashioned" or out of date, and we might therefore fail to properly appreciate it.

The obvious question for Hume's purposes is, are there any such critics? The obvious question for our purposes is, are there any such critics of *food*? In other words, even if Hume's account can provide us with a standard of taste for painting, or poetry, can it provide one for food? This is related to a question we'll take up in the next section: the question of whether food is a proper object for aesthetic appreciation. But the two questions are also importantly distinct, because what we're interested in here is the activity of making judgments about taste, and what makes one such judgment better than another; we'll defer the question of whether and how food is like other art objects until the next section.

Hume acknowledges that true critics will be difficult to find in any case, but maintains that the important lesson to be drawn from his discussion is that some taste is better than others, and that we can agree on what makes a good critic. His emphasis on practice and experience suggests that taste can be educated: through experience of comparisons between different objects and judging various works, we can educate our judgment. These characteristics of the true critic accord with our beliefs about how to acquire expertise at tasting food and wine: experience is the best education. It may not make up for a completely deficient palate, but it teaches us how to make the sorts of fine discriminations that Hume claims are essential to critical judgments.

Hume also emphasizes the need for acquaintance with a range of historical examples of beauty. This is obviously problematic with regards to food, in one sense: we can't eat the meals acclaimed by ancient Romans. Nor can we know what their ingredients tasted like: in the days before modern agriculture and processing techniques, grains, fruits, meats, and dairy all would have had different flavors. But we might also worry that because of this limitation, critics' verdicts reflect entrenched cultural values about how food ought to be and are therefore culturally bound in a way that judgments of paintings, literature, and sculpture are not. In our previous discussion of metaphysics (see Chapter One), we discussed the ways that a social-constructionist account risks unwittingly reinforcing normative assumptions about how we ought to eat. Similarly, a Humean account of aesthetic value may end up reinforcing cultural preferences about food, elevating these into aesthetic truths; this is a concern we'll address at the end of this chapter.

4. FOOD AS AESTHETIC EXPERIENCE

Having identified both the characteristics of aesthetic experience and what qualifies someone to be a good judge of it, we can now look at the question of whether food can be art. We'll start with the question of whether food can ever give rise to genuine aesthetic experiences. That's because the ability to cause an aesthetic experience is one of the requirements on a work of art. If we can't have aesthetic experiences of food, it isn't art. However, while the possibility of genuine aesthetic experiences of food may be *necessary* to establish that food can be art, it isn't sufficient. In other words, even if we establish the possibility of such experience, food might still fail to qualify as art. This is because "being the object of aesthetic experience" is only one possible way of classifying art, and many philosophers argue that it's too broad—we need an additional definition to distinguish art from other aesthetic objects. For example, as we saw in Section 2 above, natural beauty generates aesthetic experience, yet it is false to say that the Grand Canyon is a work of art. To understand why, it will help to look at some attempts to define art, and see how they apply to food.

5. DEFINING ART

First, we should acknowledge that defining art is a tricky business, and some philosophers have concluded that it can't—and shouldn't—be done.[12] These skeptics point to the wide range of works that are considered art, and to the fact that even the sorts of things that are considered art (e.g., sculpture, music, dance, video) are constantly evolving. Even if art can't be defined, we might analyze it using the twentieth-century philosopher Wittgenstein's idea of family resemblance concepts. Wittgenstein invites us to

> consider for example the proceedings that we call "games." I mean board-games, card-games, ball-games, Olympic games, and so on. What is common to them all? Don't say: "There must be something common, or they would not be called 'games'"—but look and see whether there is anything common to all. For if you look at them you will not see something that is common to all, but similarities, relationships, and a whole series of them at that. To repeat: don't think, but look![13]

Wittgenstein goes on:

---

12   For example, see Dean (2003) and Adajian (2005).
13   Wittgenstein (1953, para. 66–67).

The result of this examination is: we see a complicated network of similarities overlapping and criss-crossing: sometimes overall similarities. I can think of no better expression to characterize these similarities than "family resemblances"; for the various resemblances between members of a family: build, features, color of eyes, gait, temperament, etc. etc. overlap and criss-cross in the same way. And I shall say: "games" form a family.[14]

If we take Wittgenstein's suggestion, we should approach food by comparing it to other members of the art family and seeing what resemblances we can find. One way to do this will be by looking at more traditional definitions of art and seeing which of these characteristics are present in food. In the remainder of Section 5, we'll survey a number of definitions of art; as we'll see, all of them have their shortcomings.

5.1 Traditional Characteristics of Art: Form, Expression, Representation

FORM

Traditionally, painting and music are appraised in terms of their form and structure. The composer and conductor Leonard Bernstein explains, "Anyone can hear and enjoy a tune or a rhythm. But a true listener hears much more. That listener hears the form of a piece."[15] By way of illustration, here's how Bernstein describes a piece by the twentieth-century composer Stravinsky: "There are elements less classic than Mozart and Bach in the score of Capriccio: especially the ballet style of Tchaikovsky. And other elements less classic still, like a certain French salon atmosphere recalling Chaminade or Offenbach. All these, together with a hint of jazz rhythms, combine to make a piece of delicious artificiality, an essay in wit."

These examples illustrate the importance of formal elements in artistic appraisal and appreciation. Food and drink, skeptics like Kant claim, lack these elements: there's no formal complexity, no structure on the basis of which to critique and appreciate food. A piece of music can draw on established formal elements; even if it departs from tradition, it nonetheless evokes it. Food can't do this (or so skeptics claim).

I suspect that many chefs would take issue with this point, however, and would respond that food can be immensely complex and embody many formal elements. Just as there are established forms and conventions in Western classical music, as Bernstein describes, there are established culinary traditions. For example, there are four "mother sauces" with which all classically trained chefs are familiar: bechamel (made

---

14   Wittgenstein (1953, para. 66–67).
15   Bernstein (1962/2005, p. 243).

from milk, flour, and butter), veloute (stock, butter, and flour), espagnole (tomato and stock), and allemande (stock, egg yolk, and lemon). In the same way, a musician might play on the form of a sonata to subvert the listeners' expectations, an unexpected flavor or technique can play on the established formal conventions of classical cuisine. It isn't just tradition that gives food formal elements, either: food demands certain substances and relations in order for tastes to come together. Acid and salt, for example, play off one another; the amount of salt also affects the perception of bitterness versus sweetness in a dish, as we saw in Chapter One.

In the wine world, "structure" is often cited as a characteristic of good wines. When wine critics talk about a wine's structure, they refer to the relationship between sweetness, acidity, tannins, and body. In addition to the structure and formal elements of taste and flavor, certain formal elements are required to instantiate a dish. A pavlova requires a meringue, or at least, a meringue-like substance; a strawberry shortcake is traditionally some sort of biscuit-like cake along with berries and cream. This doesn't mean any shortcake will have these exact elements, but if we order a shortcake that substitutes, say, a plate full of cake crumbs atop a swipe of thick yogurt, we will understand the dish in terms of the traditional shortcake form—as a play on a shortcake. Or consider the "eggs benedict" served at the (now-closed) New York City restaurant WD-50: cylinders of slowly cooked egg yolks surrounded by cubes of fried hollandaise sauce coated in English muffin crumbs and "wisps" of Canadian bacon.[16] The dish contains the elements of traditional eggs benedict, but reinterprets both their form and the way they combine to create the dish.

EXPRESSION

Tolstoy writes that art is "a human activity consisting in this, that one man consciously, by means of certain external signs, hands on to others feelings he has lived through, and that other people are infected by these feelings and also experience them."[17] The twentieth-century philosopher R.G. Collingwood also defines art as the expression of emotion: "By creating for ourselves an imaginary experience or activity, we express our emotions; and this is what we call art."[18] On this view, art is characterized by the artist's intention to convey something—an emotion, an idea—to the audience. Some critics have denied that food can do this.[19] To these critics, food is importantly different from, say, music, since music can be sad or happy, and food cannot. One might object that certainly food can *make* us happy, or sad, just as music does. It's true that we use the phrase "sad song" more often, perhaps, than the phrase "happy hamburger," but is this reflective of a fact about food, or a fact about our language? But the fact that food makes us happy is not enough to meet the criteria; the definition requires that food itself express emo-

---

16   Dufresne & Meehan (2017, pp. 76–80).
17   Tolstoy (1996, p. 51).
18   Collingwood (1958).
19   See, for example, Telfer (1996, p. 59).

tions like joy or sadness. And this seems more difficult. While we can express emotion in the act of cooking; whether the emotion is transferred to and present in the food itself is debatable—does a cake made in a joyous mood, or on a sad occasion, itself contain or express sadness or joy? We'll say a bit more about food's expressive powers in Section 8 below, for as we'll see, they play an important role in determining whether food and recipes are entitled to certain kinds of legal and intellectual protection. For now, note that even if food has trouble meeting this requirement, art does as well. While music seems to be capable of expressing emotion, other works of art—for example, certain paintings and sculptures—are less obviously expressive, and their emotional component is unclear or absent. For example, Ellsworth Kelly's "Colors for a Large Wall" is a large square composed of 64 smaller squares of various solid colors, arbitrarily placed. The work does not clearly express emotion or express any idea. However, visual arts possess another characteristic which food is said to lack: they represent.

REPRESENTATION

This claim that representation distinguishes food from art is problematic for (at least) two reasons. First, food can quite vividly resemble other things: animals, nature, castles. The great eighteenth-century chef Carême constructed elaborate models out of marzipan and spun sugar—Chinese pavilions, ancient Greek ruins—going so far as to classify pastry as a branch of architecture. Food can even represent works of art themselves: a quick Internet search yields plenty of instructions for how to make a Mondrian cake, for example. But perhaps this kind of imitation is not what critics mean when they argue that food is not representational—the claim can be read not as a claim about appearance (that food represents by resembling something else) but a claim about what it conveys to the eater (that food represents by communicating something). On this reading, the objection is not that food can't resemble something, but that food can't convey content. This is also false. Food plays a number of symbolic roles, and the very existence of some dishes is due to their ability to represent and stand in for another symbol: Carolyn Korsmeyer cites the example of 'the pretzel', whose shape represents hands clasped in prayer.[20] She points out that in addition to this sort of representation by resemblance, food can also come to *exemplify* meanings, via a complex relationship between taste properties and their expressive functions. So, for example, chicken soup exemplifies care, both because of its cultural significance and its comforting and restorative properties. And foods have enduring cultural meanings and associations: as we'll see in Chapter Four, in much of Western culture, meat eating is associated with man's domination over nature, and is symbolically opposed to femininity. Among the Hua of New Guinea, red soft fruits are treated as feminine (and as having a kind of feminizing effect on men), because of their supposed resemblance to the female anatomy.[21]

---

20   Korsmeyer (2002, pp. 119–20).
21   Meigs (1984, pp. 31–37).

In ritual meals like the Passover Seder, foods stand in for and symbolize emotions and experiences (the bitterness of slavery, the emergence of spring). Chefs give their dishes titles and their menus themes. Anthony Bourdain recounts a meal he had at Thomas Keller's restaurant, The French Laundry, in which Keller, knowing Bourdain to be a heavy smoker who would (at that point in the meal) want a cigarette, sent out a dish called "coffee and cigarettes": a coffee tuile served with a tobacco-infused custard. The dish both represents (its namesake items) and expresses a sense of humor.[22]

5.2 Institutional/Conventional Definitions of Art

Even if we decide food lacks the characteristics of form, expression, and representation, it may fare better according to other definitions of art, such as institutional definitions like this one from the philosopher George Dickie: "A work of art is an artefact which has had conferred upon it the status of candidate for appreciation by the artworld."[23] The term "artworld" comes from Arthur Danto's 1964 paper of the same name; Danto defines it as "an atmosphere of art theory." This definition is more expansive than traditional definitions in that it allows for works that are problematic according to traditional criteria, such as Duchamp's readymades—a series in which the artist installed urinals, shovels, and other everyday objects in art galleries—to count as works of art based on their (eventual) reception into artworlds. But figuring out whether institutional theories can accommodate food raises a tricky question: does the artworld include a "foodworld"? Is there such a thing as "an atmosphere of food theory"? And perhaps a foodworld would not suffice to call food *art*, in which case we are faced with a slightly different question: if the artworld begins to appreciate food, and take it seriously as an object of theory and contemplation, would food therefore be art? This is not a purely hypothetical question. At various times in the past, food has been appreciated and theorized as art. For example, the Italian Futurist movement that lasted from 1910 to the mid-1940s embraced all artistic media, including food; they published a cookbook in which they attacked traditional foods and proclaimed their intention to radically change the practice of eating.[24]

5.3 Aesthetic Definitions

Functional definitions of art invoke the creator's intention to bring about a kind of experience or response in the work's audience—typically, an aesthetic response. Monroe Beardsley offers "an aesthetic definition of art" as "something produced with the

---

22   In Ruhlman (2009).
23   See Dickie (1974).
24   Marinetti (1932/1989).

intention of giving it the capacity to satisfy the aesthetic interest."[25] Here it seems we have found a definition of art that can happily accommodate food! In fact, one criticism of Beardsley's definition is that it is *too* accommodating: my iPhone was carefully designed to satisfy aesthetic interest, as were many of the apps on it. But we wouldn't call my iPhone a work of *art*. (Or would we? Visitors to New York City's Museum of Modern Art will find an entire wing devoted to design, containing items from telephones and toasters to cars and a helicopter.) Beardsley is aware of the expansiveness of his definition and emphasizes that the aesthetic intention needn't be the sole reason for the object's creation—he gives the example of a tale written to teach children a lesson, but which might nonetheless have certain literary features that cause us to classify it as art. Likewise, a dish of food which is intended to achieve critical acclaim, or to nourish, or to entertain guests at a party could still count as art, as long as its creator also intended to achieve certain aesthetic goals.

Others have criticized the definition as being too narrow, citing its exclusion of conceptual art like that of Duchamp, who reportedly chose a urinal to hang on the wall of a gallery precisely because of its lack of aesthetic properties. But Beardsley argues that such criticisms miss the point, because Duchamp's choice of a urinal was intended to force critics to rule the piece out as artwork—it was a comment on the definition of art, rather than a work of art itself. Its intention was not to serve aesthetically but indeed the opposite—to show that we do require aesthetic interest in order to classify something as art. To place an everyday object into the contexts usually associated with art is to comment on art, not to create it.[26] A useful comparison here might be with Alice Waters' Berkeley restaurant, Chez Panisse, where the dessert course might consist of a single peach: perhaps she is best understood, not as claiming that the peach itself is cuisine, but as commenting upon the relationship between raw ingredients and cuisine. Adopting an aesthetic definition of art therefore allows us to explain why some food is art and other food is not, without necessarily confining the label of "art" to high cuisine or expensive restaurants. Anyone can turn food into art with the right intentions—the intention to satisfy our aesthetic interests. This expansiveness has caused controversy as a theory of art, but seems appropriately democratic in the case of food. Still, even if we accept this as a definition of art, some additional criticisms and questions remain, and we'll turn to these next.

6. FOOD AS ART: OBJECTIONS

Our judgments about taste are sensitive to matters of context—perhaps too sensitive to truly count as aesthetic judgment. According to this complaint, food is not really an aesthetic object because our response to food is influenced not just by the

---

25   Beardsley (1983/2004, p. 58).
26   Beardsley (1983/2004, p. 60).

properties of the food in question, but by the contextual features of our experience. It's hard to deny the influence of context on our aesthetic judgments of food, but it's also hard to deny that context plays a role in other aesthetic judgments as well. Our appreciation of a painting or a symphony depends on our inner state and on the external circumstances in which we encounter it. And some contemporary art is aimed specifically at creating a certain context to which each individual will bring their own experiences; consider the performance artist Marina Abramovitch's work at the Museum of Modern Art in New York City, "The Artist Is Present," in which she sits in a gallery, with viewers entering a room and sitting facing her in silence. In this work, the presence of the viewer is part of the very nature of the piece: the piece is predicated on an element of unpredictability, of the viewer's presence; as each viewer leaves the room and a new one enters, the piece changes completely (or remains unchanged?).

A second objection concerns the transience of food. Food is necessarily impermanent. It is organic, so it decays (mostly urban legends about Twinkies notwithstanding[27]); moreover, it's something that we must destroy in order to appreciate.[28] Does this disqualify it as art? This is tricky, because especially in contemporary art, works are not always permanent. Consider land art or site-specific art, which uses natural materials such as clay, dirt, and stone, making it necessarily impermanent. The artist Andy Goldsworthy works with twigs, ice, snow, and mud; he says of his work, "When I make an ephemeral work, when it's finished, that's the moment that it ends, in a way."[29] One might argue that there is nonetheless a crucial difference between these cases and the case of food. First of all, land art doesn't require that the work be destroyed in the very act of appreciating it. Secondly, and relatedly, the transience of food is much more momentary than the transience of the cases cited here—in the case of food, one enjoys it only fleetingly, and it can't be prolonged for more than a few hours, at most—a far cry from the days or weeks or years in the cases above. But this seems to be a difference of degree, rather than kind; to the extent that art decays and is affected by our involvement with it, this is no obstacle to considering food to be art.

7. FOOD: THE ART AND THE ARTWORK

At this point, if we have successfully responded to challenges to food's role as art, it's time to ask: when we ask if food is art, which food are we talking about? We appreciate a painting for being that particular painting (no one travels halfway around

---

27   Roger Bennatti, a science teacher in Maine, has had an unwrapped Twinkie in his classroom since the 1970s, when he placed it there as part of a lesson on food additives. Aside from some dust and light mold on the surface, it's remained intact. Bennatti was interviewed about the project on the August 1, 2005 episode of NPR's *All Things Considered* (Norris 2005).

28   See Telfer (1996), Chapter 3; also Korsmeyer (2002), Chapter 4.

29   Gross (2015).

the world with the intention of seeing a reproduction of the "Mona Lisa"), but we appreciate a performance of a symphony in part because it is a performance of that composition. In the case of food, what is the artwork: a particular dish, an instantiation of that dish, or the recipe for the dish? Or is it all three? This is a question for art (and food) theory but it's also a practical one, since we typically treat a "copy" or reproduction as less valuable than the original work itself.

When thinking of a dish—a risotto, for example—we have, first, the recipe for it. There are also the dishes made according to that recipe on different occasions, using different ingredients and materials, in different kitchens and for different eaters. Which of these is "the dish" may be beside the point; as Telfer points out, we can never recreate a dish exactly.[30] Even if we prepare it precisely according to the original recipe, the ingredients we use will be different (perhaps because the recipe dates from a time when produce and spices were different; perhaps simply because, of necessity, we will be using physically distinct ingredients from the "original"). Telfer doesn't mention equipment—the heat sources, the pots, pans, knives, and cutting boards—but, of course, this will also be different, and so may the eaters themselves.

The question of what constitutes the relevant work of art here—the particular dish or the recipe—is partly a question about the *ontology* of food, that is, what kinds of things exist: is there such a thing as "the" dish, independently of the printed recipe and any particular instance of it? Here a comparison with music and theater is useful. We often talk of a piece of music—Stravinsky's "Rite of Spring," for example—and make claims about the properties of the piece. When we do this, what exactly *is* the object to which these properties belong? It does not seem that we are describing some particular performance, nor are we talking about a printed score. Rather, we seem to be trying to evaluate something over and above these things: the piece that a performance instantiates, which is represented by, but not identical to, the written score. But it seems that we only have access to the work of music through particular performances. This is puzzling: on the one hand, the work is not identical to any particular performance, or even to the totality of its performances. On the other hand, we experience the work by experiencing performances of it, and if there were a sense in which "the music" existed independently of any and all performance, it would be mysterious what exactly this thing was, and how we could evaluate it when we were unable to experience it.[31]

To return to food, we might say that a recipe is like a musical score, and a particular plate of food cooked from that recipe is like a performance. Beyond these two things, there is something else—"the dish"—which exists, perhaps, as a kind of ideal. We can only experience an instantiation of the dish, just as we can only experience a performance of a type of music. We can appraise the execution of a particular

---

30   See Telfer (1996), Chapter 3.
31   See Goodman (1968), Kivy (1983), and Levinson (1980) for discussion.

"performance" of the dish, but we can also critique the dish independently of any particular execution of the recipe: for its balance of flavors and textures, or the way it plays on familiar concepts. The ability to understand and appraise a dish without experiencing it is partly responsible for our enjoyment of reading restaurant reviews and browsing cookbooks for recipes we'll never cook, and underwrites much of our aesthetic discourse about food. One lesson of the previous chapter's discussion of testimony is that we can come to know about the tastes of foods without directly experiencing them ourselves, and if we accept that a dish's aesthetic properties are not solely determined by how it tastes, but include its appearance, we ought to be able to appraise dishes as we appraise musical works—not just by evaluating particular performances, but by evaluating the thing those performances are instances of.

Another argument to the effect that dishes aren't necessarily transient comes from comparing the status of a single dish of food to a work like a painting. In the case of the painting, when that particular object is destroyed, we say that the work of art itself is destroyed; if the "Mona Lisa" is lost to a fire, we might say we still have evidence of what it looks like in the form of prints and reproductions, but we wouldn't say we have a million more "Mona Lisas"—the work is gone. But in the case of a musical work, while the original score may be destroyed, or all recordings of a particular performance lost, we do not say that the work itself has been destroyed. In sculpture, painting, and other visual arts, the physical object is essential to the work; this is not so in the case of music or theater. A *particular* dish of food, like a particular performance of music, is transient—even more so in the case of food, since we cannot "record" it. But the work itself is durable, a fact which has implications for its ownership and its status as a piece of intellectual property.

8. FOOD AS ART, RECIPES AS PROPERTY?

If food is art, this would seem to make chefs the artists, and dishes the artworks. Like all artists, chefs influence one another, making references to other dishes, and borrowing from shared traditions. But can food also be plagiarized? If cooking is a creative act, can credit for the creations be stolen? As cookbooks and food blogs proliferate, the question of when a dish can be considered intellectual property has become increasingly relevant. Flavors themselves—the chemically produced kind— are highly guarded secrets, since, as we've seen, they're big business. And some chefs, especially those working in so-called "molecular gastronomy," have gone on to copyright their innovations: the Chicago chef Homar Cantu held more than 12 patents on his kitchen utensils and creations, including a printer that yielded edible paper made from corn and soy.[32] But what about dishes themselves? Certainly, chefs can

---

32   Rousseau (2012, p. 21).

pay homage to each other. The menu of In Situ, the restaurant in the San Francisco Museum of Modern Art, curates "exhibits" of famous dishes from other restaurants around the world (including the aforementioned WD-50), attributing each to the chef and restaurant where the dish originated. But there have been other cases of chefs imitating dishes without giving credit: an Australian restaurant drew Internet ire when its website posted pictures of dishes that looked exactly like dishes from two top US restaurants. Indeed, complaints about recipe plagiarism—and the lack of protection against it—go back at least as far as the grandfather of French Cuisine himself, Auguste Escoffier, who wrote in his *Guide to Modern Cookery*, "The painter, sculptor, writer, and musician are protected by law. So are inventors. But the chef has absolutely no redress for plagiarism on his work; on the contrary, the more the latter is liked and appreciated, the more will people clamour for his recipes."[33]

Things haven't changed since Escoffier's day; legally, recipes are not subject to copyright protection. The government explains:

> Copyright law does not protect recipes that are mere listings of ingredients. Nor does it protect other mere listings of ingredients such as those found in formulas, compounds, or prescriptions. Copyright protection may, however, extend to substantial literary expression—a description, explanation, or illustration, for example—that accompanies a recipe or formula or to a combination of recipes, as in a cookbook.[34]

So, a recipe in the traditional "list of ingredients and instructions" form won't be legally protected. But if its description contains "substantial literary expression," it might qualify. The idea of expression plays a key role in discussions of food's legal status. If recipes describe, or are statements of fact, they're not entitled to any special consideration; no one can claim intellectual ownership of the facts. I can't copyright the statement that to cook rice, you combine it with water in a 1:2 ratio. That's just a basic piece of information about the world, and no one created or invented it—it's determined by the nature of rice, water, and the interaction between the two. Here we can see a sense in which recipes are more like scientific formulae than like creative inventions. On the other hand, when we reflect on some of the dishes discussed in this chapter—WD-50's eggs benedict, Keller's coffee and cigarettes—they don't fit this description. These dishes reflect an interpretation or expression of an idea, rather than a simple set of instructions. The qualification "expression" is important here, because legally, ideas themselves can't be copyrighted, but their expressions can. So, a plot element of a book isn't subject to legal protection, but the words used to express it might be.

---

33   Escoffier (1907, p. vii).
34   United States Copyright Office (2012).

Whether food has expressive content also determines whether it receives other kinds of legal protection. In the recent case of *Masterpiece Cakeshop v. Colorado Civil Rights Commission*, the US Supreme Court considered whether a baker's refusal to make a wedding cake for a same-sex couple constituted illegal discrimination. In concluding that it did not, the court admitted that, "few persons who have seen a beautiful wedding cake might have thought of its creation as an exercise of protected speech," but in writing their rulings, several judges described it as just that, writing that, "The use of his [the baker's] artistic talents to create a well-recognized symbol that celebrates the beginning of a marriage clearly communicates a message" and that baking a cake (or refusing to bake one) could qualify for "legal protection" as a "sincere act of faith."[35]

Showing that food is (or isn't) legally protected doesn't itself settle the moral question of whether it ought to be: should we consider recipes and dishes to be intellectual property and therefore deserving of some kind of protection against copies? Here we aren't talking about the exact words used on the page of a cookbook (these will be protected as part of a book), but about the concept behind a dish—its ingredients, techniques, and plating. There are a number of justifications for considering a person's ideas or creations to belong to that person and to protect those ideas from being copied by someone else. The first is that protecting people's creations—their intellectual property—encourages creativity and innovation. Therefore, rules against copying without attribution benefit everyone. Whether this sort of argument succeeds in the case of food and recipes is another question. On the one hand, it may be that everyone benefits when a new dish or recipe is invented, but few people will be likely to try it. On the other hand, if the dish is widely copied, more people will have a chance to experience it, but people may be less likely to introduce techniques and products if they know they're unlikely to receive credit—and profit—from it. Whether this is true is an empirical question, of course, but chefs themselves (including Homar Cantu) have made similar arguments, pointing out that innovations in cooking techniques have potential to help alleviate hunger, food waste, and other problems, but that chefs will only pursue these innovations if there is a financial reward.[36]

The question of who owns a recipe becomes yet more complex when we consider that recipes are also tied to, and express the beliefs and values of, a culture or tradition. Food has always traversed national boundaries. Dishes travel from one place to another and are shaped by their journeys; contact between cultures yields contact between cuisines. The *taco al pastor* was an innovation brought by Lebanese immigrants to Mexico; many of the most popular Indian and Chinese dishes in Western countries, such as General Tso's chicken and chicken *tikka masala*, are really adaptations for Western palates. And there are certain elements that are virtually universal:

35 *Masterpiece Cake Shop, Ltd. v. Colorado* (2018).
36 See Wells (2006).

noodles, dumplings, roast meat. But cultures also claim certain dishes or foods as their own possessions, tied to a geographic region or group of people. Sometimes this is for economic reasons: if the title "Champagne" is prestigious and valuable, it makes sense to claim ownership of it and restrict its use. Allowing anyone to use the term diminishes its prestige. But there are also reasons having to do with cultural pride and identity.

9. CUISINE AND CULTURAL APPROPRIATION

The term "cultural appropriation" refers to the use of certain styles, art forms, experiences, or practices characteristic of one culture by members of another culture. Whether cultural appropriation is always wrong or inappropriate is a controversial question; some authors argue that it is wrong because it takes away the appropriated group's means of expression, while other authors argue that it is wrong when a dominant group appropriates the culture of a marginalized group.[37] Most of the attention paid thus far to cultural appropriation has focused on cases where a writer adopts the perspective of a narrator from a marginalized group (not their own), or where fashion designers have adopted traditional patterns or styles from indigenous groups. But can food be appropriated too?

The philosopher James Young distinguishes several types of cultural appropriation, depending on what is being appropriated: objects (such as a work of art or artifact), styles and motifs, content (such as a song or story), subject or voice (when one culture borrows the experiences or narratives of another).

We can see all of these types of appropriation in food and cooking. The adoption of certain types of artifacts and ingredients from one culture by another is widespread: many Mexican restaurants in the US serve guacamole in *molcajetes*, the Mexican version of a mortar and pestle, and the tool has become popular in American home kitchens. In the 1990s, banana leaves began to appear on menus in the West, wrapped around steamed fish or rice. This is also an example of the third of Young's types, *style* appropriation: the technique of wrapping and steaming in banana leaves is traditional in Southeast Asian cuisines. Allegations of appropriation have also been raised in contexts where chefs cook recipes and cuisines of other cultures. Here we might identify both the recipe itself and a chef's claim to authority or expertise about a culture—the claim to speak on behalf of that culture's cuisine—as the things being appropriated. To take the headline of a recent magazine article on the topic, it's what happens "when chefs become famous cooking other cultures' food."[38]

---

37   The discussion here is drawn largely from Chapter 1 of Young's *Cultural Appropriation and the Arts* (2010); see also Young (2005) and Matthes (2016).

38   Godoy & Chow (2016).

One objection is that appropriation is a kind of theft, either of particular objects or of intellectual property. Since food and ingredients are rarely *completely* singular or unique, theft in cases of food appropriation is more likely to involve theft of intellectual property: of the use of an ingredient, technique, or of a specific recipe. This argument is complicated by the question of who owns a recipe, technique, or cuisine. In the case of objects themselves, collective ownership is a complex issue: can a culture own an artifact? The question is even thornier when the possession in question is not a clearly defined item but a changing, evolving practice such as cooking. Two other objections to appropriation are that it harms the culture appropriated, and that it causes offense to that culture. How might culinary appropriation harm or offend the cultures appropriated from? One possibility involves the way in which expertise and economic benefits accrue to chefs, restaurant owners, and other culinary professionals: if appropriation leads members of one culture to profit from the dishes, cuisines, or techniques of another, the dominant culture might seem to be engaging in a kind of cultural appropriation that disenfranchises and even colonizes the culture appropriated from, claiming cultural (culinary) property as their own.

Young characterizes cultures—both appropriated and appropriating—in terms of "insiders" and "outsiders." But individuals move between cultures and take their foods with them, and cuisines are fluid, too. The very definition of a cuisine is challenging: cuisines are made up of dishes and techniques, but they're also cultural constructions that change over time and across space and time. The anthropologist Sidney Mintz notes that, "ethnicity, like nationhood, is also imagined ... and associated cuisines may be imagined, too. Once imagined, such cuisines provide added concreteness to the idea of national or ethnic identity."[39] The idea is not that cuisine, ethnicity, and nations are fictions, but that, like food itself, they are partly constructions, and that they reinforce one another: we construct our cuisine out of our national and ethnic identity, but that identity is itself reinforced by our cuisine. This may be more readily observed in other countries—several scholars have expressed doubt that there exists any such thing as "American" cuisine, partly because the country is so geographically big, partly because it's so culturally diverse, and partly due to its lack of history and tradition. Perhaps this explains why so much of our cuisine does seem to be borrowed and modified from other traditions.

The ingredients and dishes we associate with various nations and cultures are often (if not always) the product of exchange and amalgamation. Thus, the difference between assimilation and appropriation might not always be clear: when the British adapt chicken *tikka masala* and other Indian dishes, resulting in a new version of Indian cuisine, is this appropriation? It certainly fits one condition: a dominant group adopting the styles or traditions of a marginalized group. Indeed, the fusing of cuisines often follows patterns of colonialization and imperialism: tomatoes, so

---

39   Mintz & DuBois (2002).

closely associated with Italian cuisine, originated in Mexico; many historians argue that pasta was brought back to Europe from China by Marco Polo. Whether this necessarily makes it wrong is a tricky question, and one we won't be able to do justice to here. But we can note that one problem with cultural appropriation is that it often misrepresents cuisines, distorting what people view as "authentic" representations. A second, related problem with cultural appropriation is that by allowing members of one culture to speak on behalf of another, it affects whom we see as representatives of that culture, and who we view as possessing expertise in the relevant area. In the case of cooking and cuisine, high-end and expensive restaurants have typically been the domain of American or European men, while so-called ethnic restaurants are viewed as less prestigious. "Ethnic" restaurants (the term itself is problematic—every cuisine is ethnic, and the term runs together a wide and diverse array of cuisines by dubbing them "other") are unable to charge as much money as their Western counterparts; there are, in London and New York City, a few high-end Indian, Mexican, and Chinese restaurants (and sushi is also an exception to this rule), but for the most part these cuisines are viewed as the domain of inexpensive dinners, takeout and delivery, or they are sought out as opportunities to have "authentic" cultural experiences. The philosopher Lisa Heldke has written self-critically about her "penchant for cooking and eating ethnic foods":

> The unflattering name I chose for my activities was "cultural food colonialism," which made me your basic colonizer. As I saw it, my adventure eating was motivated by an attitude that bore an uncomfortable resemblance to the various ideologies of western colonialism.... I was motivated by a desire to have contact with and to somehow own an experience of an Exotic Other to make myself more interesting.[40]

The food studies scholar Krishnendu Ray has argued that certain cuisines face a dilemma when they arrive in the West: they can be perceived as authentic, or as expensive, but not both, because Americans equate expense with inauthenticity. He notes that

> astonishingly, only 3 Chinese restaurants and 7 Mexican restaurants are counted by Zagat among the top restaurants in the USA in 2014, compared to 59 Japanese, 84 French, 85 Italian, and 139 American. There is not one Chinese or Mexican restaurant among the top in Los Angeles, San Francisco, New York, or even San Antonio.[41]

---

40   Heldke (2001, pp. 77–78).
41   Ray (2016, p. 104).

Where these cuisines are served in high-end restaurants in US cities, the chefs are often American. Some critics object to the attention paid to American chefs who study in Thailand, or Mexico, and bring the cuisine back to restaurants in New York City and Portland, arguing that these chefs are the (unwitting, perhaps) beneficiaries of systemic discrimination that allows them to receive business loans, investments, and media attention where minority chefs might not. As Ray notes, the career paths followed by these chefs

> are usually unavailable to cooks confined to the "ethnic" corner of the field, who have to trade more in the domain of authenticity than the realm of innovation in haute cuisine.... The chef occupies the heights of the culinary field in the USA today, just as the ethnic cook inhabits the bottom rungs of the hierarchy.[42]

We will talk more about the ways in which food and issues of social justice interact in the final chapters of this book, and the reader might at this point be thinking that we have gone quite far afield from our discussion of aesthetics! But the point of this discussion has been to draw attention to the fact that the ways we assign both aesthetic and economic value to food, and the ways we judge which foods are properly appreciated as works of art and which as authentic representation of ethnic cuisines, are themselves normative exercises, subject to biases and prejudices. Food reflects our values, for better or worse; to treat something as food is to assign it a certain normative status. In the next few chapters, we will examine the ethics of what we eat, looking at the moral consequences of our food choices from various philosophical perspectives.

CONCLUSION: FOOD AS ART, AND AS CULTURAL ARTIFACT

Our experiences of food range from the everyday to the aesthetic; in this, food is like many of the other material objects we encounter in our daily lives. But food is also something we need and can't do without, so we engage with it both as art and as a kind of artifact: a useful, practical object. Like other art forms, food is a way of expressing and engaging symbolic values, emotions, and rituals; like other art forms, food is something we assign both cultural and monetary value to. I hope I have convinced the reader that food is worthy of being considered art, but, if not, I have at least shown that we can have genuine aesthetic experiences of food. And the debate about whether food can ever be art shows that categories like art—and food

---

42   Ray (2016, p. 179).

itself—are not fixed or given, but constantly negotiated. To return to the theme with which we began this section of the book, these categories are socially constructed. In the next section, we'll turn from aesthetic value to moral value, examining the ethical implications of our food choices. As we'll see, there are no simple answers here either, but in the case of moral value at least, we must justify our choices to others—unlike matters of art and beauty, the ethics of eating cannot be left up to personal taste.

Chapter Four

THE
ETHICS
OF
EATING
ANIMALS

INTRODUCTION

Is it morally permissible to eat animals? In this chapter and the next we'll look at various answers to this question. The arguments in this chapter approach the issue from the perspective of animal ethics and our moral obligations to animals: in eating meat, do we wrong animals? If so, how and why? These are not the only considerations relevant to whether or not we ought to eat meat, though, and the next chapter will address some of the environmental impacts of animal agriculture. Our survey of the various philosophical objections to eating meat will also serve as an introduction to the ethical theories we'll use in the remainder of the book.

The discussion in this chapter isn't conducted explicitly in the language of veganism and vegetarianism. We will engage in a discussion of these terms, and their significance for food ethics, at the end of the book. For now, our focus will be more specifically on the circumstances—if any—in which it's morally permissible to eat animals. Most readers already know that a vegetarian is someone who does not eat animal flesh and a vegan is someone who doesn't eat or use animal products (including eggs and dairy, usually honey and leather, and sometimes wool and other animal fibers). I encourage the reader to think about, and work through, the implications of the views discussed below for the question "Should we be vegan?" but the aim of this chapter is not to defend a single principle by which to guide our food choice. Rather, it's to illuminate the various challenges and complications that arise as we try to arrive at such a principle.

We'll begin by looking at two moral theories, both of which think it's wrong to eat animals, but for very different reasons. The first argues that it is wrong because it causes animal suffering. The claims that suffering is bad and that we oughtn't cause unnecessary suffering are uncontroversial; most of us do not need philosophical argument to convince us of the badness of pain, and few of us would be able to watch an animal suffer or die without significant psychological distress. Why, then, do we continue to eat meat? After introducing and discussing the argument from suffering and examining some philosophical views about the relationship between suffering and moral obligation, we'll look at how, exactly, the act of eating meat contributes to the suffering of animals. As we'll see, certain types of animal agriculture do clearly cause animals to suffer. But other cases are less clear; philosophers argue over whether there is really any such thing as "happy meat." Even if such a thing is possible, the question remains whether we, as consumers, could ever be in an epistemic position to know that we were eating this kind of meat. We'll also look at arguments that suffering, while bad, is not the fundamental wrong of eating animals: using animals for food involves reducing living, sentient beings to objects consumed for our pleasure. No alteration to the way we treat the animals while they're living can change the fact that ultimately, we will kill them and eat them. After contrasting these two approaches, we'll look at some alternatives: feminist care ethics offers us a way of understanding our relationship to animals in terms of our feelings of sympathy and empathy; pluralist approaches acknowledge a number of diverse and competing moral claims and values at work in our relationship with animals.

1. EATING ANIMALS: THE PROBLEM OF SUFFERING

Virtually everyone agrees that pain and suffering are bad. This is such a fundamental observation that someone who didn't understand the badness of suffering would, it seems, fail to possess the very concept of suffering itself. If eating animals causes unnecessary suffering, do we really need a philosophical argument to convince us that it's morally wrong? It seems we could simply point out the link between food choices and animal suffering and thereby convince people that it's wrong to eat animals. For example, the philosopher Mylan Engel gives an argument for veganism with the following premises:

1. Other things being equal, a world with less pain and suffering is better than a world with more pain and suffering.

2. A world with less unnecessary suffering is better than a world with more unnecessary suffering.

3. Unnecessary cruelty is wrong and prima facie should not be supported or encouraged.

4. We ought to take steps to make the world a better place. Or at least we ought to do what we reasonably can to avoid making the world a worse place.

5. A morally good person will take steps to make the world a better place and even stronger steps to avoid making the world a worse place.

6. Even a minimally decent person would take steps to help reduce the amount of unnecessary pain and suffering in the world, if she could do so with very little effort.

7. I am a morally good person.

8. I am at least a minimally decent person.

9. I am the sort of person who certainly would take steps to help reduce the amount of pain and suffering in the world, if I could do so with very little effort.

10. Many nonhuman animals (certainly all vertebrates) are capable of feeling pain.

11. It is morally wrong to cause an animal unnecessary pain or suffering.

12. It is morally wrong and despicable to treat animals inhumanely for no good reason.

13. We ought to euthanize untreatably injured, suffering animals to put them out of their misery whenever feasible.

14. Other things being equal, it is worse to kill a conscious sentient animal than it is to kill a plant.

15. We have a duty to help preserve the environment for future generations (at least for future human generations).

16. One ought to minimize one's contribution toward environmental degradation, especially in those ways requiring minimal effort on one's part.[1]

Engel argues that there is nothing controversial about these premises—most if not all people already endorse them, even if they don't realize it. And it follows, from these premises and various facts about the practice of raising animals for food, that eating animal products is morally wrong, "regardless of your views on speciesism, animal equality, and animal rights."

It seems our work here is done: if we can advance an argument against consuming animal products that doesn't depend on a controversial philosophical theory, why

---

1   Engel (2000, pp. 888–89).

not rest content with that argument? What work is left for moral theory to do, when we already hold the moral convictions on which the argument is based?

Perhaps we don't need a particular moral theory to see that there are reasons not to eat animals. But philosophical argument can nonetheless be useful here, because it allows us to examine the exact nature of the link between the badness of suffering and the moral wrongness of eating meat. It also helps answer questions about how we should understand the causal role of our own food choices in the context of a system as vast and complex as current industrial animal agriculture. And competing views about the moral status of animals, and our obligations to them, offer different prescriptions about how we ought to reform our current food system.

2. UTILITARIANISM

Utilitarianism is the view that we ought to act in such a way as to bring about the greatest balance of pleasure over pain: the rightness and wrongness of actions is measured by the amount of pleasure and pain they create. Utilitarianism is a form of *consequentialism*, a family of views that assess the morality of actions in terms of their consequences. For consequentialists, the right action is the one that brings about the best outcome. Utilitarianism is also *hedonistic*. For the utilitarian, the only things that are intrinsically valuable are pleasure and pain; all other states of affairs have value only insofar as they contribute to, or detract from, these states. In addition to being hedonistic and consequentialist, utilitarianism is *aggregative* and *impartial*. Aggregative, because it assesses actions by taking into account their consequences for all affected, and looks at the total balance of pleasure and pain that results from the act. Impartial, because it weights everyone's pain and pleasure equally. Mill, one of the earliest utilitarians, explains, "As between his own happiness and that of others, utilitarianism requires him to be as strictly impartial as a disinterested and benevolent spectator."[2] The fact that an act would bring lots of pleasure at the expense of a small amount of pain is reason to perform that act; the fact that the pleasure in question belongs to you and the pain to me is no reason not to. Everyone's pleasure and pain gets equal weight, regardless of what other characteristics they might have, and the process of aggregating pain and pleasure erases other morally irrelevant distinctions between individuals.

Partly because of these two features, utilitarianism is historically associated with advocating on behalf of oppressed and disenfranchised groups. Early utilitarians were actively involved in abolition and the women's rights movement. And they recognized that if the basis for moral rightness or wrongness is pleasure and pain, there could be no grounds for refusing to extend moral consideration to all beings capable

---

2   Mill (1879/2009, pp. 31–32).

of experiencing those states. As the founder of utilitarianism, Bentham, famously wrote:

> The day has been, I grieve it to say in many places it is not yet past, in which the greater part of the species, under the denomination of slaves, have been treated by the law exactly upon the same footing as ... the inferior races of animals are still. The day *may* come, when the rest of the animal creation may acquire those rights which never could have been withholden from them but by the hand of tyranny. The French have already discovered that the blackness of skin is no reason why a human being should be abandoned without redress to the caprice of a tormentor. It may come one day to be recognized, that the number of legs, the villosity of the skin, or the termination of the *os sacrum*, are reasons equally insufficient for abandoning a sensitive being to the same fate. What else is it that should trace the insuperable line? Is it the faculty of reason, or perhaps, the faculty of discourse? But a full-grown horse or dog, is beyond comparison a more rational, as well as a more conversible animal, than an infant of a day, or a week, or even a month old. But suppose it were otherwise, what would it avail? The question is not, Can they reason? nor, Can they talk? but, Can they suffer?[3]

The capacity to feel pleasure and pain is also known as *sentience*, and for the utilitarian, it is sentience that is the morally relevant feature of an individual. If an individual is sentient, we must take its suffering into account; since animals are sentient, we must include them in our moral calculations. However, Bentham explains in the same passage that this doesn't mean it's wrong to *eat* animals:

> There is very good reason why we should be suffered to eat such of them [non-human animals] as we like to eat: we are the better for it, and they are never the worse. They have none of those long-protracted anticipations of future misery that we have. The death they suffer at our hands commonly is, and always may be, a speedier, and by that means a less painful one, than that which would await them in the inevitable course of nature.[4]

The justification he offers here is instructive, because it acknowledges that our differences with animals are morally relevant insofar as they contribute to our ability to experience suffering differently: because we can anticipate future suffering, and be made worse-off by it, we would suffer from being used for food. Because animals don't have this capacity, Bentham claims, they don't suffer from being used in this

---

3   Bentham (1780/1970, Chapter XVII fn b/p. 283).
4   Bentham (1780/1970, Chapter XVII fn b/p. 283).

way. And we can offer animals a speedy and relatively painless death. So, it would seem that we can justify eating animals—under some conditions. This highlights the fact that, for utilitarians, the rightness or wrongness of an act is contingent on its consequences, and not determined by the nature of the act itself. So, as our methods of raising animals for food change, so too does the moral permissibility of eating meat. We can't ask about the morality of eating animals without knowing the practices involved, so before proceeding further, it's worth spending a moment to discuss exactly what we mean when we talk about factory farming.

2.1 Factory Farming: Some Facts and Figures

First, there are the staggering numbers involved. In the first six months of 2017 alone, over five billion chickens were killed in the US.[5] Around 30 million cows and 100 million pigs are killed for food each year.[6] And the vast majority of these animals spend their lives in cramped conditions, with little concern given for their welfare: they have almost no freedom of movement and spend little time outdoors. Sows are subjected to confinement in "gestation crates" so small they can't move (to prevent them from crushing their piglets) or lie on their sides. Partly as a result of this confinement and crowding, animals are subjected to painful medical procedures, and subject to diseases and other medical problems—chickens whose bones break because they grow so heavy so fast that their frames can't sustain their weight; pigs whose tails must be docked so that they won't be bitten off by other pigs in their crowded quarters. After enduring these conditions, the animals are transported to the slaughterhouses where they're killed. This can mean a long journey in a crowded truck where animals may or may not have access to food and water. Since the passage of the 1978 Humane Slaughter Act, the law requires that "livestock must be slaughtered in a humane manner to prevent needless suffering." This means that, in practice, cows, pigs, and sheep are stunned first (by a bolt to the head, or an electric shock) so that they're unconscious when they die; in reality, animals sometimes survive this initial stunning and are conscious when their throats are cut.[7] Chickens and other poultry aren't covered by the humane slaughter act, but are typically stunned before their throats are cut. When one multiplies this suffering by the numbers given above, we have billions of animals each year living painful lives and experiencing painful deaths. To outweigh this suffering, meat eaters would have to experience very high levels of

---

5   See United States Department of Agriculture (2016b).

6   According to the United States Department of Agriculture's livestock slaughter summary report (2016a), the numbers for 2016 were 30.6 million cattle and 118.2 million hogs.

7   Singer & Mason (2006) offer a comprehensive overview of the conditions under which animals are raised and killed for food.

pleasure—pleasure that could only be gotten from eating meat. And this seems false, empirically. While we may sometimes get pleasure from eating steak, or ribs, or duck breast, much of the meat eaten every day goes unnoticed and unremarked upon, and could be replaced with a meat substitute without significant loss of pleasure—especially as meat substitutes become more and more similar to meat itself. If this is true then, at least in many cases, the pleasure humans experience when eating animals does not outweigh the suffering experienced by animals raised for food.

It may not even be necessary to establish that animal suffering outweighs the amount of human pleasure—perhaps we only need to show that eating animals causes significant amounts of pain. Richard Ryder coins the term "painism" to describe the view that

> the pains and pleasures of each sentient individual are calculated, but they cannot be totaled across individuals. So it may be justifiable to cause or tolerate mild pain for one individual in order to reduce the greater pain of another individual, but it is never permissible to add up the pains or pleasures of several individuals in such calculations. A better way to rate the badness of a situation ... is by the quantity of pain experienced by the most affected sufferer. The suffering of each individual really means something, whereas totals of sufferings across individuals are meaningless.[8]

The most significant difference between painism and utilitarianism is that painism is not aggregative, so it avoids a kind of counterexample to utilitarianism in which the utilitarian is forced to say that it's right to inflict gross suffering on a single individual in order to bring moderate pleasure to a large number of others. For example (to take a case from Ryder), suppose 20 police officers are investigating a crime and can close the case immediately by torturing a suspect's young child. Closing the case will allow the police officers to spend the weekend with their families, thereby creating 10 units of pleasure for each police officer, but will cause 100 units of pain to the child. Ryder objects to the fact that the utilitarian seems forced to condone, or even prescribe, the torture; this kind of case shows the problems raised by aggregating across individuals. The painist therefore avoids the worries raised above about whether the aggregate pleasure brought about by the practice of eating meat outweighs animal suffering. The question is no longer even an empirical one; regardless of how much human pleasure is involved, the relevant quantity is the suffering of each individual animal, not the pleasure of all humans.

---

8   Ryder (2009, p. 87).

2.2 Animal Suffering and the Causal Impotence Objection

On both the utilitarian and the painist views, causing animal suffering is bad. But what remains to be shown is that eating meat *causes* unnecessary animal suffering. It might seem obvious that it does: if no one ate meat, then animals would not be raised for food, and the factory farming processes described in the previous paragraph would not exist, nor would animal suffering. So, if we are asking whether the widespread cultural *practice* of eating meat causes unnecessary suffering, the answer is a straightforward "yes." But it's a different question whether my (or your) individual choice causes unnecessary suffering: how can a single individual act make a difference to such a widespread, pervasive, and entrenched practice as animal agriculture? Given the millions and billions of animals killed each year, it seems unlikely that one person's abstinence from consuming animal products could have any impact on the number of animals raised and killed for food. In addition to the question of scale, there is the question of causality. Most of us do not raise and kill our own animals, so the meat we consume is that of animals who have already been killed. In that case, whether or not I buy and eat a particular steak can't make any difference to the suffering of the animal from which it came, because that specific animal has already been killed.

One response is to note that even if there's only a small chance my individual choice will make a difference, the amount of suffering I could prevent is significant enough to warrant taking that chance. And while it's true that no single act of refraining from eating meat can be correlated with a single animal life saved, our choices can affect the number of animals raised and killed for food in the future. This may be so even if there is only a possibility of having an effect. Consider the following hypothetical (but not far-fetched) scenario:

> For each group of 10,000 who give up chicken, a quarter of a million fewer chickens are bred per year. It appears, then, that if you give up eating chicken, you have only a one in ten thousand chance of making any difference to the lives of chickens, unless it is certain that fewer than 10,000 people will ever give up eating chicken, in which case you have no chance. Isn't a one in ten thousand chance small enough to render your continued consumption of chicken blameless? Not at all. While the chance that your behavior is harmful may be small, the harm that is risked is enormous. The larger the numbers needed to make a difference to chicken production, the larger the difference such numbers would make. A one in ten thousand chance of saving 250,000 chickens per year [based on the assumption that the average meat-eater consumes 25 chickens per year] from excruciating lives is morally and mathematically equivalent to the certainty of saving 25 chickens per year.[9]

---

9   Norcross (2004, p. 233).

Given that through the relatively minor sacrifice of foregoing meat (or just reducing my consumption from, say, five to two times a week) I will possibly prevent massive suffering on the part of even two or three animals, I ought to do so. Even if my choice on its own has no effect on the number of animals killed for food, it may influence others to alter their behavior, either by influencing them to give up meat, or less directly by influencing them to make meatless meal options available, which in turn influences others' attitudes towards vegetarianism and veganism.

Responding to this objection also offers us an opportunity to return to the classical utilitarian views of Bentham and Mill. Both these authors describe utilitarianism as the view that acts are right or wrong in virtue of their *tendency* to produce pleasure or pain. In other words, it needn't be the case that we can identify, on a strict case-by-case basis, the individual act as producing more pain than pleasure (or vice-versa); if what matters is some sort of overall assessment of how conducive an act is to pleasure or pain, we can say that the act is wrong even if on a particular occasion it doesn't actually produce the typical result. Using this understanding of the view, we could say that eating meat has a tendency to produce greater pain than pleasure, since the act tends to cause animal suffering. Alternatively, we might say that refraining from eating meat tends to reduce suffering, even if we can't point to a specific instance of reduced suffering that's the result of a specific act of refraining from eating meat.

2.3 Critiques of the Argument from Suffering: Happy Meat, Engineered Animals?

Our discussion so far has focused on the wrongness of eating meat produced by factory farming; we've been arguing that eating this type of meat is wrong because of the suffering involved. (It's worth noting again that factory farming might be wrong for other reasons as well, including that it may cause human suffering, a point we'll take up in the chapters to come.) However, this is not the only way to eat animals; not all meat or animal products are produced on factory farms. Some farmers do produce meat, eggs, and dairy products from animals that spend most of their lives outdoors, grazing on grass. If these animals' lives aren't characterized by suffering—if they're actually enjoyable—and if their deaths are painless, then what if anything is wrong with eating them?

This question illustrates our earlier point about the contingency of the utilitarian objection to eating meat, a contingency that is a feature of most consequentialist views. Because the moral wrongness of eating meat is a feature of consequences the practice has—namely, causing animal suffering—if we can avoid these consequences, the act is no longer wrong. Indeed, one might even argue that if these animals enjoy their lives, then eating meat is actually a good thing, since the animals would not exist, and therefore would not experience this pleasure, were it not for our decision to raise and then eat them.

However, whether such a scenario is ever really possible is controversial. First, most animals raised for food live much shorter lives than they would otherwise. If their lives are pleasurable, then cutting them short is a bad thing, insofar as it reduces the overall amount of pleasure they experience. And regardless of how much space to roam or grass to graze on we offer animals, practices like dairy farming always involve some degree of stress to animals, since calves must be weaned early from their mothers, and the milk that would ordinarily be given to their calves is then mechanically taken from the mothers twice a day. And because of federal regulations, in the United States, meat sold commercially cannot be slaughtered or processed on a farm, but must be taken to a federally inspected slaughterhouse, which means that most animals end their lives by undergoing a stressful and frightening trip in a truck to a place where they may be painfully killed.[10] But what if we could kill animals painlessly, on the farms where they lived out their long lives?[11] Would this make a difference to the ethics of eating meat? It seems that it must, but the utilitarian could respond that very few consumers, if any, are able to purchase meat produced this way. Epistemic concerns about the transparency of meat labeling arise because terms such as "grass fed" and "natural," along with pictures of cows roaming freely through bucolic pastures, are often used to suggest a kind of happy animal, but there is no relationship between the terms and pictures and the actual conditions under which the animal lives out most of its life. Furthermore, meat produced by small farms is both difficult to find and expensive, meaning that the ability to eat ethically becomes a commodity in itself. (This is related to concerns raised in Chapter Two about the transparency, or lack thereof, of food labeling, but in this case the information being obscured is not just about the content of the package, but its moral status.)

A very different approach would be to eliminate the problem of animal suffering not by altering farming practices to better accommodate the nature and needs of animals, but by altering the animals themselves. For example, we might genetically alter animals to better withstand certain conditions, or to eliminate the need for certain painful procedures. Cattle might be genetically altered to eliminate the need for dehorning. Chickens bred to be blind would be more docile, potentially eliminating the need for painful debeaking procedures. Going even further, we might one day be able to alter animals' brains so as to eliminate the capacity to experience certain kinds of pain and stress, by altering the neural pathways that allow for the experience

---

10   This is true for cattle, goats, pigs, and sheep; for poultry, it depends on how many animals are being slaughtered—if it's more than 20,000, the slaughter must take place in a federally inspected facility. For a helpful explanation and diagram, see Harris & Tan (2004).

11   In fact, the Processing Revival and Interstate Meat Exemption Act, currently before Congress, would allow states to decide for themselves how to regulate the slaughter of animals whose meat is sold in-state. Perhaps unsurprisingly, the act has faced significant opposition from large meat processors.

of pain, or eliminating the hormones associated with stress responses.[12] We might even produce animals with no brains whatsoever: as early as the nineteenth century, scientists were experimenting with removing the cerebellum from birds; it's not a stretch, then, to think that we might soon be able to produce birds that lacked the brain structures to maintain conscious experience.

These scenarios—about which we'll say more when we discuss GMOs in Chapter Six—can be read either as suggestions to make factory farming more palatable or as counterexamples to the argument from suffering. It seems that by fundamentally altering the nature of animals and their conscious experience, we do them some wrong. It's not obvious how to explain the nature of this wrong in utilitarian terms, though. It's possible that animals will have to suffer in the process of developing and perfecting the sorts of alterations discussed above; perhaps the experiments needed to figure out whether animals' capacity to feel pain will involve a certain amount of suffering. But this is a relatively insignificant amount of pain compared to the amount we will prevent once the technology is fully developed. And yet many people still have the intuition that altering animals' nature in this way is wrong, even if it doesn't cause any pain at all. If this intuition is correct, then utilitarianism cannot account for the wrong we do animals by eating them. Even if we remove suffering from the equation, eating animals is still wrong. That's not to say that causing unnecessary suffering *isn't* wrong—few people would want to deny that it is. But the next argument we'll look at claims that the wrongness of eating animals is not contingent on the way animals are raised or killed, but is an intrinsic aspect of eating animals.

3. DEONTOLOGICAL OBJECTIONS TO EATING ANIMALS

A second way of explaining what's wrong with eating animals is associated with a family of philosoph   ical views known as *deontology*. These views are best understood by contrasting them with consequentialism: whereas consequentialism evaluates actions in terms of their outcomes, deontological views evaluate them in terms of the principle or rule with which the act accords or from which it comes. The views agree on the rightness and wrongness of many actions (and disagree about others), but differ on the property that makes the act right or wrong. So, a utilitarian might explain the wrongness of theft in terms of the unhappiness it causes the victim; a deontologist would point to the fact that it violates a rule such as "do not steal," or to the fact that it violates an individual's right to property. There are a number of views that fall under the umbrella of deontology, and not all of them agree on our obligations to animals. Kant, the philosopher most commonly associated with the view,

---

12   See Shriver (2009) and Thompson (1997).

rejected the idea that humans have any moral obligations to animals. Kant based his argument on the claim that humans have rationality, self-awareness, and understanding—qualities which render us "altogether different in rank and dignity from *things*, such as irrational animals, which we can dispose of as we please."[13]

Here we'll discuss two of the most influential contemporary deontological approaches to the question of how to treat animals: rights views and contractarian views. Both are deontological in that they maintain that it is the principle or process that determines an act, rather than its outcome, which makes it morally right or wrong. But, as we will see, they have different answers to the question of whether it is wrong to eat animals and why.

3.1 Animal Rights

Animal rights views maintain that our obligations to animals are not simply a matter of pain and pleasure. They don't deny that suffering is bad, but they deny that this is the fundamental wrong involved in eating animals. Because animals are living, experiencing subjects of a life, killing and eating them is wrong because it deprives them of their right to life and objectifies and disrespects them. It is a violation of their rights, but it is also a violation of the respect we owe them as fellow morally significant beings. To treat animals as food is to use them as things, whereas, since animals are moral subjects, we ought instead to treat them as worthy of moral consideration in their own right. Animals have inherent moral value as living things, according to rights views; their value is not dependent on us, nor reducible to our feelings about or interests in them.

Animal rights proponents often argue in favor of their view by pointing out the flaws in the alternatives. As we saw above, utilitarianism seems unable to account for the intuition that there is something wrong with treating animals as mere objects and reducing them to lumps of flesh, even if doing so eliminates any pain or suffering. It seems that there is some additional obligation we have to animals, over and above the obligation not to cause them pain, which is violated when we modify their nature in order to make them more convenient to us. (One might object that we've been doing this since we first began domesticating animals, a point we'll discuss further in Chapter Six.)

We invoke the language of rights to explain this intuition: that what is wrong with such modifications is that they reduce a living creature with its own nature, interests, and desires to a mere object to be used as a resource. One way to explain this point is in terms of the concept of *integrity*. The idea of "bodily integrity," which is discussed in more detail in Chapter Six, is that our bodies should be free from

---

13   Kant (1798/1974, 7: 127).

unnecessary alteration; if there is a right to bodily integrity, it is a right against inter-ference with the shape, form, and features of our bodies. Altering animals' bodies, whether in the form of docking pigs' tails, dehorning cattle, or modifying their genome itself, is a violation of this right. While we can (arguably) justify violations in cases where it significantly benefits the animal—as when we perform surgery to remove a tumor, or an abscess—we can't justify violations on the grounds that they benefit *us*. Infringing on the bodily integrity of creatures that can't give their consent has to be justified with reference to their welfare, not our convenience.

Bodily integrity is just one of the rights assigned to animals; others include a right to life, a right to liberty, and a right not to be harmed or used as a means. While the rights view is sometimes characterized as granting animals *equal* rights, it would be a caricature of the view to portray it as advocating, say, animals' right to vote. Rather, most rights theorists argue that animals have equal moral *standing* and that therefore their rights must be granted equal importance to human rights. The claim is not that animal rights are equal in content, but in priority, because they share the characteristics that place all humans on equal moral footing. Tom Regan explains,

> The really crucial, the basic similarity, is simply this; *we are each of us the expe-riencing subject of a life, each of us a conscious creature having an individual welfare that has importance to us whatever our usefulness to others* ... all these dimensions of our life, including our pleasure and our pain, our enjoyment and suffering, our satisfaction and frustration, our continued existence or our untimely death—all make a difference to the quality of our lives as lived, as experienced by us as individuals. As the same is true of those animals who concern us ... they too must be viewed as the experiencing subjects of a life with inherent value of their own.[14]

One might worry that the rights view is nonetheless unacceptably strong, because it is inevitable that animal rights and human rights will conflict, and when they do, we must prioritize human rights. Defending this claim requires some explanation of why we should assign greater priority to humans and their rights: what's morally spe-cial about being human? The next few sections will examine this question in greater detail. We'll begin by looking at a form of deontological view on which participa-tion in morality requires a kind of rationality that only humans possess, in which case the rights of animals are indirect, at best; they exist only insofar as humans choose to grant and defend them. We'll then look at an important objection to such views: that they exclude too many creatures (including some humans) from the moral community. Lastly, we'll look at alternatives to consequentialist and deontological approaches to animal ethics.

---

14   Regan (1985, p. 24).

3.2 Contractarianism and the Moral Status of Animals

According to contractarian theories, morality consists of a set of rules or principles that would be arrived at by rational agents negotiating under certain hypothetical conditions. The view is most closely associated with the twentieth-century philosopher John Rawls, who imagined a set of rational, informed, and impartial agents who negotiated moral principles from behind what he called a "veil of ignorance":[15] the agents do not know what position they will hold in the resultant society, so they will be unable to negotiate rules that give them any unfair advantage. In a contractarian morality, morality is identified not as a set of specific rights or rules, but as the set of rules arrived at by such a process. Because the negotiators are rational and impartial, the rules they arrive at are fair. Since they do not know what place they will hold in the resultant society, they are in a sense negotiating on behalf of everyone, because they could be anyone. The view is often used in political theory and as an account of justice, and we'll return to it in these contexts in Chapters Seven and Eight. For now, our focus will be on its adequacy as a theory of moral obligation to others—and particularly to animals. Though contractarianism differs from Kant's moral theory in many ways, it shares the emphasis on rationality, universalizability, and impartiality as the basis for morality. The moral rules derive their authority from the fact that we can justify them to any rational being. This creates a difficulty in accounting for obligations to animals: since rationality is a key feature of the negotiating parties who determine morality, animals lack a seat at the table. Contractarianism seems forced to deny that we have any obligations to animals. If that's true, any reasons we have to refrain from eating them must come from our obligations to other humans (for example, involving the environmental costs eating meat imposes on other humans) and not to animals themselves.

The contractarian can avail herself of a move similar to one that Kant makes on behalf of animals: we grant them some moral consideration because people will negotiate for protection of the things they care about, and people care about animals. This gives animals *indirect* moral status: they don't get consideration for their own sake, but by virtue of being important to us. One problem with this gambit is that *which* animals we care about seems to be a somewhat arbitrary matter; we would accord more protection to puppies, say, than to pigs or rats, despite the fact that there seems to be no morally relevant distinction between the two—the only difference is that one is more appealing to us than the other. Our hypothetical negotiators might also want to live in a society without gratuitous cruelty, and would therefore grant animals

---

15   Not all contractarians (for example, Gauthier [1987]) agree that the bargaining should take place behind such a veil; I discuss Rawls (1971) here because of the influence his account has had, though it is worth noting that Rawls offers this as a view of political theory and not morality. It will also become clear below why the veil of ignorance may be especially useful in applications of contractarianism to animal ethics.

protection from abuses like the ones described at the beginning of this chapter. There is also Kant's claim that cruelty to animals cultivates a corrupt moral character and a propensity to be cruel to other humans. Perhaps the negotiators would grant moral protection to animals for self-interested reasons, to discourage the development of cruel characters.

For rights theorists, these responses are unsatisfactory, because they make moral status contingent on whether animals matter to us. If the negotiators were to decide that they preferred a world with cheap meat to a world without animal cruelty, there would be nothing *wrong* with such a decision—indeed, there couldn't be, since whatever the contractors agree to is, by definition, right. Protections based on our concerns, or how eating meat affects our moral character, grounds animals' moral status in our interests, so that status will always be contingent, subject to change as our interests, desires, and feelings change. The rights theorist maintains that animals must be granted direct moral status, and accorded rights and respect in virtue of their inherent moral worth. For the contractarian, this is difficult if not impossible: since animals cannot enter into the hypothetical negotiations, they cannot be parties to the creation of morality. Someone else must negotiate on animals' behalf. This is also how the contractarian accounts for moral obligations to children and those who lack the cognitive capacities to deliberate: just because these beings don't have the capacity necessary to be moral *agents* doesn't mean they can't be moral *patients*—they can still be wronged, even if we don't view them as morally responsible actors themselves. A small child can't fully participate in moral reasoning and deliberation, and we don't expect them to grasp concepts like "right" and "wrong." But we still think it is morally wrong to harm children: we are morally obligated to them, and think of them as beings with moral status.

Another strategy for incorporating animals into a contractarian framework is to restrict the information negotiators are allowed to consider—specifically, with regard to species. In his formulation of contractarianism, Rawls introduces the veil of ignorance as a kind of thought experiment, a tool to eliminate biases and injustices based on morally irrelevant factors. If we don't know whether we'll be male or female, we'll negotiate a morality that is gender blind. If we don't know the color of our skin, our abilities or disabilities, we'll likewise try to arrive at a morality in which everyone enjoys certain basic protections and opportunities. Might we also therefore include species membership as one of the factors to which we're blind in the negotiations? If so, the contractarian might find a place for animals' interests in the moral negotiations as objects of direct moral value, and not merely indirect participants. If we didn't know what species we'd end up as, we'd negotiate a morality that protected all species as much as possible—and not only insofar as humans had an interest in them.[16] (Some might object that we don't have enough of an understanding

16   See Rowlands (1997).

of animals' interests to negotiate for them, but surely we could agree that animals have an interest in avoiding unnecessary pain and suffering. At the very least, such a process should rule out factory farming and other cruelty to animals.) Finally, we should note that the negotiators might rule out eating animals for reasons unrelated to animals themselves; as we'll see in the next chapter, animal agriculture has significant environmental impacts, so the contractors might have self-interested reasons to forbid it.

4. THE MORAL STATUS OF ANIMALS

The difference between the contractarian view and the rights view turns in part on what is required for something or someone to be considered worthy of moral consideration. The contractarian maintains that we only have direct moral obligations to rational agents, because to engage in morality requires engaging with a rational agent; animal rights theorists and utilitarians deny this. For both these views, being a creature with subjective experience is enough to secure moral standing: to be in possession of rights, or to have one's suffering weighed equally in moral consideration. The argument for moral equality for animals often takes a form known as the argument from *marginal cases*. We'll look at this argument, and its implications, before moving on to look at some additional critiques and analyses of the moral complexities of eating meat.

Both the utilitarian and the rights theorist argue that animals are, by virtue of being sentient creatures—that is, creatures with conscious experience of pleasure and pain—entitled to equal moral consideration to humans. There is no morally relevant difference between humans and animals, according to these views, and to treat animals differently simply because they are not human amounts to a form of discrimination they call *speciesism*. Like Bentham before him, the contemporary utilitarian Peter Singer sees the animal rights movement as part of a broader historical movement:

> Our concern for others ought not to depend on what they are like, or what abilities they possess—although precisely what this concern requires us to do may vary according to the characteristics of those affected by what we do. It is on this basis that the case against racism and the case against sexism must both ultimately rest; and it is in accordance with this principle that speciesism is also to be condemned. If possessing a higher degree of intelligence does not entitle one human to use another for his own ends, how can it entitle humans to exploit nonhumans?[17]

---

17   Singer (1989, p. 151).

Another term sometimes used to describe views that place humans above all other species is *anthropocentrism*. Anthropocentric value systems place humans at the center of morality, and accord greater weight to their interests than those of any other species (we'll talk more about anthropocentrism in the next chapter, when we discuss the environmental impacts of agriculture).

The contractarian—and other defenders of speciesism—might respond that there is a property that entitles humans to a place at the negotiating table, and which animals lack: rationality. As we've seen, the contractarian view places rational deliberation at the very heart of morality. Some rights theorists, too, grant that animals have some rights, but deny that they have the same rights as humans, because humans are rational, and animals are not:

> Between species of animate life, however—between (for example) humans on the one hand and cats or rats on the other—the morally relevant differences are enormous, and almost universally appreciated. Humans engage in moral reflection; humans are morally autonomous; humans are members of moral communities, recognizing just claims against their own interest. Human beings do have rights, theirs is a moral status very different from that of cats or rats.[18]

But the defenders of animal equality will respond by observing that some humans lack rationality, or the capacity to reflect, or to be morally autonomous, and we do not therefore exclude them from receiving any moral consideration—we don't think it's okay to cause them to suffer, or to ignore their interests (if anything, we often accord special consideration to the interests of the most vulnerable humans, such as infants and the severely disabled).

4.1 Animal Equality and the Argument from Marginal Cases

The argument from marginal cases is designed to show that there is no morally relevant characteristic possessed by all humans, and lacking in all non-humans, which would justify different moral treatment for humans. The fundamental idea behind the argument is that, in the absence of any relevant non-moral difference in two beings, there ought to be no moral difference in how they are treated: if A and B are the same in all relevant non-moral respects, then they deserve equal moral consideration. Failure to accord that consideration amounts to a kind of discrimination; we are according different moral worth based on arbitrary or superficial characteristics. This is why Singer draws parallels between the civil rights movement, the women's

---

18   Cohen (1986, p. 97).

liberation movement, and the animal rights movement: in all three cases, what was once seen as a significant difference between the groups, warranting different moral treatment, has been (or, in the case of animals, will someday be) revealed to be a merely superficial, morally irrelevant difference.

The argument from marginal cases challenges us to identify some morally relevant characteristic shared by all humans and lacked by (non-human) animals; it aims to show that there is no such characteristic. Any morally relevant property will either be lacking in some humans or present in some non-humans. For example, take the property of rationality, which philosophers such as Kant have suggested is what gives humans their distinctive moral status. Suppose the claim is that we are justified in withholding moral status from animals because they lack rationality. The problem is that not all humans are rational—for example, infants. One response to this is that infants will, given the opportunity, develop into rational beings, while puppies will not. So, we might say that infants are potentially rational, and that this suffices to give them moral status. But now we are faced with the problem of what to say about those who are born with or develop severe cognitive disabilities, and will never develop the ability to reason. Should we include such individuals in the moral community? If we do, we are acknowledging that rationality, whether actual or potential, is not actually a necessary condition for inclusion. But then we must find some other way to justify our refusal to include animals in this community. Or, we can be consistent by excluding such humans, relegating their moral status to that of animals. The argument points out this inconsistency; it doesn't tell us how to resolve it. But many of us would feel uncomfortable claiming that it would be okay to use those with severe cognitive disabilities for food, or as subjects in laboratory experiments, the way we do animals. And it's not just the consequences of the comparison that critics of Singer and the anti-speciesist argument object to: writers such as Kittay[19] have pointed out that it fundamentally mischaracterizes the disabled and our relationships to them, a point we'll come back to below.

Rationality is just one of the characteristics we can plug into the argument; we can repeat the argument for any candidate property, because the claim being defended is that there is no characteristic or property that is both morally relevant and maps neatly onto the human/non-human divide. Therefore, there can be no justification for extending moral status to all and only humans. We can represent the argument as follows:

1. If we are justified in considering the interests of all and only humans over those of animals, there must be some morally relevant characteristic shared by all humans and lacked by (non-human) animals.

---

19   Kittay (2005).

2. There is no morally relevant characteristic shared by all humans and lacked by (non-human) animals: any such characteristic will be lacking in some humans or present in some animals.

3. So, we are not justified in considering the interests of all and only humans over those of animals.

One thing to notice about the argument is that it tells us we can't consistently grant moral status to all humans while withholding it from animals. But it doesn't tell us how to resolve this inconsistency. For example, suppose one takes the position that what justifies treating humans and non-humans differently is that humans possess reason and non-human animals do not. Faced with this argument and the fact that some humans don't possess reason, one might resolve the tension in either of two ways: by conceding that reason isn't a necessary condition for moral status, and granting said status to some animals, or by maintaining that reason is a necessary condition, and therefore denying moral status to some humans. The argument above doesn't tell us which of these responses is correct, it only points out that we cannot consistently draw the line of the moral community around all and only humans.

4.2 Speciesism

Responding to the argument's challenge requires identifying some morally significant characteristic shared by humans and lacked by non-humans. The allegation of "speciesism"—indeed, the word itself, with its "ism"—presumes that basing moral status on species membership alone is no more than a prejudice, since species membership itself is morally irrelevant, unless it is accompanied by some additional abilities or characteristics that distinguish its members from all others. But some philosophers deny that species membership is morally irrelevant, maintaining that an individual's species determines facts about that individual's nature and interests which determine what is good for that individual. Other philosophers argue that our obligations to animals can be understood in terms of our relationships to those animals. Since we have different relationships with different animals—due, in part, to their species— we have different moral obligations to them.

There can be no question that we do take different attitudes towards different species. Americans tend to be protective of animals such as horses and dogs, which we view as pets, rather than food: when a chef in Philadelphia served a tasting menu that included a horse tartare, the Internet responded with outrage and even death threats. Alistair Norcross draws attention to the fact that "before the 2002 World Cup, several members of the England team sent a letter to the government of South Korea protesting the treatment of dogs and cats raised for food in that country. The same players have not protested the treatment of animals on factory farms in England."[20] Other animals are rejected as food because they're deemed too lowly: most Americans would not eat a raccoon, or a rat, or insects. As the anthrozoologist Hal Herzog puts it, to be food, an animal must neither be too close nor too far from us.[21] We treat some animals as pests or vermin, others as cuddly companions, and yet others as meat to be farmed, killed, and eaten. The question is whether there can be any justification for this differential treatment.

While most of the animals we have discussed so far in this chapter are clearly sentient, there are also more difficult cases. Do fish feel pain? What about lobsters? These animals have quite different nervous systems to those found in mammals, but difference itself is not decisive: the octopus lacks a central nervous system, but instead has decentralized neural systems in each of its arms, and is capable of advanced learning and extremely intelligent behavior. Scientists who work with octopuses say that they are more intelligent than many mammals, and few doubt that they are sentient.[22] The case of fish is less clear; scientists disagree over whether they are capable of experiencing pain. They exhibit pain *behavior*: they learn to avoid areas of their environment associated with painful stimuli (like electric shocks) and if injected with bee venom, they'll rub the site of the injection. But skeptics argue that these are reflexive behaviors and don't tell us anything about the fish's subjective experiences.[23] Still, the defender of the argument from marginal cases can argue that we ought to err on the side of caution: given that species membership is irrelevant, if a creature seems to be sentient, we should accord it moral consideration.

5. VALUE PLURALISM

Value pluralism is the idea that there is no single or overriding source of value. It contrasts with consequentialism and deontology insofar as it denies that morality can be reduced to a single rule or principle; for the pluralist, there are a number of ways things can be morally valuable and a number of moral goods. This means that for the pluralist, we can identify a number of features that make a being worthy of moral consideration, as well as a number of sources of moral obligations to other creatures. The pluralist agrees with the utilitarian that suffering is bad, and pleasure is good; she agrees with the rights theorist that being an experiencing subject of a life entitles one's interests to consideration; she also agrees with the contractarian that being able

---

20   Norcross (2004, p. 235).

21   Herzog (2010).

22   The philosopher Peter Godfrey-Smith has done extensive research on octopus cognition; see his (2016) for a discussion of his findings.

23   For two contrasting views of the fish pain issue, see Sneddon (2003) and Rose et al. (2012).

to enter into rational deliberation entitles one to participate in morality to a greater degree than one who is not so capable. The pluralist can agree with all these views, while also maintaining that being a member of the human species, or being able to enter into relationships with members of the human species, entitles a creature to a distinctive type of moral consideration. As Elizabeth Anderson writes, explaining the intuition behind pluralism:

> I find myself moved by some of the considerations advanced by all three perspectives ... How can I do justice to the values upheld by all three, given their conflicts? I shall argue that, while each perspective has identified a genuine ground of value, none has successfully generated a valid principle of action that does justice to all the values at stake. The plurality of values must be acknowledged.[24]

Pluralism is attractive insofar as it captures the complexity of our relationship to animals. The utilitarian and rights theorist might object that it allows for discrimination between groups of animals. Another objection is that the view doesn't offer enough guidance: the existence of a plurality of values explains the moral phenomenology—our feeling that there are genuinely multiple, competing values at work in our relationship with animals—but it doesn't offer a conclusive answer to fundamental moral questions such as whether, by treating animals as a source of food rather than as fellow sentient beings, we do them wrong. However, we can also view this criticism as an advantage: we relate to animals in various ways, and our theory of value should capture that. We'll run into pluralism again in later chapters, because its ability to acknowledge multiple genuine sources of value makes it an attractive characterization of many of the moral issues and debates we'll be discussing.

6. FEMINIST AND CARE ETHICS

Feminist ethical theories also reject the traditional dichotomies and rule-based approaches of deontological and utilitarian views. While it would be a mistake to speak of "the" feminist approach to animal ethics, since there are a number of feminist ethical theories that diverge from each other in important ways, we can nonetheless identify some themes in feminist critiques of traditional ethics and their approaches to animals.

Before entering into a discussion of feminist approaches to animal ethics, a word about feminist attitudes towards vegetarianism and veganism are in order. At the beginning of the chapter, I said we wouldn't be discussing these terms, but they're

---

24 Anderson (2005, p. 279).

important here, because some feminists object to these terms precisely because they are rules about what we can and cannot eat. The objection is that when we talk of a moral obligation to be vegetarian or vegan—on any of the grounds discussed in this chapter—we are telling women what they can and cannot put into their bodies, and therefore continuing the objectionable tradition of policing women's bodies and consumption, a tradition that feminists identify as part of Western philosophy specifically and Western society more generally. These feminists don't necessarily disagree with the substance of the critiques discussed below, but they disagree about whether these critiques give us grounds for issuing dietary proscriptions to women, or whether we ought to reject any dictates about diet, on the grounds that they stem from problematic conceptual hierarchies. To understand what that means, let's turn to the substance of the feminist critique in more detail.

6.1 Feminist Critiques of Traditional Discourse

Feminist philosophers critique traditional approaches to ethics—such as the rights-based and utilitarian approaches described above—as emphasizing reason and abstract concepts while overlooking the role that relationships and emotions play in our ethical life. Arguments based on claims about rights (deontology) and rules (utilitarianism) appeal to reason to convince us that there is no basis for treating animals and humans differently. But by relying entirely on reason and leaving out the emotional aspects of our relations to animals, such arguments reveal the philosophical tendency to separate reason from emotion and value the former more highly than the latter. This tendency is implicated in the oppression of both animals and women, since men tend to be associated with rationality while women, and animals, are associated with emotion. Indeed, many feminists see speciesism as one facet of a more broadly problematic worldview; for these critics, speciesism, sexism, racism, and classism all share important conceptual underpinnings. The human/non-human dichotomy, and the value judgment attached to it, is just one of a number of problematic dualisms, such as nature/culture, reason/emotion, and mind/body. The problem with all of these distinctions is that, historically, men have been associated with the "superior" rational, cultural, and mental aspects, while women, animals, and minorities, have been associated with the supposedly inferior, emotional, natural, and bodily aspects. If this is correct, then animal issues (and environmental issues, about which more in the next chapter) are feminist issues—the same value system that leads to the mistreatment of animals is implicated in the subjugation of women. More specifically, the attitude that licenses violence towards animals and views them as objects for our consumption also licenses sexual violence towards women:

It is not simply that the Western dualistic worldview has divided us from each other, from animals, from a sense of self that thinks and feels in a continuous, related way.... Nor is it only that the dominated side of the dualism is in service to the dominant kind. It is also—and very specifically—that the inequality attributed to the colored-female-body-animal side is *sexualized.* That is, the colored, female, animal is the body that is available for sex.[25]

As an alternative, some feminist philosophers have put forward an ethics based on the relationship of caring as an alternative way of understanding our ethical obligations and relations. In place of general concepts such as justice, which are abstract and universal, care ethics emphasizes particular relationships between individuals as central to our ethical lives. These theories argue that caring is a fundamental moral value, and one of the most fundamental forms of human relationships, and that it grounds what we owe to one another—we should treat others in certain ways because we care for, and are cared for, by them. In other words, it is our particular relationships to, and emotions for, other individuals that ground our moral obligations to them. Whereas the framework of rights focuses on individuals and their autonomy, the ethics of care focuses on the relationships between socially situated individuals.

6.2 Feminism and the Ethics of Care

Care ethics criticizes traditional approaches to animal ethics for several reasons: both the utilitarian and rights approaches are too abstract and emphasize reason while devaluing emotion. These traditional approaches also rely on similarities between animals and humans as the basis for animals' moral status; in doing so, they ignore important differences—between humans and animals, but also between different types of animals and different types of humans. Indeed, while both utilitarians and rights theorists argue for animal equality, proponents of care ethics, because of their emphasis on relationships, can point out that all animals are not equal, nor are our obligations to them:

> The feminist ethic of care regards animals as individuals who do have feelings, who can communicate those feelings, and to whom therefore humans have moral obligations. An ethic of care also recognizes the diversity of animals—one size doesn't fit all; each has a particular history. Insofar as possible, attention must be paid to these particularities in any ethical determination concerning them.[26]

---

25 Adams (1995, p. 203).
26 Donovan & Adams (2007, p. 3).

We have special obligations to domesticated animals, for example, because they are dependent on us—we've made them dependent on us. This allows care ethics to answer questions that rights or welfare views struggle with: if we have obligations to protect domesticated animals from suffering, does this also apply to wild animals? Do wild animals have rights? Should we interfere with predation to protect prey? Because care ethics says that our obligations to animals depend on our relationship to them, it can consistently say that we have no obligations to wild animals, but do have obligations of care to domesticated animals. By denying that a single rule governs our obligations to all animals, care ethics opens the door for treating different animals differently.

Critics seize on this aspect of the view as a weakness, rather than a strength. They question whether the view can account for, or move us to acknowledge, moral obligations to those outside our existing circle of relations. Given, as we've seen above, that we tend to accord more protections to certain animals based on their appearance or their value as domestic companions, does care ethics have any resources to change the status quo, or does it merely underwrite arbitrary distinctions in our treatment of other species? The defender of care ethics might respond that, once we understand our obligations to others in terms of relationships, species distinctions are no longer arbitrary: we have an obligation to infants and severely cognitively disabled humans that we don't have towards animals, by virtue of being in social or familial relationships with the former. This echoes Anderson's point about our ability to enter into relationships with some animals but not others, and is a marked departure from the sort of egalitarian impartial calculus that the utilitarian advocates.

7. PRACTICAL IMPLICATIONS: OUGHT WE EAT ANIMALS?

As will be clear by now, the extent to which each of the views discussed above allows for eating animals differs and may depend on the specific sorts of practice involved. According to animal rights theorists, it is never permissible to kill animals for food. This raises the question of whether one might eat animals that died by other means: what about roadkill, for example? In 2016, Washington State became the first to legalize and regulate the consumption of roadkill; according to their Department of Fish and Wildlife, almost 1,600 deer and elk were salvaged and eaten.[27] On the one hand, given that such animals are dead regardless of whether or not we eat them, we don't violate their right to life in order to eat them (though of course this right is violated by being run over). On the other hand, the rights theorist might still object that eating an animal, regardless of how that animal died, reduces it to a mere thing or

---

27   Dining on Roadkill (2017, July 27).

resource, a means for our enjoyment, and is therefore disrespectful of the animal and impermissible. We don't eat humans who have been killed by cars, the rights theorist might point out, because we have respect for human bodies. Therefore, we ought to show respect for animals by refraining from consuming their corpses, no matter how they die. (This point will be especially relevant in Chapter Six when we discuss the possibility of in vitro, or lab-grown, meat.)

Utilitarians would have no such objection. For the utilitarian, the contractarian, and the care ethicist, whether it is permissible to eat animals depends on the details of how that animal lives and dies. Almost all views would agree that factory farming of the sort practiced by large-scale chicken, cow, and pig farmers today is morally impermissible. Whether there is truly such a thing as happy meat is an empirical question, but if it were possible to raise and kill animals with a minimum of pain, the utilitarian might allow that such meat was morally permissible. This is a theoretical matter, however, since there is currently no possibility of replacing all or even most of the meat consumed today with non-factory-farmed animals (although we'll discuss other possibilities in Chapter Six). Whether or not killing and eating an animal is compatible with having a caring relationship with it is also controversial. On the one hand, that an animal will be killed and eaten does not preclude our attending to its needs, but whether it is possible and appropriate to kill and eat a creature with which one has formed an emotional bond is a more complicated question. Several years ago, Green Mountain College in Vermont found itself embroiled in controversy after one of a pair of oxen on its campus broke its leg; the college announced plans to kill the animal and serve its meat in the dining hall. Many people were outraged, not because they objected to eating meat per se, but because they felt that killing an animal that had become part of campus life was a violation of the relationship between the community and the animal. Similarly, many people would find the idea of eating a pet abhorrent. Perhaps, then, truly caring for an animal in a way that involves empathy and emotional attachment rules out the possibility of viewing that animal as a source of food.

CONCLUSION

Our discussion here of the permissibility of eating animals—and particularly of factory farming—has focused on the issue from the perspective of our obligations to animals. But there are additional ethical issues involved; factory farming, in particular, has significant impact on humans and their environment. Factory farms are prone to disease outbreaks, and there are concerns that keeping animals in such close confinement increases the likelihood of outbreaks of new strains of flu that could spread to humans. Because of the frequency of disease in crowded factory farms, the use of antibiotics is widespread—with some figures suggesting that factory farms account for three quarters of the antibiotics used in the United States—and some scientists have cautioned that factory farms may be a leading cause of antibiotic resistance. In the next chapter, we will look at the environmental effects of industrial agriculture more generally.

Chapter Five

AGRICULTURE
AND THE
ENVIRONMENT

INTRODUCTION

In the previous chapter we examined the ethics of eating animals through the lens of our obligations to animals: do we wrong them by farming, killing, or eating them? As we saw, one of the main tasks for animal ethics is to explain and justify the moral status (or lack thereof) of animals. In this chapter, we will examine the impact of agriculture on the environment, and in doing so, we'll see whether we can extend the moral community beyond sentience to include non-sentient life and even things like species, rivers, and ecosystems.

1. ENVIRONMENTAL IMPACTS OF FOOD
PRODUCTION: SOME FACTS AND FIGURES

Agriculture is a major consumer of land and water in the US and worldwide. In the US, it accounts for about 40 per cent of land use and 80 per cent of water use.[1] Animal agriculture, in particular, is often criticized as environmentally unsustainable; many vegetarians and vegans cite environmental concerns as one of the reasons (in addition to animal welfare) for their dietary choices. Critics point to the fact that

---

1   Land usage is based on numbers from the 2012 agricultural census (United States Department of Agriculture [2014]), which actually represents a decrease from previous decades. Water usage is based on figures from the United States Department of Agriculture, Economic Research Service (2018, July 19).

animals consume more energy than they produce: estimates vary, but it takes *at least* seven pounds of grain to produce one pound of beef.[2] Pigs are slightly more efficient at four to one, and chickens even more so at about two to one. Animals also require a lot of water. Here again, numbers vary, "ranging from 441 gallons to about 12,000 gallons per pound of beef."[3] All of these resources could be used to produce food for humans; alternatively, the land used to graze or raise food for animals could instead be devoted to conservation or small-scale farming. For all these reasons, critics argue that devoting our limited resources to meat production is unjustifiable when there is not enough food and water to go around. This is a point we'll return to briefly in Chapter Six, since it bears on the motivations for developing GM crops.

In addition to the resources they consume, animals also produce lots of waste. A dairy cow produces around 100 pounds of manure per *day*. That's a ton and a half per month. On small-scale farms, some of this waste can be used as fertilizer. But the specialization of industrial agriculture has led to a separation between the farms that grow animal feed and the farms that feed and grow animals: because farmers are guaranteed a minimum price for their corn that's often more than the cost of feed, it's more profitable for them to sell their corn as animal feed than to feed it to cows themselves. The cost of animal feed is less than the price farmers receive for selling corn, so even if a farmer did raise cows and grow corn, feeding that corn to cows would mean losing money. The result is that on most large farms, animals and crops are no longer grown in the same place—animal feeding operations are concentrated in one area; corn and grain farming in another. This means that animal waste is no longer integrated into the cycle of a farm where it's used as fertilizer, so cattle feedlots and pig and poultry farms must find a way to dispose of large amounts of waste. This is often accomplished by placing the waste in "lagoons": large ponds adjacent to the farms. In addition to smelling terrible, and emitting fumes that cause respiratory problems, headaches, and other physical symptoms in nearby residents, runoff from these lagoons can contaminate groundwater. The Environmental Protection Agency estimates that the runoff from these farms is the biggest cause of water pollution in the United States.

1.1 Pesticides and Pollutants

Pesticide and fertilizer runoff from farms finds its way into lakes, rivers, and streams. Fertilizer drainage from farms in Illinois and Indiana ends up in the Mississippi river,

---

2   The numbers here are based on a Food and Agriculture Organization report (van Huis et al. [2013]). As Singer & Mason (2006, p. 232) note, estimates for beef have been as high as 21 pounds of feed per pound. Some of the variation depends on how we measure the weight of the animal—in terms of edible beef or the whole cow. The numbers have changed, too, as production has gotten more efficient.
3   See Singer & Mason (2006, p. 235), which also includes a useful discussion of why estimates might vary and the ways various cattle-rearing and grazing practices impact water use.

which feeds into the Gulf of Mexico, causing a condition known as hypoxia: algae feed off the fertilizers (in particular, nitrogen and phosphorous) and these in turn feed bacteria, which deplete the oxygen supply, causing fish to die off or move. Pesticides also end up in waterways, including those that provide drinking water; water treatment plants spend millions to clean pesticides out of the water supply. Certain types of pesticides called neonicotinoids are toxic to honeybee populations, which play an important role as pollinators, fertilizing plants to allow them to produce fruits and nuts. As honeybee populations decline, some farmers have been forced to truck in bees to pollinate almond trees and other crops (in China, some farmers have reportedly resorted to pollinating apple trees by hand). There is evidence linking pesticide exposure to birth defects and childhood cancer among farmworkers and their families—whether the exposure comes through airborne drift or from residue on workers' clothing.[4] Pesticides also affect birds, insects, and butterflies, as well as wildflowers and other native grasses. Lastly, we should note that agriculture is detrimental to animal welfare, too: land used for agriculture means a loss of habitat for wildlife, and tilling and plowing of fields kills small animals such as mice and rabbits. This complicates the idea that there is truly any cruelty-free diet.

1.2 From Land to Sea

Seafood also has significant detrimental impact on the environment. Overfishing is a major problem: over 90 million tons of fish are pulled from the water each year. Practices such as "bottom trawling," in which nets are dragged across the ocean floor, picking up all kinds of shellfish, coral, and seaweed, result in the destruction of marine habitats despite the fact that much of what's caught is inedible and will be thrown back or thrown out. Part of the problem is a lack of oversight, especially in international waters: unlike agriculture and land, it's unclear who owns the fish in these seas. Managing the problem will require international cooperation, but it's difficult to police illegal fishing.

Aquaculture—farming fish and shellfish—can take some of the pressure off wild fish stocks, by offering an alternative source of seafood, but it too has environmental costs. First, the feed used in these farms contains fish meal and fish oil, meaning that one kilo of farmed fish might actually use up to two kilos of wild fish (typically smaller fish such as anchovies and sardines, which could be consumed directly by

---

4   Carson (1962/2002) is one of the earliest and most influential discussions of pesticides' effects on wildlife. See Estabrook (2011) Chapter 3 for a discussion of how pesticides affect workers on Florida's tomato farms. See also Beamer (2011), Engel et al. (2005), and Chen, Chang, Tao, & Lu (2015) for discussion of the link between pesticide use and disease.

humans).[5] Farmed fish are often raised in sea cages, which are open, meaning that waste is released into the sea, as is feed and the medications the fish receive. Because fish farms are situated in open water, when disease or parasites break out, it is difficult to stop the outbreak from spreading to nearby rivers; many rivers in Norway and Scotland are therefore now infected by parasites affecting salmon. These issues mean that fish farms degrade the environments around them even after they've moved on. Shrimp farms, in particular, tend to be located around mangrove forests in Southeast Asia and South America; these ecosystems recover slowly, if at all, from the pollution of the farms. The United Nations estimates that since 1980, one-fifth of the world's mangroves have been destroyed by shrimp farming. In other areas, coastal ecosystems are cleared or destroyed entirely to make room for shellfish farms. We should note that shellfish is not all bad news, environmentally; oysters tend to be beneficial to their ecosystem, as they filter out pollutants from the water. And when alternated with rice production, fish farming can be beneficial: the fish consume insects and weeds, and their waste fertilizes the fields. But these systems are typically found on small-scale farms. Some scientists have suggested that fish farms could be used as a way of recycling waste water, especially in urban areas, since fish can feed on human and animal waste. Whether consumers would accept this is a different matter, one we'll touch on in the next chapter.

1.3 The Problem of Waste

A less obvious environmental cost of agriculture is food waste. It is estimated that between one quarter and one half of all the food produced in America is wasted— sometimes plowed under in the field because of cosmetic deficits, sometimes thrown away by stores and businesses, and sometimes left to rot in the vegetable drawers of our refrigerators.[6] This is doubly costly: first, the resources that go into the production of wasted food, and its processing and transport, are wasted; if less food were thrown away, less food would need to be produced, and fewer resources consumed. But secondly, the waste itself is an environmental problem: degrading food emits methane, a greenhouse gas. (Food surplus can itself be costly in other ways, as we'll see in Chapter Seven, insofar as it has to go somewhere, thereby incentivizing the production and consumption of highly processed, calorie-dense food.)

This is just a brief survey of some of the environmental effects of our food system. The processes described above aren't fully understood, and new research emerges daily about the relationship between agriculture, pesticides and fertilizers, land use, climate change, food waste, and so on. The philosophical question concerns how we

---

5   Naylor et al. (2000).
6   For a detailed discussion, see Bloom (2010).

should understand the moral significance of these effects: does it make sense to say of a non-sentient entity, like the environment, that it can be harmed, or should we understand the harm as something that is done to humans and animals?

2. ENVIRONMENTAL ETHICS: ANTHROPOCENTRIC VS. ECOCENTRIC APPROACHES

Anthropocentric approaches explain our moral obligations involving the environment in terms of their effects on us: harming the environment is bad not because the environment has intrinsic moral value and is therefore wronged, but because humans have an interest in preserving and conserving the environment, so that harming the environment wrongs humans. On anthropocentric views, the environment has no direct moral status. We'll return to these approaches later in this chapter, when we discuss the relationship between environmental ethics and traditional ethical theories in more detail, but the first part of the chapter will focus on ecocentric theories of environmental ethics instead.

Ecocentric views deny that the environment has moral value only instrumentally, as a means to human ends. Instead, they argue that it has *intrinsic* moral value: its moral worth is independent of its usefulness for human or any other ends. Ecocentric views also argue against the widespread tendency to justify environmental conservation in terms of human interests; we should stop thinking of what's best for the environment as what's best for us. In fact, as we'll see shortly, some philosophers maintain that human interests must be subjugated to the interests of the environment as a whole.

Ecocentric ethics cannot rely on similarities with humans to ground the environment's moral status—the environment isn't rational, or even sentient—so they face the challenge of explaining why we should think the environment is worthy of consideration for its own sake. This is an important and controversial question, especially in the case of agriculture where human interests and environmental ones are often assumed to be at odds with one another. According to the "productionist paradigm" of agriculture, the overriding goal is to feed as many people as possible, which means producing as much as food as possible.[7] Understood this way, the goals of agriculture conflict with the goals of environmental conservation, though these too are often justified in anthropocentric terms—for example, by pointing to the enjoyment people gain from natural beauty, or to the threat extinctions pose to humans' quality of life. Given that so much of our debate about agriculture and the environment takes place

---

7   The term is from Thompson (1994), Chapter 3, who introduces (and quickly dismisses) it as a possible ethical standard for agriculture.

in anthropocentric terms, the ecocentrist faces a rather challenging task: to convince us that the environment, non-sentient though it is, has moral standing of its own.

2.1 Ecocentrism: Arguments and Interpretations

Not all philosophers accept the terms of this challenge. Some have argued that plants have a kind of sentience, drawing on studies that show that plants send out chemical "alarm signals" when injured, thereby communicating distress to one another. But while there is evidence that plants can behave in certain ways in response to stimuli, this is not the same as showing that plants have a certain kind of conscious experience that would include pleasures and pains, or desires and fears. The idea of plant sentience remains extremely controversial, and most philosophers dismiss it.

2.2 Ecocentrism and the Last Person Argument

One way to argue for the intrinsic value of nature is to imagine its destruction in a scenario where no humans or animals are harmed by its loss. The last person argument asks us to imagine that there is only one human left on earth; this last human goes around systematically destroying every living thing—forests, wildflowers, fungi, and so on. Faced with this example, most people have the intuition that the destruction is wrong, but this can only be explained if we grant that non-human life has intrinsic moral value. One might object that this doesn't show that nature itself has value, because in the example as described, some of the things destroyed are sentient. A variation on the example involves a similar scenario where, after all animals, insects, and fish have gone extinct, the last person sets fire to the last tree, or destroys the last flower. In this variation, if something of value is lost, it must be because the boundaries of intrinsic value extend beyond sentience.[8]

Using a similar example, one might also argue that intrinsic value can extend beyond the boundaries of individuals. Consider an endangered species of which only one member remains. When that last member dies, we feel something of value has been lost—over and above the individual itself. For example, when the last remaining elephant dies, we will feel that the loss extends beyond the life of one elephant—this is shown by the fact that the death of the last elephant seems so much worse than the death of the twenty-seventh-to-last elephant. One way to explain this feeling is to say that the species itself has intrinsic value, and the sense of loss we feel reflects our intuition that the loss of the species is a loss of value.

---

8   The argument is introduced in Routley (1973, p. 207); see also Peterson & Sandin (2013, pp. 121–33).

2.3 Ecocentrism and Holistic Ethics

These examples address apparently puzzling aspects of ecocentrism: first, how non-sentient beings could have intrinsic value; and second, how a biota—an ecosystem composed of, but not reducible to, individuals—could be a locus of intrinsic value. One might deny the intuitions generated by the examples above, or argue that while the intuitions are real, we shouldn't grant them any evidential value (perhaps because there is some other explanation for them—we are responding to the bad character of the last person rather than wrongness of their act itself, or we are confusing aesthetic for moral value and intuiting the loss of the former). But the fact that many people have found these cases compelling suggests that the idea that the ecosystem could be a source of intrinsic value is not as implausible as it might initially appear, and that the reasons for preserving our environment go beyond economic utility or even the desires, enjoyment, or welfare of other humans.

Many environmental and agricultural ethicists emphasize the interdependence of humans and their environment. Wendell Berry argues that the very terms in which we conduct the discussion reveal our tendency to objectify the environment: "To talk about 'the environment' as something apart from us is to separate us from the environment. We were, after all, made from the environment. We are maintained by it. The subject-object dualism has given us the notion that it is possible to isolate parts of the environment we don't like."[9] The two views we'll look at next both adopt a holistic approach, taking the relevant subject of moral significance to be ecosystems as a whole, not just as collections of individuals.

DEEP ECOLOGY

One approach that accords moral standing to non-sentient beings is known as *deep ecology*. Introduced by the Norwegian philosopher Arne Naess in the 1970s, deep ecology contrasts with what Naess dubs "shallow ecology," which is mainly concerned with pollution and conservation. Naess critiques the environmental movement's "shallow" priorities, arguing that these reveal an underlying bias in favor of tackling issues that affect humans, and managing nature to make it more accommodating of humans, rather than any real respect for the environment for its own sake. A true environmental ethic would need to recognize that human needs are just one set among many, and should not be given any higher priority than the needs of other aspects of the ecosystem. Deep ecology also rejects any separation between humans and nature, and indeed between individuals, viewing everything as connected. As such, the view is metaphysically quite radical: it demands that we rethink the catego-

---

9   Quoted in Heldke (2001, p. 366).

ries into which we usually classify the objects around us, and cease seeing ourselves as beings existing independently of the natural world and of each other.

THE LAND ETHIC

Aldo Leopold's *land ethic* also accords direct moral standing to the environment (and originated at roughly the same time as the deep ecology movement). According to the land ethic, "a thing is right when it tends to preserve the integrity, stability, and beauty of the biotic community; it is wrong when it tends otherwise." Leopold advocates changing our view of "the role of *Homo Sapiens* from conqueror of the land-community to plain member and citizen of it ... man is, in fact, only a member of a biotic team." He broadens the scope of the moral community to include "soils, waters, plants, and animals, or collectively: the land."[10] We must also shift the way we view land and nature: as having moral value in its own right, and not just as an economic resource. He points out that historically, arguments for conservation have tended to invoke economic threats or benefits, and that where protecting resources can't be justified in economic terms, we treat them as "monuments" or "refuges." What is needed instead, according to Leopold, is an admission that land should be preserved "as a matter of biotic right." The criterion for moral consideration is no longer rationality, species membership, or sentience, but rather being part of the biotic community: being alive or sustaining life (soil is arguably not itself alive, but it is teeming with microorganisms, so it at least falls into this latter category).

The land ethic is consequentialist but not utilitarian. It locates the rightness or wrongness of acts in their consequences—specifically, their effects on the stability of the biota—but not in any kind of pleasure, pain, or felt state (since the thing being affected is not sentient). Together with holism, the result is that an act might be right (because it benefits the biota or community as a whole) despite adversely affecting the individuals in a community.

This feature yields the main objection to Leopold's view, and to holistic ethics more broadly: that it subjugates and even sacrifices the interests of (human) individuals, if doing so preserves the stability of the community as a whole. So, if eliminating a species would contribute to the stability of the ecosystem, according to the land ethic, it would be the right thing to do. In practice, attempts to intervene with ecosystems by introducing or eliminating species have tended to have unforeseen consequences (another pitfall of consequentialist views is the difficulty of predicting an act's outcomes). But the bigger concern is not with the predictability of outcomes, but with the subjugation of individual interests, both human and animal, to those of the ecosystem as a whole. Regan has argued that the view threatens to lead to a

---

10   Leopold (1949, pp. 224–25).

kind of environmental fascism—an "ecofascism."[11] The analogy is obviously imperfect, since most environmentalists don't advocate for an authoritarian, militaristic government; nonetheless, the charge of ecofascism highlights concerns about how to manage conflicts between individual property (and other) rights and environmental conservation. This concern is not an historical artifact, but is very much alive today, as governments weigh the environmental costs of agriculture (the water it requires, the waste it produces) against farmers' and ranchers' rights.

Writing almost 25 years ago, Zimmerman cautions that the language of ecological conservation might be harnessed by anti-immigration movements: "If resurgent tribalism were harnessed by a charismatic leader who urged his people to recover their 'homeland' and to protect it from environmental ruin, and if that leader had access to modern military equipment and communication facilities, he (or she) might generate a tribal ecofascism."[12] This scenario may seem far-fetched; a more pressing concern is weighting individual rights and human well-being against conservation. This is a concern for ecocentric systems of ethics generally, since it's inevitable that, at our current population levels, human interests and environmental interests come into conflict. But Zimmerman also draws attention to the relationship between ecological crises and immigration: as sea levels rise and droughts become more common, communities will relocate to escape floods and famine, creating new political conflicts. Thus, there is also the sense that ecological stability and conservation enhance political stability and human interests. But while this convergence of interests mitigates the objection from ecofascism, it is not enough to satisfy the defender of an ecocentric ethics, who wants to grant the environment moral standing for its own sake, and not just because it furthers human interests, whether individual or collective. If we take seriously the claim that we are just one part in a system, each member of which has intrinsic value, we will be forced to admit that, at least in some cases, our interests take a backseat to those of the environment. Indeed, we may be forced to admit that from the perspective of an ecocentric ethic, it would be better for many of us not to exist at all.

One response to the ecofascism objection invokes the value pluralism discussed in the last chapter. Just as we are members of several communities (our families, our nations, our species) so we have several sets of moral obligations. The land ethic sets out one of these, but it's not the only one, and it's not intended to trump the others. Rather, it's meant as an addition to our moral communities and their attendant obligations—Leopold is asking us to see ourselves as a member of the ecological community just as we see ourselves as members of families, nations, religions, and so on. Thus, the response argues, we won't end up confronting ecofascism, because we can maintain our obligation as members of a community of humans, or as residents of a

---

11   See Regan (1985, pp. 361–63).

12   Zimmerman (1995, p. 210).

nation, and these obligations will take precedence over our membership in the ecological community.

Whether this response succeeds depends in part on how one views competing identities and obligations in other spheres of our moral lives. Many of the most difficult moral dilemmas involve cases of conflict: choosing between a job that allows one to provide for one's family and a job that would help society; choosing whether to protect a close friend and lie under oath, or tell the truth; risking arrest and separation from one's children to protest an unjust law. These cases illustrate that the problem of adjudicating competing moral obligations isn't unique to environmental ethics; the fact that we have obligations to humanity in addition to the ecosystem doesn't guarantee that we'll never have to put humanity second to environmental concerns. Still, this response does help rebut the ecofascism objection insofar as it demonstrates that the interests of the biota needn't be our only moral concern; there's room for our identities as individuals, and the moral obligations and values they imply, to play a significant (if not the determining) role in our moral judgments and actions as well.

2.4 Ecofeminism

As in our discussion of animal ethics in the previous chapter, it would be a mistake to speak of a single feminist approach to environmental ethics. Some feminist philosophers have developed views within the frameworks described above, but others have argued that while these rightly draw our attention to the ways in which we are connected with nature and non-human animals, they do not go far enough in recognizing and repudiating the problematic conceptual structures and dichotomies that enable oppression of women, animals, and nature.

Like feminist approaches to animal ethics, ecofeminists draw our attention to the ways in which our conceptual framework creates a (mutually exclusive) dichotomy between the categories reason, male, culture, and human; and emotion, female, nature, and animal.[13] Understanding the way this conceptual framework operates in our social and philosophical thought enables us to understand our treatment of nature as a symptom of a broader framework that seeks to oppress and dominate women, animals, and nature, justifying their subjugation with the oppositions mentioned above. This conceptual framework is also at work in the methodology and substantive beliefs of much of Western philosophy itself, with its emphasis on rationality over emotion; the dualisms enable oppression and domination by linking membership in a dominant group (such as men or humans) with the possession of certain characteristics that justify that membership (such as rationality). We also see it in

---

13 For a detailed discussion of the ways these dichotomies reveal themselves, and an overview of the different ways feminists have interpreted and analyzed them, see Plumwood (1986).

our everyday language and the metaphors with which we approach both nature and animals: when humans are angry or emotional, we invoke animalistic descriptions ("going wild," "howling with rage,"); nature itself is something to be "tamed" and "mastered"; soil is "fertile" and unlogged forests are "virgin."

Not all ecofeminists go so far as to embrace the radical egalitarianism of deep ecology; many wish to retain a distinction between the ways social structures oppress and dominate sentient and non-sentient beings. But all agree that we cannot begin to critique traditional attitudes and practices regarding nature without understanding the systems of oppression and domination in which these are embedded: both the linguistic and conceptual apparatus described above, but also the social, political, and material systems that these apparatuses support and justify, which encourage viewing women, animals, and nature as resources to be managed and exploited for benefit.

3. ENVIRONMENTAL ETHICS, AGRICULTURAL ETHICS

The critiques above emphasize the problem of viewing nature as something distinct from humans, something for us to master. Yet while these views critique our current practices, none is necessarily opposed to agriculture. Some of the most influential twentieth-century conservationists—such as Leopold and his (rough) contemporaries Wendell Berry and Wes Jackson—were themselves farmers and landowners and viewed these roles as essential to the development and implementation of conservation practices. Historically, Leopold argues, farmers and other landowners have relied too heavily on the government to manage and subsidize their land. And he cautions that policies must be made and executed with the interest of the environment in mind, not just economics. There is nothing wrong with agriculture per se, but its current emphasis on maximizing the productivity of land for the sake of food production, rather than on considering what is best for the land itself, is a problematic facet of how agriculture is currently practiced. Some environmentalists view the emergence of agriculture as the beginning of humans' problematic exploitation of and relationship with the earth, but most object to the way agriculture is practiced and viewed today, and not the concept itself. Agriculture and environmentalism needn't be incompatible, but we need an ethical system that can incorporate both practices—an agrarian ethic.

3.1 Stewardship: Towards an Agricultural Ethic?

The concept of stewardship refers to the idea that humans are caretakers of the environment and its resources. Originally, this idea is based in religious doctrine—the idea that the earth is given to us to use and care for—but in recent decades some writers have developed a secular version of the concept to characterize our relationship to the environment in a way that encourages and guides ethical agricultural practices. Paul Thompson explains:

> Farmers have long been thought to be natural stewards of the land. The ideal of good farming has been expressed in terms of care for the soil, water, plants, and animals under the farmer's supervision. Although there have always been bad farmers who ruin their farms, the practice of stewardship has traditionally been thought characteristic of an ideal to which all farmers aspire. Common wisdom has taught that the farmer unskilled in the care of nature inevitably fails in the task of proper farming.[14]

Stewardship need not be motivated solely (or even at all) by care for the land itself, or out of a respect for the intrinsic value of nature:

> Stewardship is not something that farmers undertake altruistically, nor is it a religious duty that farmers perform at the expense of their personal, earthly betterment. Stewardship requires the conservation of nature, and enjoins against the waste and abuse of land or water. Stewardship is an integral component of agricultural land use. Stewardship duties do not oppose use, but are components of wise use ... agricultural stewardship is entirely compatible with self-interested, anthropocentric use of nature.... The farmer's dependence on soil fertility and clean water creates a biological basis for the marriage of stewardship and self-interest.[15]

The concept of stewardship promotes conservation, while appealing to and satisfying humans' own interests. But if its justification is purely self-interested, one might doubt that stewardship is truly an ethical view at all: typically, an obligation is something we would undertake whether or not it benefits us. If the only motivation for stewardship is self-interest, we might think it an insufficient basis for an agrarian ethic.

3.2 Stewardship and Future Generations

One non-self-interested argument for stewardship rests on our obligation to leave future generations with resources to sustain themselves. By ensuring the ongoing health of land and water, the farmer who practices stewardship is keeping land and

---

14 Thompson (1994, p. 94).
15 Thompson (1994, pp. 94–96).

water healthy and available for future generations. Why think any such obligation exists? One reason would be a principle like the following: whenever we can choose to act so as to significantly harm or help someone, we have an obligation not to harm them (for another application of this principle, see Engel's argument against eating animals on pages 58–59). This is similar to the utilitarian principle that tells us to act so as to minimize suffering and maximize pleasure, although it is weaker in that it tells us only to avoid significantly harming others. This principle seems to require us to leave enough resources for future people to ensure that they don't suffer from, and aren't significantly harmed by, starvation and drought. The utilitarian's commitment to impartiality is also relevant here: Singer and other utilitarians have argued that the distance at which suffering takes place is no excuse for inaction: there is no morally relevant difference between walking past a starving person at my doorstep without offering help and omitting to contribute money to famine relief that would save a starving person thousands of miles away.[16] In both cases I am equally morally blameworthy; geographic distance doesn't lessen my moral obligation to help the hungry person. Perhaps the same principle applies to distance in time: there is no justification for refusing to take an action that would prevent someone's starving, just because that person is temporally distant from me.

Another consideration in support of obligations to future generations can be found in care ethics: just as we have obligations to our children because of our relationship to them, future generations exist as a result of our actions, and so we're obligated to ensure that their basic needs can be met. This is complicated by the fact that our relationship with more distant generations is necessarily one-sided; we can't meet and interact with them, so it's doubtful that we can actually engage in caring and empathic relationships with them except through imagination.

There are a number of additional challenges to the idea of obligations to future people. The first challenges the assumption that there exist any future people to whom we could be obligated. While we generally accept that we have obligations to actual people, future people are merely possible. How could we have obligations to people who don't—and might never—actually exist? Derek Parfit has pointed out that the actions we take now will affect which people exist in the future; if we adopt a policy aimed at helping future generations, we thereby take actions that result in different future people existing. To talk of harming future people can be misleading, because it implies that there is a fixed set of people who will exist at some future time and who we can make better or worse off. Instead, Parfit explains, our actions now result in some people existing and others not existing—we're not affecting the welfare of a single set of people, but rather affecting which people come into existence. Parfit does not take this to imply that we have no reason to consider the effect of our actions on future generations; he argues that if a policy would make living conditions worse for future people than alternatives, we have reason to avoid that policy. In other words, we can compare the living conditions of the two groups that would come into existence if we pursued two different policies and, if one is significantly worse than the other (and the numbers of people are roughly comparable) we have reason not to choose it. What Parfit denies is that this reason takes the form of an *obligation*.[17]

One can also make deontological arguments for obligations to future generations, drawing on a kind of contractarian picture of our moral obligations. Recall that the contractarian views morality as stemming from a kind of hypothetical negotiation between rational individuals who don't know their place in the resultant society. We might extend the contractarian negotiations to include members of different generations. So, in addition to imagining that we are negotiating behind a "veil of ignorance" as to the particulars of our situation, talents, and resources (and perhaps, as was suggested in the last chapter, species membership) we can also imagine that we do not know, as we negotiate the rules governing the use and distribution of resources, which generation we will belong to. When considering policies that will conserve or deplete resources, on this picture, we might ask ourselves whether, if we were to live three generations, or five generations from now, we would still endorse this policy. If the policy can only be endorsed from the perspective of someone living now, and not someone living in the future, it would not, on this deontological picture, be just.[18]

Nor does there seem to be any obligation to bring people into existence. We accept that whether or not to have children is an individual choice, not a moral obligation, so it would seem that there is no obligation to make possible future people actual.[19] However, this argument may seem problematic when we consider that many people take an interest in the future of humanity: we pursue current projects in the expectation that humanity will continue to persist for generations. Many people feel that, were the human race to die out soon after their death, something would be lost, even if it did not directly affect them.[20]

A further worry about obligations to future generations is whether we can accommodate them while also meeting obligations to present generations. Many of the defenses of industrial agriculture and its use of fertilizer, pesticides, and other technologies (about which we'll say more in the next chapter) point to the need to feed an ever-growing population. Stewardship for future generations is not itself problematic, this argument goes, but if it requires us to compromise our ability to feed existing people, it is unsustainable. If forced to choose between meeting our obligations to current versus future people, we should prioritize those who already exist.

---

17   See Parfit (1986), Chapter 16.
18   See Barry (1978).
19   For an argument *against* bringing more people into the world, see Benatar (2006).
20   See, for example, Scheffler (2016).

Stewardship thus raises as many questions as it promises to answer. Ecocentric philosophies might well object that the idea of man as caretaker of, and responsible for, the environment is unacceptably anthropocentric. But even if we accept this picture, we still need an explanation of why we have these obligations to land, and how we ought to weigh these against other, possibly conflicting obligations.

4. ENVIRONMENTAL ETHICS THROUGH TRADITIONAL APPROACHES

As mentioned above, incorporating the environment into ethical theory by granting it direct moral status isn't the only option. We can also assess the environmental impact of various actions—specifically, here, agriculture—through the lens of the moral theories introduced in the previous chapter.

4.1 Utilitarianism and Environmental Ethics

Utilitarianism will have little to say about the environment as a direct object of moral concern since its moral calculus is based on pleasure and pain, and non-sentient life is capable of neither. But it can assess environmental impacts in terms of their tendency to produce pleasure and pain in other sentient creatures. As we saw above, factory farming causes enough suffering to animals that the utilitarian condemns it on that basis alone; asking about its environmental impact might therefore seem unnecessary. On the other hand, examining the impact of factory farming and industrial agriculture on humans is still a worthwhile exercise, especially since if we were to one day face a scenario where sentience was "engineered out" of animals—would factory farming still be morally wrong, according to the utilitarian? If it requires or results in agricultural practices that are themselves objectionable, it would. In the remainder of the discussion, then, I'll put animals to one side, having already discussed utilitarian analyses of factory farming and eating animals, and focus on utilitarian analyses of agricultural practices more broadly.

Above, we saw that Leopold objects to the tendency to reduce the environment's value to economic value, or to its effects on humans. And this is perhaps the most obvious way to construct a utilitarian objection to agriculture: to point to the effects it has on humans' environment and quality of life. Above, we discussed the potential harms caused by pesticides. There is some evidence that they cause disease in farmers and their families, as well as those who live near fields where pesticides are used. We also discussed the effects of runoff from farms on groundwater and waterways. Insofar as these effects cause suffering to people and to animals, the utilitarian will have to weigh them against the benefits of agriculture, pesticide, and fertilizer use.

And as we'll see in the next chapter, there is something to be said for these benefits. Recall, too, that because utilitarianism is aggregative, it does not take into account whether costs and benefits are distributed fairly across persons and communities. As we'll see in Chapter Eight, one concern about the pollution from large farming operations, especially factory farms, is that its effects tend to be felt disproportionately by poor and minority communities. This leads many to object that such a distribution is unjust. But this objection is not available to the utilitarian; they must weigh the total benefits against the total costs, without taking into account whether these are fairly distributed. However, as we saw on page 63, a painist consequentialist does not aggregate, and so might be able to offer a more robust objection to the unfair distribution of pollution and other environmental harms.

In addition to these impacts, the utilitarian will have to consider how agriculture affects the habitats and lives of other animals. Some philosophers have argued that even (and perhaps especially) a vegan diet is morally problematic because to grow vegetables requires plowing and tilling fields, thereby causing the deaths of field mice, voles, and other mammals. Cultivating fields also destroys the habitat of birds and butterflies. These might be at the border of sentience, so perhaps the utilitarian need not weigh them, but insofar as their disappearance affects other sentient beings, they may be worth considering. In sum, the utilitarian can make some case for an environmental ethic, but it will be limited and, like the case against factory farming, contingent on the effects these practices actually have. There is no basis in utilitarianism for affording the environment moral consideration for its own sake, only insofar as its destruction affects the lives of sentient beings.

4.2 Deontological Approaches

Traditional deontological approaches are anthropocentric or at least "rationality-centric"; these views can incorporate the environment as a source of moral value instrumentally, insofar as it matters or is necessary to humans. In our discussion of future generations, we saw that environmental resources are one of the goods that can be distributed or protected by the moral contract; as the hypothetical contractors negotiate the rules of morality, they can determine what obligations, if any, we have to protect and conserve the environment and its resources. But they will not, according to traditional contractarian views, be doing so for ecocentric reasons. The environment will only be protected insofar as it serves human interests to do so. Likewise, the traditional rights view, because it holds being an experiencing subject to be the basis of rights, will not accord any rights to the environment. But we may nonetheless have an obligation to preserve the environment insofar as creatures that do have rights depend on it—if a policy damages environmental resources on which a creature depends for its well-being, then arguably that policy infringes on that creature's rights.

Paul Taylor develops what he calls a "life-centered system of environmental ethics," according to which "we have prima facie moral obligations that are owed to wild plants and animals themselves as members of the earth's moral community." Taylor does not explicitly say that his view is deontological—indeed, he says it is neutral as between consequentialism and deontology—but because he uses the language of duties towards and respect for nature, it is often described as a deontological environmental ethics. Taylor argues that each living thing has a good: it can be benefited or harmed. "What is good for an entity is what 'does it good' in the sense of enhancing or preserving its life and well-being. What is bad for an entity is something that is detrimental to its life and well-being."[21] Taylor points out that to have a good in this sense doesn't require sentience or any kind of subjective experience; things can be good for plants and species in this sense (whether the view can accommodate things like rivers or rock formations is another issue). Taylor goes on to argue that any entity that has a good also has inherent worth, and that therefore its good must be taken into consideration whenever we are deliberating on actions that will affect it, and that it is to be treated as having intrinsic value and not merely instrumental. The realization of its good is an end in itself.

This last point has seemed, to many, unacceptably strong: just because an entity has some good does not mean that we are obligated to realize it or even assign it any positive moral weight. For example, viruses have goods—things can be beneficial or detrimental to viruses. Does this imply a moral obligation to help HIV, or Ebola, or Zika, flourish? Some critics have argued that Taylor is confusing the descriptive sense of "good" with a normative sense: just because something is good for a being in the descriptive sense does not mean it is good in the moral sense. A bomb may be good for ending lots of innocent lives; neither the bomb nor ending lots of lives is good in any moral sense. Others argue that, like the land ethic and deep ecology, the view's actual prescriptions for behavior are ambiguous at best and unacceptable at worst. As the virus example illustrates, we will inevitably confront cases where human interests conflict with the interests of other living things. What we want from an environmental ethics is a view that tells us what to do in such cases. A view that tells us to respect all living things and realize their good is a view on which we seem destined to fail.

4.3 Virtue Ethics and Agrarian Ethics

Much of the moral critique of agriculture assumes what Thompson describes as "an industrial philosophy of agriculture."[22] Implicit in the industrial philosophy is the

---

21   Taylor (1981, p. 199).
22   Thompson (2012, p. 175).

view that humans' relationship with the environment is one of cause and effect—human actions bring about environmental outcomes—and our moral evaluation of agricultural practices proceeds by weighing costs against benefits. Agriculture is just one form of economic activity among many, and the moral issues it raises are the familiar ones raised by any other kind of technology and industry; if it plays a role in climate change, so do other activities, such as transportation. If it raises issues about labor conditions, so do other types of factory work. Critics of agriculture make their case by pointing to hidden or external costs of food production, whether these are environmental, consequences for animal welfare, or obesity and malnutrition. By focusing on problematic outcomes of agriculture, these criticisms entrench the industrial philosophy, asking us to consider whether the costs of our current practices are unacceptably high.

The industrial philosophy also reinforces the idea that nature is something that humans act *upon*, by using technology and industrial practices to alter it. In contrast, Thompson advocates an "agrarian philosophy of agriculture," one which views agriculture as "performing a social function over and above its capacity to produce food."[23] The agrarian philosophy offers a more dynamic understanding of agriculture and our relationship with the environment, in which we act on and are acted upon by the environment and our agricultural practices. Specifically, our practices surrounding the production, purchasing, and consumption of food "establish patterns of conduct that are conducive to the formation of certain habits. These habits become "natural" to people who engage in them repeatedly and become the stuff of personal moral character."[24] The agrarian philosophy views agriculture as a component of individual and community moral development; the farmer is not just defined by her job, but by her character and as a citizen of her community. As Thompson notes, this idea has roots in the early American view of farming; Thomas Jefferson thought that farmers were the ideal citizens, because farmers were uniquely invested in—literally, rooted in—their land and their community. The idea of farmers as uniquely good citizens goes back much further: in the *Politics*, Aristotle writes, "The best material of democracy is an agricultural population; there is no difficulty in forming a democracy where the mass of people live by agriculture or the tending of cattle ... having the necessaries of life they are always at work, and do not covet the property of others."[25]

This agrarian philosophy is neither consequentialist nor deontological; it's a kind of virtue ethics, a view on which our actions are formed by and evaluated against the character traits from which they stem. This approach will be familiar, since we applied it to epistemic evaluation in Chapter Two. As we saw there, part of what distinguishes the virtuous person is a kind of practical wisdom: she can evaluate a

---

23   Thompson (2012, p. 175).
24   Thompson (2012, p. 181).
25   Aristotle (1984b, 1318b8–12).

situation and see which acts and feelings are called for, and conduct herself accordingly. We don't begin by inquiring into which acts or principles are right or wrong and aiming at these acts; rather, we begin by inquiring into the nature of good and bad character, and evaluating actions as expressions of character. We start by doing the kind of acts that a kind or courageous person does, and thereby become kind and courageous. Since our characters are formed by our actions, we must be careful to form the right habits. Thompson's point is that rather than viewing our food choices as independent choices made in an economic framework of costs and benefits, we ought to view them as forming habits that affect how we relate to our environment and each other, and as expressions of and contributions to our characters as individuals and as citizens. Understood through this lens, the moral implications of our food and agriculture are wide-ranging and extend far beyond the act of eating itself: what we eat and how determines what sort of characters we form and what sorts of communities we create.

Critics might argue that this is an unrealistic picture of our food system and its possibilities; the ubiquity of industrial agriculture forces most of us to engage with food in economic transactions, and few of us have opportunities to engage with land and the environment on a regular basis. We'll look more at local food movements, and concerns about their viability, later in the book. The agrarian philosophy needn't be entirely opposed to industrial agriculture, however; we can explain what industrial agriculture leaves out, and what is lost when we focus on environmental impacts as costs, without jettisoning industry altogether. Another criticism might be that the empirical claims about agriculture's impact on character are unrealistic, and that our food choices don't really impact the way we view and interact with our environment. This might be a critique of the agricultural philosophy, or it might be a critique of our current food system—perhaps our alienation from the sources of the food we eat is preventing us from realizing a certain kind of civic virtue—a point we will return to in the context of local food and urban farms in the concluding chapter.

CONCLUSION: RECONCILING THE VIEWS— PLURALISM AGAIN?

We've seen arguments that the environment has moral value in its own right, such as, the "last person" example. But it is also of tremendous value to humans—and to other animals. For humans, ecosystems affect our health, serve as a resource (providing food, water, and other resources), and are objects of aesthetic appreciation. In the first case, we can see from our discussion above that agriculture affects the water we drink and the air we breathe. It is a major source of our food supply, and without industrialized agriculture, food would arguably be much more expensive. But industrialized agriculture, and especially animal agriculture, also consumes enormous amounts of resources, and may deplete resources for future people, since some of the farming practices deplete soil quality and the runoff kills ocean life, including fish we eat. Finally, people place aesthetic value on the environment. We derive aesthetic pleasure from looking at landscapes, including rock formations, mountains, streams, plants and trees, and wildlife, including songbirds and insects. Agriculture changes the landscape around us in obvious and less-obvious ways: it requires land, lots of land, and it alters that land in ways that affect the wildlife and plant life surrounding it. This is not to deny that farmland is beautiful; however, as agriculture consumes more and more of the available land, diverse landscapes are lost—such as the coastal ecosystems given over to aquaculture.

These values often conflict: we want clean air; cheap, abundant food; and beautiful views. Which is most fundamental? Value pluralism answers that all of these values may be equally fundamental and yet irreconcilable. In evaluating the environmental impacts of agriculture, we may run into cases where our fundamental moral values conflict with one another. Perhaps agriculture is one such case: for health and environmental reasons, we would prefer to avoid industrial agriculture; for reasons of need, we can't abandon it altogether. The concepts of stewardship and Thompson's agrarian ethics promise to reconcile economics with ethics by telling us that what is good for the land is good for the farmer and the eater. But this is not always so: many farmers need to make money and may already be invested in an industrial system. A move to local farming is perhaps desirable, but incurs significant economic costs. For example, for a farm to move from conventional to organic farming—which, from an environmental perspective, means less pesticide and fertilizer use—requires that land not be conventionally farmed for three years. While farmers can command a higher price for organics, during those three years they're investing in the lower yields and more labor-intensive methods without seeing any of the accompanying profit. It also remains to be seen whether consumers are really happy to pay the additional cost of organic food, and whether they can afford to. So, there may be a genuine conflict between what's good for the environment, what's good for producers and consumers, what's good for humans as eaters and consumers, and what's good for us as inhabitants of an ecosystem on which we depend.

Likewise, we can see conflicts between future and present people and their needs, and between different communities. Those who enjoy the benefits of cheap food aren't always those who bear the costs. Lagoons of animal waste aren't distributed evenly across America (an observation we'll explore further in Chapter Eight); they're concentrated in low-income areas and disproportionately affect people of color. Depletion of fish populations has a greater impact on small-scale fishermen, who can't afford sophisticated equipment to help them locate fish, or bigger boats to take them further out to sea. And all of the environmental effects of agriculture described in this chapter will have an impact on the resources available for future people to use. In the next chapter, we will look at some of the ways technology has had and will continue to have an impact on our food supply, from animals to agriculture—can technology offer a solution to some of the environmental problems outlined above, or does it simply introduce new risks and concerns?

Chapter Six

FOOD
AND
TECHNOLOGY

INTRODUCTION

This chapter discusses technology's role in our food system. Understood in one sense, this is redundant: our food system is and always has been a form of technology, whether using tools to hunt and fire to cook, applying fertilizer to lands, designing irrigation systems, or using selective breeding techniques to domesticate animals and plants. But in the last century, humans have made significant advances in our ability to modify organisms for food consumption, and to influence their growth through the application of chemically engineered pesticides and fertilizers.

Throughout the chapter, I'll use GM as an abbreviation for "genetically modified" and GMO to abbreviate "genetically modified organism." This is arguably misleading, since all the food we grow is genetically modified from its original origins. "Genetically engineered" is another term that's sometimes used for these foods, and perhaps that's more accurate insofar as many objections to GM food are based on the role technology plays in the process—the engineering rather than the modification per se (a point we'll discuss in Section 4 below). But GM has become the dominant term, so much so that it is common for writers to begin papers on the topic by acknowledging its inadequacy and then continue using it—just like I'm doing right now.

The disagreement that begins with the name extends to virtually every aspect of these foods: the motivations for their invention, their safety and effects on the environment, and whether and how to sell and market them. In addressing these disagreements, we find ourselves confronted with conflicting and potentially irreconcilable values. But unlike in earlier chapters, where we found some areas of agreement (on, say, the badness of suffering), here there is little common ground. That's partly because GMOs originate out of the industrial food system, a system that has aroused suspicion since well before the invention of GM crops. And it's partly because of a more general unease about the role of technology in our food supply. It makes sense, then, to begin by looking at the history of industrial agriculture in the twentieth century, so we'll start by describing some of the technological innovations that precede GMOs. We'll then look at arguments in favor of and against GMOs, before turning to questions about the role of GM in animal agriculture.

1. THE GREEN REVOLUTION

The "green revolution" has its origins in research conducted in Mexico in the 1940s and the Philippines in the 1960s. Funded by the Rockefeller foundation, scientists began breeding new, high-yield, disease-resistant varieties of wheat (Mexico) and rice (the Philippines). The timing of this research closely followed one of the most significant innovations in human agriculture (for better or worse): the discovery of chemical fertilizers. In the early twentieth century, scientists developed a method for producing fertilizers out of thin air—literally. Plants rely on nutrients to grow, and they're particularly reliant on nitrogen, which is essential for photosynthesis. Prior to the invention of chemical fertilizer, farmers returned nutrients to depleted soil using traditional approaches—applying manure as a fertilizer or rotating animals through the fields, planting other crops that return nitrogen to soil (so-called nitrogen-fixing crops, such as alfalfa), or adding compost. Sources of nitrogen fertilizer were limited, and most of the supply came from saltpeter mines or as a byproduct of other processes. The new Haber-Bosch method allowed scientists to capture nitrogen from the air and, by combining it with hydrogen to form ammonia, "fix" it into a stable chemical form, which farmers could then buy and add to their soil. This meant that farmers were no longer limited by the natural fertility of soil or by traditional methods (which require time). Instead, they could grow crop after crop of, say, corn (which is a real nitrogen hog—it uses up to half a ton of nitrogen per acre)[1] without worrying about how to replenish the soil.

Nitrogen doesn't just fertilize, though—it explodes. The discovery of nitrogen-fixing just preceded the outbreak of World War I, and enabled Germany to manufacture its own explosives without relying on supplies from overseas. In 1924, a Cambridge, Massachusetts newspaper explained, "America's entrance into the World War in 1917 found us dependent upon Chile for nitrates with which to manufacture explosives.... Hence the federal government decided to construct a federal nitrate

---

1   This discussion of Haber-Bosch, and the statistic about corn, is drawn from Roberts' *The End of Food* (2008, p. 20).

plant of its own." This plant, located in Muscle Shoals Alabama, was still under construction when the war ended; nonetheless, the article goes on to report, it "did not become useless at the signing of the armistice.... Nitrogen compounds can be made into either explosives or fertilizer."[2] During World War II, the plant was used for the former; after the war, it shifted to manufacturing fertilizer. This turned out to be a pivotal moment for twentieth-century agriculture: the development of artificial fertilizer, combined with pesticides, new irrigation practices, and the new hybrid crops developed by green revolution breeding programs meant that farmers became much more productive. The new varieties of wheat and rice were hardier and yielded more food per acre; as a result, productivity skyrocketed. Between 1961 and 1970, China's rice production doubled. Between 1940 and 1999, US corn production went from 56 to 240 million tons—while the amount of land devoted to corn actually *decreased*. The green revolution is often credited with saving millions of lives; Norman Borlaug, often called "the founder of the green revolution," won the Nobel Peace Prize in 1970.

But the green revolution has its critics, too, and the debates begun by its innovations are still playing out today, in the context of genetically modified organisms and other applications of biotechnology to food production. The current interest in GM crops is motivated by many of the same concerns that drove the green revolution; critics of GM foods are likewise motivated by many of the same fears and objections. Still, while the debates are not new, there does seem to be something dramatically different about the technology itself—genetically modified organisms (GMOs) have elicited strong responses from consumers and activists. In this chapter, we'll look at debates about the ethics of genetically modifying crops and animals. We'll see that the technologies themselves might be new, but the disagreements are familiar, and possibly irresolvable.

2. THE DEBATE OVER GM FOODS

Proponents of genetically modified crops point out that for as long as humans have engaged in agriculture, we have been engaged in genetic engineering: domesticating plants and animals has involved an ongoing process of selective breeding, modifying crops and livestock to encourage desirable traits (such as docility, or size of fruit) while weeding out undesirable ones. However, as we saw above, the advent of twentieth-century technologies such as synthetic fertilizer removed previous limitations on what kinds of crops could be grown and to what extent. At the same time, using conventional breeding methods (in other words, without editing genomes—we'll say more about what this means in a moment), scientists such as Borlaug were engineering new strains of crops such as wheat, corn, and rice. These new strains had a number

---

2   Sherman (1924).

of advantages: they were resistant to disease and drought, and they were smaller, producing higher yields on smaller plants (hence their label, "dwarf" varieties—because the plants don't invest energy in growing tall, they have sturdy, short stalks and bigger seeds or grains). This major revolution in agriculture was accomplished without genetic engineering per se, although one might argue that it depended on the ability to engineer the soil itself, by adding nutrients back in via fertilizer.

The discussion of fertilizer above is significant, because it can be seen as laying the groundwork for the current generation of GM crops and as a kind of litmus test for how one views GMOs: these fertilizers were a huge breakthrough for agricultural productivity, ushering in a new age of industrial agriculture. But they also turned fertilizer itself into a product, one that was always in demand regardless of how the prices of various crops might fluctuate. Separating fertilizers from farming laid the groundwork for a new kind of agricultural industry: one whose products and profits were not food itself, but the technologies on which farmers increasingly rely to produce that food.

This is important to bear in mind as we discuss genetically modified crops, because there are two quite different narratives we will encounter. The first depicts GM crops as the technological innovation that has allowed us to feed a growing population (population growth and hunger will be discussed further in Chapter Eight). Bill Gates has claimed that two out of every five people on earth owe their existence to the invention of synthetic fertilizer.[3] If that's true, then GM crops are the logical next step: once those people exist, they need land to live on, and food to eat; these new crops promise to yield more food from less land, require less water, and tolerate the more extreme conditions brought on by climate change.

The second narrative is significantly less optimistic: GM crops are designed to maximize profit first and foremost, by requiring farmers to invest in expensive seeds, fertilizers, and pesticides. By modifying the genomes of plants and animals, GM crops turn food into technology, and subject it to patents and intellectual property laws, taking it out of the hands of farmers and placing it into the hands of multi-national corporations. While the process of selecting plants and animals for desirable traits might not itself be radically new, the fact that the process is now largely concentrated in the hands of a few powerful private corporations marks a radical and threatening departure from the past. Furthermore, GMOs threaten biodiversity, by encouraging farmers to grow a narrow range of crops; because GM crops are designed to withstand the application of certain pesticides, they also encourage greater pesticide use and can therefore actually lead to pesticide-resistant weeds, insects, and disease.

The remainder of this chapter will proceed as follows. First, we'll look at the use of GM crops in agriculture. We'll discuss the motivations for GM, as well as the

---

3   Gates (2013).

arguments against GM crops, contrasting the two narratives outlined above. Then, we'll look at the issue of GM animals. We'll discuss these separately for two reasons: first, while general concerns about power and technology are the same, many of the arguments concerning GM crops are different from those that apply to GM animals, since the fact that animals are sentient arguably entitles them to special moral consideration (as we've seen in Chapters Four and Five).

3. GM CROPS: BACKGROUND AND USES

As used in this context, "genetic modification" typically refers to recombinant deoxyribonucleic acid (rDNA) techniques: processes that identify and isolate the genes that code for a desirable trait in one organism and then transfer those genes into the genome of another organism. The most controversial cases involve *transgenic* rDNA, where the gene is transferred from one species into the genome of another species. So, the gene(s) that make one species tolerant of cold might be transferred into another. The species need not be closely related; the media eagerly seizes on stories of fish genes placed into tomatoes as evidence of a kind of "Frankenfood."

The most common GM food crops are more prosaic and less sensational: corn and soy. These crops typically undergo GM either to make them pesticide or herbicide resistant, or to reduce or eliminate the need for pesticides—two dramatically different approaches and outcomes. For example, Monsanto's "Roundup Ready" seeds (which include soy, corn, sorghum, and cotton) contain genes from bacteria that make the plants resistant to glyphosate, a commonly used pesticide (which Monsanto also manufactures). This means that farmers can spray their entire field with Roundup without worrying about killing their crops. On the other side of things, so-called *Bacillus thuringiensis* (Bt) crops incorporate genes from a bacteria toxic to caterpillars, the result being that farmers don't have to apply (at least some) pesticides to these crops; the plants make their own. These two examples point to one important feature of the debate over GM foods and crops: the environmental costs and benefits of the technology differ enormously from crop to crop! In just these two examples, we see one case where GM results in a significant *increase* in the use of herbicides, and another where GM promises to significantly *reduce* the use of pesticides. In both cases, proponents of GM point to increased efficiency for the farmer, which in turn benefits consumers.

Another application of GM is engineering crops to better withstand adverse growing conditions, such as drought, heat, and disease. In the 1990s, the ringspot virus spread throughout Hawaii's papaya crops, reducing the yield by almost 50 per cent. By injecting a bit of the virus into a papaya's genome, scientists were able to develop a variety of papaya—the Rainbow—that's immune to ringspot, and which now accounts for nearly 80 per cent of the papayas grown on the islands. This means that if you've eaten a papaya in the last decade, you've probably eaten GM fruit. (Technically, this is only true if you've eaten non-organic papaya, since the organic label can't be applied to GM foods, but some anti-GM advocates have pointed out that thanks to pollen drift, even organic papayas in Hawaii tend to test positive for Rainbow papaya genes—a point we'll return to below).

Finally, scientists have used GM to modify the nutritional profile of foods. The most famous example is "golden rice": rice that is genetically engineered to contain high levels of beta-carotene, which is converted by the body into vitamin A. Rice doesn't usually contain any beta-carotene, and in areas where rice makes up a large part of the diet, there are high rates of vitamin A deficiency, which can lead to childhood blindness and death. So, golden rice has been touted as a humanitarian breakthrough.

The potential to relieve hunger and prevent malnourishment is the strongest argument for GM crops. Proponents argue that without GM, we will be unable to feed a rapidly growing population (for a more detailed discussion of population growth worries, see Chapter Eight). GM crops promise to be resistant to disease, therefore offering a food supply that is less susceptible to fluctuation and disruption. Advocates also point out that while we can't increase the amount of land, we can increase the amount of food each acre of land yields by breeding more productive crop varieties. This is another environmental argument for GM crops: by making existing farmland more productive, we can avoid having to destroy ecosystems and displace wildlife in order to create new farmland.

4. GM CROPS: OBJECTIONS

Critics don't necessarily deny these benefits, but raise a number of additional objections. We can divide these into two categories. *Intrinsic* objections to GM are based on the very idea of genetically modifying or engineering crops. These are objections that apply to GM regardless of how it is practiced; according to intrinsic objections, we should never pursue GM because the very idea of it is morally wrong. *Extrinsic* objections, on the other hand, are based on possible (or actual) consequences of, or motivations for, GM. Extrinsic objections are contingent insofar as the aspects of GM they object to are not the very act itself, but to a cause, consequence, or corollary of GM. Most extrinsic objections rest on matters of empirical fact, which we won't have time to fully explore, but we can say a bit about the general concerns at work: GM food is bad for the environment; GMOs threaten biodiversity; GM food increases social inequality and reliance on the industrial food system; GM food is unsafe. We'll discuss each of these before turning to the main intrinsic objection to GM foods: that they are unnatural.

4.1 Extrinsic Objections to GM Foods

OBJECTION 1: GM IS BAD FOR THE ENVIRONMENT

In response to the argument that GM crops can increase yields, thus allowing us to feed the world using less land, critics point out that we already have plenty of farmland—but we're using it to grow food for animals, not humans. The claim that we need GM to feed a growing population is based on our current food system, in which over one-third of the grain we grow is fed to livestock (and much of this is GM).[4] Since, as we saw in the previous chapter, cows and pigs are relatively inefficient at converting grain and water into meat, it would be much more efficient to simply feed this grain directly to humans. So, GM is not necessary to feed the planet, or to reduce the amount of land devoted to agriculture—we could address both hunger and environmental concerns by reducing our consumption of animal products. The fact that proponents of GM rarely mention these alternatives is evidence, to opponents, that their primary concerns are neither humanitarian nor environmental, but profitability.

Some of the most prevalent GM crops are engineered to withstand the application of pesticides and herbicides. The same companies that manufacture and sell GM seeds often sell the complementary pesticide. So, Monsanto makes Roundup-Ready seed, engineered to withstand applications of Roundup—an herbicide they also manufacture. More recently, some weeds have evolved a resistance to Roundup, so the company has added a new herbicide, dicamba—and a new form of seed, engineered to withstand Roundup *and* dicamba. This illustrates one concern about the use of herbicides on GM crops: that it will eventually lead to weeds that have evolved a tolerance for those herbicides (likewise for Bt corn and caterpillars). This will in turn require even more or stronger chemicals, which will in turn create further resistance, and so on—a kind of arms race between pesticide manufacturers and plants. In other words, the respite that GM crops offer is only temporary, and in time, they will in fact require even more pesticides and herbicides—or, worse, lead to the evolution of pests that can't be controlled. And, of course, the increased use of herbicides, pesticides, and fertilizers leads to more runoff entering the water supply and increased human exposure to pesticides.

OBJECTION 2: GMOS THREATEN BIODIVERSITY

A related concern is the extent to which GM crops threaten biodiversity. GM crops might "escape" into the wild, where they could conceivably replace wild plants, because they have been bred to outperform other strains. Both GM plants and the

---

4   See Roberts (2008) Chapter 8 for a discussion of the increasing demand for meat and its impact on grain supply and fertilizer use.

pesticides applied to them can drift into neighboring fields, though there is disagreement over how big an actual threat this drift actually poses: proponents of GMOs argue that there are few if any documented cases of GM crops escaping into neighboring areas; opponents argue that the threat is real. (Pesticide drift, on the other hand, is real enough that some states in the US initially banned the use of dicamba to protect farmers who weren't growing resistant strains of soy from being affected by neighbors' use of it.) And even without this scenario, if farmers choose to plant GM crops at the expense of others, we might end up with only a few strains of corn, or wheat. If these strains then end up failing, we will face major famine. Thus, this is not only an environmental concern; it's also a concern about food security. There are a number of "seed banks" worldwide which aim to combat this possibility by storing varieties of seeds from around the world. The Svalbard global seed vault is one of the most remote and secure of these. Located inside a mountain on an island in Norway, it contains seed samples from around the world—currently, almost a million samples, but with the capacity to store up to 2.5 billion—and boasts the world's most diverse collection of seed samples. It does not accept genetically modified seeds.

OBJECTION 3: GMOS PERPETUATE SOCIAL INJUSTICE

While proponents of GMOs argue that they will benefit farmers in developing nations by improving crop yields and disease resistance, opponents reply that GM crops will mostly benefit wealthier farmers, whether in developed or developing nations, since these are the farmers who can afford GM seeds; they are also the farmers who can afford the fertilizers and pesticides needed to get the most from these seeds. Poorer farmers will be left unable to compete with the yields and lower prices that result, and may lose their farms as a result. Alternatively, they can take on debt to invest in new products such as GM seeds, fertilizers, and pesticides, but this puts them in a vulnerable position, as we'll see in the next chapter when we discuss ways that global food aid and trade policies disadvantage farmers in developing countries.

Critics also argue that GM crops encourage monocultures (growing large areas of a single crop), because they're designed for use alongside herbicides and pesticides. You don't want to grow GM crops next to something else, because then you won't be able to spray the field with Roundup—you don't want to risk it drifting across and killing your non-GM crops. GM seeds are also often patented and are engineered to be sterile, so farmers can't save seed from their crops to plant in following years. This means farmers are forced to buy new seeds every year. These two features make GM incompatible with many traditional farming practices, such as polyculture (growing several types of crops next to one another) and seed saving. In response, GM proponents point out that most farmers in industrialized nations stopped practicing seed saving decades ago. Even if it's true, this response only underscores the point that asking how GMOs affect farmers frames the question too broadly; like any technology, it will affect farmers differently depending on their circumstances and resources.

GMOs are just one example of the way agricultural technology can create a kind of dependency of farmers on corporations, and particularly farmers in developing and poorer nations. This kind of dependency hinders farmers' autonomy, and critics worry that it creates opportunities for exploitation. Dependence on GM threatens farmers' and even nations' *food sovereignty*: their ability to make their own decisions about food production and supply (we'll talk more about these issues in Chapter Eight, since they take us beyond GM into a discussion of the food system as a whole). And this is another aspect of GM that critics find problematic: it extends the reach of industrial agriculture, fostering even more dependency on pesticides, herbicides, and fertilizer, and encouraging the practices of industrial agriculture in areas where farmers have historically used traditional practices. As a result, the problems of industrial agriculture—both environmental and social—are exacerbated, and traditional knowledge and practices (and crops) are lost, which in turn increases dependence on corporations that produce GM seeds, fertilizers, herbicides, and pesticides. The idea that power over global food production might rest in the hands of a few corporations makes many people uneasy.

One response to these concerns is that they aren't really concerns about GM foods, they're concerns that apply to all forms of industrial agriculture. Industrial agriculture itself, with its reliance on technology and its emphasis on large-scale farming and maximizing crop yields, exacerbates social inequalities: the innovations agricultural research brings about benefit those with the means to adopt them. The use of pesticides and herbicides means that farmers already depend on corporations for their supplies and technology. Is all dependence bad? If so, the problems with the agricultural system pre-date and outstrip GM foods. Indeed, as stated above, many of the external critiques of GM foods go back at least as far as the green revolution and are applicable to all forms of industrial agriculture. That doesn't show them to be unfounded; perhaps critics are right that we should move away from large-scale industrial agriculture and return to more traditional methods of small-scale polyculture. But this brings us back to concerns over whether such methods can produce enough food to feed our growing population. We'll look at other farming methods, such as hydro- and aquaponic farming, in the concluding chapter; for now, we'll look at another objection to GMOs: the unknown risks they pose.

OBJECTION 4: SAFETY, RISK, AND PRECAUTION

The increasing reliance on technology in our food system raises concerns about safety, some of which emerged alongside the green revolution itself: in the 1960s and 1970s, environmentalists rallied against pesticide use based on its harm to wildlife and to humans, and controversy persists over the safety of commonly used pesticides. There are also concerns about packaging materials, preservatives, and additives; concerns about food safety have followed the industrial food system since its inception. We will talk more later in the chapter about the psychological reasons why GM food might seem especially concerning or dangerous. For now, we'll look at some of the ways we manage and negotiate the inevitable risks of our food system.

Packaged and processed foods have alternately been seen as dangerous—there is a long history of adulterated food products, from spices mixed with wood and almond shells, to watered down milk, to chalk in flour—and safe. In post-war America, processed food became a symbol of American prosperity. For example, processed baby food was seen as safer and superior to homemade versions; because it was produced in a factory, it was viewed as sterile and scientific. Fast food, too, was initially marketed as a safe, standardized, and rigorously controlled product, entering the market at a time when ground beef was regarded with suspicion as likely to contain contaminants and spoiled meat.[5] This is in marked contrast to current attitudes towards homemade versus processed foods, especially the ones we feed to our children!

While our attitudes towards industrially produced food have shifted over time (and may well shift again), our attitude towards risk tends to be consistent: our goal is to avoid it when possible and minimize it otherwise. The *precautionary principle* captures this attitude; it says that when a product or activity carries a risk of harm, we can reject it until we have proof that it is not harmful. This is significant because, in many cases, we expect proof *of* harm. It took a long time for the government to impose restrictions and taxes on tobacco because the cigarette companies argued that there was insufficient evidence linking smoking to cancer; many in the United States (and abroad) resist regulation of greenhouse gas emissions because there is no conclusive proof that these are contributing to global warming. The precautionary principle says such proof is not necessary. The principle has been stated in various ways over the years. The following are the three statements that have had the biggest impact on the debate over GMOs and environmental policy:

- 1992—United Nations Rio Declaration on Environment and Development: "In order to protect the environment, the precautionary approach shall be widely applied by states according to their capabilities. Where there are threats of serious or irreversible damage, lack of full scientific certainty shall not be used as a reason for postponing cost-effective measures to prevent environmental degradation."[6]

---

5   For an excellent and entertaining overview of food scares generally, and our attitudes toward meat in particular, see Levenstein (2012).

6   See article 15 of the United Nations Conference on Environment and Development (1992).

- 1998—Wingspread Conference on the Precautionary Principle: "Where an activity raises threats of harm to the environment or human health, precautionary measures should be taken even if some cause and effect relationships are not fully established scientifically."[7]
- 2000—Cartagena Protocol on Biosafety: "Lack of scientific certainty due to insufficient relevant scientific information and knowledge regarding the extent of the potential adverse effects of a living modified organism on the conservation and sustainable use of biological diversity in the party of import, taking also into account risks to human health, shall not prevent that Party from taking a decision, as appropriate, with regard to the import of the living modified organism in question ... in order to avoid or minimize such potential adverse effects."[8]

These three formulations of the precautionary principle have different implications, which illustrates the difficulty of using it as the basis for a specific prescription for action. The Rio Declaration sets the bar fairly high: there must be a threat of serious or irreversible damage, and the measures must be cost effective. The Wingspread statement is less specific and sets the epistemic bar a bit lower: it doesn't require that an established cause-and-effect relationship exist in order for precautionary measures to be taken, and there's no mention of cost. And the Cartagena Protocol—the only one of the three formulations designed specifically to deal with biotechnology and food—allows nations to decide for themselves which actions they are willing to take in order to minimize risks. This formulation is also the least epistemically demanding, allowing for action in the absence of sufficient information about the effects of the technology in question. Note that in all three cases, the likelihood of risk is unknown. If we knew the risks involved in GM foods, we could collectively decide whether they were acceptable. Critics of GM point out that we can't make this assessment precisely because we don't know the risks. Defenders of GM argue that this is because GM foods are safe; the fact that we don't have evidence regarding their risks is precisely because they're not risky. Because the precautionary principle allows the possibility of risk to serve as a reason to reject GM foods, and because it's difficult to prove that there are no risks from GM, the precautionary principle is often read as giving permission to reject GM foods on the basis of fears rather than evidence.

On the other hand, the precautionary principle, at least as formulated in Rio, tells us that when we have a serious threat to the environment, lack of certainty shouldn't stop us from taking cost-effective measures to act. If GM crops promise to halt damage to the environment, it would seem that the precautionary principle

---

7   Science and Environmental Health Network (1998).
8   Secretariat of the Convention on Biological Diversity (2000), article 11.8.

requires us to pursue them. And, of course, we should not forget the promise of GM crops to relieve hunger and malnutrition: according to the Wingspread formulation, we should take precautions against activities that pose threats to human health even if we don't have all the necessary scientific evidence. Shouldn't we then take every precaution against hunger and malnutrition, even if this involves GM crops regarding whose safety we're still unsure? The precautionary principle seems ambiguous at best as a guide to action where biotechnology is concerned, because there are possible harms and safety concerns both in pursuing them and not pursuing them.

Currently, there is no evidence that GM foods are harmful to consumers. But transgenic GM foods have raised concerns about the potential for allergies. And there are, as noted above, concerns about environmental risks—loss of biodiversity, famine due to GM crops failing, or the rise of pests or diseases that resist all treatment. As we said above, GM crops lend themselves to monocultures, a fact that raises fears of vulnerability: if we come to depend on a small number of strains of seed, and these come under attack by pests or disease, the result could be catastrophic crop failure. Because GMOs can spread into areas beyond where they're intentionally planted, the concern is that they might spread even more widely than we realize or intend.

The precautionary principle tells us that the possibility of risk justifies resisting the adoption of GM crops, but it also tells us that the risks of not adopting these crops should be weighed, too. Borlaug, who we discussed at the beginning of the chapter, has said that those who resist GM crops are "anti-science," because there is no empirical evidence substantiating risks from GM crops. He argues that, in light of the growing need for food, it is irresponsible not to pursue GM crops:

> To date, there has been no credible scientific evidence to suggest that eating transgenic agricultural products damages human health, or the environment. Virtually all of the scientific debate has been [about] possible damage and the risk factor society is willing to take.... Privileged societies have the luxury of adopting a very low-risk position on the GM crops issue, even if this action later turns out to be unnecessary. But the vast majority of humankind does not have such a luxury, and certainly not the hungry.[9]

Borlaug's argument is that in the absence of empirical evidence of harm, the refusal to pursue GM food represents an unacceptably risk-averse position—unacceptable, because it has consequences for our ability to feed a growing population (though not everyone agrees with this empirical claim, a point we'll return to in Chapter Eight). But there are other objections to GM that don't turn on empirical questions of harm and risk: the intrinsic objections. We'll discuss these next.

---

9   Borlaug (2001, pp. 77–78).

4.2 Intrinsic Objections to GM

There are a number of intrinsic objections to GM, but most can be reduced to some version of the idea that GM foods are unnatural. This idea can be expressed in several ways. Some critics have argued that by engineering species, humans are "playing god."[10] But we don't need to use theological language to make the point; we can understand the objection as saying something like, by developing GM crops, humans have given themselves unprecedented power over other species, and this is morally wrong. If this objection succeeds, though, it would lead to the conclusion that many human activities—agricultural and otherwise—are wrong. After all, we've been breeding plants and animals for desirable characteristics since the very beginning of agriculture. Is that morally wrong? If so, once again, we have an objection to agriculture itself, and not just GM. The challenge is to find an intrinsic objection that identifies what's problematic about GM without ruling out too many other practices.

OBJECTION 1: GM FOOD IS UNNATURAL

A variant on this objection is that GM crops are unnatural and therefore wrong. This objection is tricky to spell out, because equating "natural" with "good" forces us to say that some pretty terrible things—rape, genocide, cancer, famine, death in childbirth—are good. Surely, we reject any ethical view that led to the conclusion that childhood cancer is good. Is there a more plausible way of understanding the objection? One thought is that unnatural interventions in the food system are bad because they have historically had bad consequences. Therefore, this intervention (GM) is likely to have bad consequences and should be avoided. This version of the objection seems better; the problem is that it, too, has unacceptable implications—namely, that we should not intervene in the food system. This is simply impossible. Given the number of interventions we've already performed, we have to remain actively involved; given the need to feed an ever-growing population with ever-dwindling resources, it seems that the consequences of failing to intervene would be as bad as, if not worse than, the consequences of intervention. The objection, if successful, is an argument against any kind of agriculture, and as such it must be rejected.

Another version of the unnaturalness objection draws on the fact that GM crops are transgenic and argues that it is this crossing of species boundaries that makes GM foods unacceptably unnatural. Unlike some of the objections discussed above, this one points to a feature that distinguishes GM from other forms of agriculture. Given that species boundaries are set by nature, the objection runs, by altering them we are taking new power into our hands and meddling with distinctions that we may not fully understand. But this objection faces two challenges. First, many philosophers

---

10   See, for example, Midgley (2000).

(and scientists) have argued that species boundaries are not as sharp and fixed as the objection makes them seem. Second, even if species boundaries were static and immutable, this is a descriptive fact about them. Why should we accord it any weight in our normative deliberations? In other words, what is the moral relevance of the fact that there are boundaries between species? We need an argument to the effect that crossing species boundaries is a bad thing to do. Absent such an argument, the objection seems to reduce either to the claim that it is bad because it is unnatural, or to the claim that crossing species boundaries will have bad consequences.

OBJECTION 2: GM AND THE YUCK FACTOR

There is another intrinsic objection to GM, which is difficult to put into words but is sometimes referred to as "the yuck factor." In essence, the objection states that there is something disgusting, repulsive, or repugnant about GMOs, and that this disgustingness is sufficient reason to be wary of the practice. Before we talk about this objection, it will be useful to discuss two more applications of biotechnology to food, since these will provide some additional examples for our discussion.

We first encountered the possibility of genetically modifying animals in Chapter Four, during our discussion of the ethics of eating animals. There, we raised the question of whether it would be ethically permissible or even desirable to genetically engineer chickens to lack certain brain structures necessary for conscious experience; the reasoning was that if raising chickens for food causes them to suffer, we ought (according to some utilitarians, at least) to replace the existing, suffering chickens with birds that would suffer less.

Decerebrated chickens might seem far-fetched, but what about chickens bred to be blind? Blind birds are more docile than sighted birds, so blind chickens wouldn't require debeaking, a painful procedure that stops overcrowded birds from pecking at one another; this means that they would be able to withstand more crowded conditions with less suffering than other birds. Such birds are well within the reach of current technology. In fact, GM animals already exist:

- Dairy cows often suffer from mastitis, a painful infection of the mammary glands; it is spread from cow to cow via milking machines. It's usually treated with antibiotics, but some strains are antibiotic-resistant. And antibiotic use in animals is cited as a source of environmental concern and as a threat to public health—it is thought that antibiotic use on factory farms increases the threat of the emergence of antibiotic resistant diseases. Researchers have found that introducing a gene from a bacterium into the cows' DNA causes them to produce a protein that kills the bacteria responsible for the infection, thereby eliminating the suffering they experience as a result of the infection—and the need for mass quantities of antibiotics.[11] GM can also eliminate the need for dehorning operations (a painful operation) by transferring genes from hornless breeds of cattle (typically raised for meat) to dairy cows. While resistance to mastitis and hornlessness can be achieved through conventional breeding, the outcomes are far less reliable. GM ensures that the cattle will have the desired traits.

- The "Enviropig," developed by researchers at the University of Guelph, contains genes from mice and from the e. coli bacteria that produce an enzyme in its saliva which enable it to break down the phosphorous in its feed better than conventional pigs. Recall that phosphorous is a major contributor to pollution from factory farms. By breaking down phosphorous with their saliva, these pigs excrete less of it. Their waste therefore contributes less phosphorous as runoff and pollution. Other pigs have been genetically modified to produce healthier meat: meat with a higher level of omega-3 fatty acids, which are thought to have health benefits.

- The AquAdvantage salmon grows faster and is more resistant to cold than conventional salmon. It contains genes from another salmon species as well as from a fish called the ocean pout (which has antifreeze-like chemicals in its blood). The AquAdvantage salmon reaches its full size in about half the time of a conventional salmon and requires less feed. They have been approved by the Food and Drug Administration (FDA) for sale in the US, but as of this writing were unavailable because of issues having to do with labeling. In Canada, the fish are not labeled as genetically modified because regulators see no relevant difference between the AquAdvantage and conventional salmon.

One objection to genetically modifying *animals* (which is not applicable to GM crops) is that it violates their rights. By treating animals as things to be modified so that they better meet our needs, we reduce them to mere objects, which fails to respect that they are living, sentient beings. However, these wrongs are already being committed on a large scale by animal agriculture: if it's wrong to modify an animal's body, then practices such as dehorning, debeaking, and trimming pigs' tails are also wrong. If asking animals to modify their natures is wrong, then feeding corn to cows is wrong, since they evolved to eat grass and can't digest the diet we feed them without medication. This doesn't mean the objection fails; indeed, many who object to GM animals on the grounds of animal rights will also object to eating animals in the first place, and certainly to the way cows are fed and raised. But applying the rights objection to GM is slightly more complicated than applying it to eating animals,

---

11   Wall et al. (2005).

because in the case of GM animals it is not clear which animal's rights are violated. Thinking back to our discussion of future people in the previous chapter might be useful here. Suppose we grant that when we modify an animal that already exists— say, by dehorning a cow—we wrong that individual by violating its rights. But when we genetically engineer a hornless cow, who or what is wronged? It cannot be the engineered cow, because that cow would not exist if we did not engineer it. Furthermore, that cow's life is better than the life of a comparable cow which was not engineered, because thanks to GM, the cow will not have to undergo a painful dehorning procedure. The engineered cow was not created out of another individual that was wronged by its creation, and it itself is not wronged by its creation—unless the life of a factory farmed cow is so bad that to bring one into existence is wrong (which is not an implausible claim). But if that's so, then the problem is not GM itself, but factory farming. The rights objection to GM animals is problematic because rights belong to individuals, and in the case of GM animals, there are no individuals whose rights we can say are violated.

An alternative way of framing the objection makes use of the concept of *animal integrity*. In this context, integrity refers to, "the wholeness and completeness of the animal and the species-specific balance of the creature, as well as the animal's capacity to maintain itself independently in an environment suitable to the species."[12] Integrity is a property of animals and their bodies, but it doesn't explicitly require that the animal in question be sentient, only that it have some nature or wholeness that's violated by alterations. So, we could extend the concept to species or even to the animal genome itself.[13] We could say that species integrity refers to the completeness of a species, such that when a distinctive trait or feature of that species is removed or altered, its integrity is violated. Likewise, we could say that genome integrity is violated when the genome is altered—when parts of it are removed, or when something is added. One problem with extending the concept of integrity to the genome is that it seems to rule out any sort of domestication, even the use of selective breeding, which alters the genome. It seems some violations of animal integrity are inevitable; there must, therefore, be a kind of scale or range of modifications, only the extreme ends of which are morally wrong. Still, it would seem that removing a creature's conscious experience (as with the decerebrated chickens) or one of its most vital senses (as with blind chickens) is wrong. Whether the same can be said for increasing an animal's growth by inserting a new gene is a trickier question. Here we run into a familiar question: perhaps violations of integrity based on GM technology are especially morally objectionable, but is this because of the violation itself, or because of a more instinctive reaction to the technology involved?

---

12 Rutgers & Heeger (1999).
13 See Vorstenbosch (1993) for discussion.

This brings us back to the so-called yuck factor and the objection based on revulsion at the prospect of eating transgenic crops or animals. Critics have argued that this is simply an emotional reaction unsupported by argument: to say that GM crops or animals are disgusting is just to express an intuitive, personal, and irrational reaction to them. In response to this dismissal, other writers have attempted to identify reasons underlying our disgust at GM foods. Mary Midgley (in an article subtitled, "Why we should pay attention to the yuk factor") argues that disgust is a reaction to the perceived "monstrosity" of GMOs: because GMOs cross species boundaries, they are creatures not found in nature—in other words, monsters. And as our oldest myths and stories reveal, we have always been cautious if not afraid of monsters. Therefore, we shouldn't dismiss disgust as irrational, because it expresses a principled objection to the project of genetic engineering: its crossing of species boundaries. Midgley also objects to the attitude with which we undertake these projects, as evidenced by the fact that we sometimes describe it as "genetic engineering":

> Cogs and sprockets can in principle be moved from one machine to another since they are themselves fairly simple artifacts, and both they and the machines they work in are more or less fully understood by their designers. Those who use this analogy seem to be claiming that we have a similar understanding of the plants and animals into which we might put new components. But we did not design those plants and animals. This is perhaps a rather important difference.[14]

This way of putting the yuck-factor objection makes it sound as though the real problem with GM is a kind of epistemic hubris: we tinker with nature as if we fully understand it, but we don't. But while epistemic hubris and overconfidence is a real concern, it's unclear why we should react to it with *disgust* rather than some other form of condemnation or caution. Midgley goes on to explain: "What they [critics of GMOs] are essentially rejecting is not any particular single project. It is this huge uncriticized impetus, this indiscriminate, infectious corporate overconfidence, this obsessive one-way channeling of energy." But while overconfidence is a practical problem, it is unclear why this is a *moral* objection, and why this kind of objection should express itself in the language and experience of disgust.

5. DISGUST AND TECHNOLOGY

Disgust is intimately linked to food and eating. It evolved as an outgrowth of our distaste response, as a way of protecting us from poisons, parasites, and pathogens.

---

14   Midgley (2000, p. 12).

Distaste occurs when we taste something bitter, or sour, or otherwise unpalatable—we withdraw from it and eject it from our mouth. Disgust is likewise a form of withdrawal, but it's more dramatic: first, we don't even have to taste something to be disgusted by it. Sight, smell, touch, and even *imagining* something might be enough to disgust us. Second, when something is disgusting, we don't just spit it out, we feel revolted by it. We might gag or even vomit. We wrinkle our nose and pull our whole face back. Disgusting foods are also contaminating and polluting in a way that distasteful foods aren't: if I simply feel distaste for broccoli, I will push it to the side of my plate and eat the other food. If I'm disgusted by it, I won't want to eat anything with which the broccoli has come into contact. I might even be unable to eat while it's on my plate.

A further difference is that disgust isn't necessarily a response to the sensory properties of a thing. Two pens might be identical in all their observable properties, but differ in disgustingness—if, for example, one has been dipped into a public toilet. This is what makes disgust such a powerful emotion: it doesn't respond just to appearances, or smells, or tastes, or feel, but also to ideas and beliefs about an object's history or origins.

This flexibility raises concerns about disgust's suitability as a basis for policymaking. Because disgust is not necessarily grounded in any observable or even empirical feature of a disgusting thing, it's subjective: we justify claims of disgustingness by pointing to our own feelings of disgust, rather than any independent or intersubjective standard. Hard-boiled eggs are disgusting to me, but not to you; there is no definitive answer to the question, are they really disgusting? Because disgust evolved to protect us from threats that are invisible to the eye (and hence especially dangerous) like bacteria and other microbes, it tends to be overcautious and result in a lot of "false positives"—it's better to reject a food that is actually safe than to accept a food that's actually dangerous. As a result, many of the foods we find disgusting aren't actually threatening at all, and we shouldn't trust our feelings of disgust as a reliable guide to threat.

5.1 Disgust, Rationality, and Labeling

This implies that we should give no weight to objections to GM based on disgust unless the feelings can be explained in terms of some other, more empirically grounded threat. But food is a very personal choice; our responses to food are often saturated with emotion. Shouldn't people have the freedom to decide what to eat, even if those decisions are based on emotion rather than reason or evidence? The idea that people should be able to exercise autonomy over what food enters their body is an argument in favor of labeling for GM foods. Foods could either be labeled to indicate that they do contain GM ingredients (this is currently the EU standard), or they might be labeled to indicate that they don't contain any GM ingredients. Proponents argue that consumers have a right to know whether or not they are eating GM ingredients—partly because people have such strong feelings about the issue. Sales of unlabeled GM salmon, or unlabeled non-GM foods, make it impossible for consumers to know whether foods have been genetically modified or not, and therefore violate their autonomy.

Opponents of labeling regulations argue that they would impose a significant, even prohibitive, cost while promoting mistaken beliefs about the safety of GM. If foods containing any GM ingredients must be labeled, then manufacturers would have to build additional facilities in order to keep GM products separate from non-GM products. These costs, argue opponents, would be passed on to the consumer, resulting in higher food prices. Furthermore, there's a risk of labeling creating a stigma against GM foods. The fact that a food says it is free of GM ingredients can be seen to imply that this is a good thing, thereby giving the impression that there is something wrong with GM ingredients. Alternatively, the fact that a food is labeled as containing GM ingredients might be interpreted as a warning. (In Europe, once labels on GM foods were required, the use of GM products decreased dramatically due to worries about consumer reactions.) In either case, opponents argue, labeling presents a major obstacle to the widespread adoption of GM crops.

CONCLUSION: AN IRRECONCILABLE MORAL DISAGREEMENT?

One reason to be pessimistic that the debate will be resolved any time soon is that the two sides seem to invoke conflicting and irreconcilable moral values to justify their positions, making it difficult to find common ground between them. Consequentialist arguments point to potential harms GM crops might cause to the environment and to farmers who adopt them (and farmers who don't). On the other hand, consequentialists must balance these possible harms against GM's promise to alleviate hunger and malnutrition. Deontological and rights-based views would point to the fact that people must be able to exercise autonomy over their food choices. These views might point out that farmers may not want to grow GM food, and consumers—even hungry ones—may not want to eat it. In 2002, Zambia refused a shipment of food aid because it contained GM corn and soy. News reports at the time suggested that the aid was refused because of fears that the mere possibility of GM contamination would make Zambia's export crops less appealing to European markets.[15] This illustrates that the attitudes we bear towards our food aren't entirely personal or private, but have consequences even for very distant people. Understood this way, the debate

---

15   See, for example, Better Dead Than GM Fed? (2002).

over GM foods involves a conflict between competing moral values: on the one hand, we have the consequentialist goal of relieving suffering, which few people would reject outright. On the other hand, we have the deontological imperative to respect people's autonomy and right to control what enters their bodies.

Conflicts between different value systems are always difficult to adjudicate, because there is no clear basis for comparing the value of suffering with the value of autonomy: the two are *incommensurable*. That is, they can't be compared or weighed against one another. This is part of what makes the debate over GM foods so difficult: it requires us to judge whether the potential benefits of the technology outweigh the (often deeply felt) values and emotions which lead people to reject GM foods.

Virtue theory does not resolve this debate, but it does offer another basis for objecting to GM foods. The virtue theorist might point to those responsible for developing and marketing GM foods as a reason to avoid GMOs. Large food producers do sometimes behave in ways that suggest they are more concerned with profit than with safety. For example, as I am writing this, the news reports that several executives at Dutch poultry companies have been arrested for producing and applying an illegal insecticide to kill mites on chickens in egg farms, a scandal which has led to the recall of eggs across Europe. The harm need not be intentional; negligence that results in contaminated or mislabeled food can itself be a sign of vice. If these companies' intentions are seen as evincing a lack of virtue, we might think that the products themselves are untrustworthy. Thompson suggests our judgments about GM are subject to a kind of "virtue-risk feedback loop":[16] because the people who develop GM foods are seen as not virtuous, their products are seen as risky; because they develop risky products, they are seen as not virtuous. This feedback loop might well operate in other areas of industrialized food production; food recalls remind us that food is inherently risky, which leads to doubts about the virtues of its producers and manufacturers; these doubts in turn feed into the perception of such foods as risky.

The virtue-risk feedback loop is not intended as a vindication of objections to GM foods. It is, instead, a diagnosis of a kind of objection—one that stems from the untrustworthiness and lack of virtues of big food corporations. One reply to this sort of objection is that people are notoriously unreliable and irrational when it comes to estimating risk, and so we should pay extra attention to intuitions about risk and be careful about using them to make important policy choices. We'll talk more about the relationship between psychology and public policy in the next chapter, when we look at our food choices and their effects on health.

---

16   Thompson (2015), Chapter 2.

Chapter Seven

FOOD,
HEALTH,
AND
FREEDOM

INTRODUCTION

According to the World Health Organization, as of 2016, nearly two billion adults worldwide are overweight; over 650 million are obese. Globally, obesity has more than doubled since 1975.[1] These statistics are controversial—there is debate over how we should define the terms involved, and whether these numbers tell us anything of significance about our diet and health—but alarm at the apparent rise in overweight and obesity has led many governments to propose new regulations on the sale and marketing of processed food. This chapter explores these policies and their psychological, social, and political implications. In particular, can we justify government interference with people's food choice, and if so, to what extent? What form will the justification take?

We concluded the last chapter with the observation that the debate over GM foods is particularly difficult because it requires us to weigh competing, incommensurable values, and that will be true of the issues discussed in this chapter as well. The debate over health and freedom is in part a debate over how to balance considerations of well-being and autonomy. But it's complicated by the fact that we may not be as autonomous as we think. While we like to think of ourselves as making choices about our food, in fact, the environment in which those choices take place is more limiting

---

1   See the World Health Organization's "Obesity and Overweight" fact sheet (2018, February 16).

and less conducive to rational reflection than it appears. Our own cognitive processes aren't as well-suited to careful weighting of evidence and goals as we might like, especially where food and pleasure is concerned.

We often think of freedom and choice as synonymous, but this chapter will question that equation. Most of us value choice because it reflects our authentic goals and desires, and not the manipulations of outside forces, so simply having options isn't sufficient to realize the value of freedom. Because the discussion below relies in part on facts about how we make choices and form preferences, we'll encounter themes first presented in Chapter Two: how information about food is presented to us and in which contexts, and how we can know what we're eating.

We'll begin our discussion by looking at one of the most influential views about when the government is justified in restricting freedom: liberalism. The view apparently precludes the government from interfering with our food choices, but as we'll see, this depends on how we understand both "choice" and "freedom." On a certain understanding of what freedom requires, restrictions on the choices available to us actually enhance our freedom, rather than limiting it. Since this claim turns on the psychology of choice and food choice, we'll discuss the sorts of cognitive biases that play a role in those choices. We'll also discuss the ways in which the language that we use to frame the debate over health can itself influence our judgments about who bears responsibility for our food choices.

I want to take a moment to acknowledge the difficulty posed by terms like "health" and "obesity." Some of the activists and critics we'll encounter later in the chapter prefer the term "fat," on the grounds that obesity is too "medicalized"—it connotes disease and ill-health. The term "healthy," used in conjunction with food is also problematic; arguably, foods on their own are neither healthy nor unhealthy, and only become so when considered in the context of diet as a whole. I'm sympathetic with this concern up to a point, but I don't think there is any sense in which Coca-Cola is healthy. The reader is free to disagree with this point, of course! The challenge of negotiating such disagreements is one of the themes of this chapter, so I hope readers will find the material below useful regardless of their views about the nature of a healthy diet.

1. LIBERTY AND LIBERALISM: THE HARM PRINCIPLE

A number of policies and approaches have been proposed to deal with the so-called obesity epidemic, including but not limited to the following:[2]

- Education: Public health campaigns have aimed at encouraging people to exercise more and eat healthier foods using advertisements, school programs, and workplace programs.
- Taxation and subsidies: a number of cities have imposed so-called soda taxes on sugar-sweetened beverages. Others have proposed taxing processed foods (one proposed definition of "processed" being anything that requires a nutrition label or list of ingredients) and taxing fast foods. To encourage consumption of healthy foods, some have proposed government subsidies of fruit and vegetable purchases, and there are programs that offer Supplemental Nutrition Assistance Program (SNAP) recipients incentives for spending SNAP money at farmers' markets on fruits and vegetables.
- Bans: In 2012, New York City mayor Michael Bloomberg proposed banning the sale of large servings of soda and other sugary drinks. (New York State's court of appeals later overruled the ban.) New York City also bans the use of trans fats in restaurants.
- Labeling requirements: The US FDA recently revised its nutritional labeling to make the total number of calories in packaged foods more prominent. The UK uses a labeling system that codes nutrition information in red, yellow, and green, to offer a visual guideline for consumers.
- Restrictions on advertising and promotion: in 2010, San Francisco banned McDonald's from giving away free toys in happy meals. The UK restricts the advertisement of certain foods during hours when children are most likely to be watching television.

Critics object to many of these proposals on the grounds that they are unacceptably *paternalistic*. Paternalism is the view that restrictions on our freedom are justified by the fact that they benefit us or prevent harm to us. Whether the above proposals actually meet the criteria of paternalism is something we'll discuss below, but there is

---

2   The Centers for Disease Control's (CDC) Division of Nutrition, Physical Activity, and Obesity maintains an excellent searchable database of all legislative efforts related to physical health and activity, whether successfully enacted or not. It is accessible via the CDC website and provides the most up-to-date information about these efforts, which are ongoing—the information cited above is current as of this writing, but subject to change.

no doubt that opponents have portrayed them as such: when Mayor Bloomberg proposed his ban on large sodas, opponents ran full-page newspaper ads, complete with a photo-shopped image of him in a dress, towering over the New York City skyline, under a banner reading "The Nanny." The tagline? "You only thought you lived in the land of the free." Notice that they didn't dispute the claim that drinking lots of soda was unhealthy; they focused on the idea of choice. As a free, informed, consenting adult, their argument went, I should be free to make unhealthy choices about my own diet. (And the ad reminded non-soda drinkers that they too should be worried: "What's next? Limiting the size of a pizza slice, a hamburger, or the amount of cream cheese on your bagel?") To these critics, telling adults how much soda they can drink represents an infantilizing infringement on freedom.

The idea that government is not justified in interfering in our actions for our own good, but only to prevent us from harming others, is known as *liberalism*. In his famous essay *On Liberty*, Mill lays out the central principle of liberalism—the *harm principle*:

> The sole end for which mankind are warranted, individually or collectively, in interfering with the liberty of action of any of their number, is self-protection. That the only purpose for which power can be rightfully exercised over any member of a civilized community, against his will, is to prevent harm to others. His own good, either physical or moral, is not a sufficient warrant.... The only part of the conduct of any one, for which he is amenable to society, is that which concerns others. In the part which merely concerns himself, his independence is, of right, absolute. Over himself, over his own body and mind, the individual is sovereign.[3]

But this does not mean we can never interfere with someone's behavior for their own good. Mill gives the following instructive example:

> If either a public officer or any one else saw a person attempting to cross a bridge which had been ascertained to be unsafe, and there were no time to warn him of his danger, they might seize him and turn him back, without any real infringement of his liberty; for liberty consists in doing what one desires, and he does not desire to fall into the river.[4]

This last qualification introduces a host of complications, especially in cases involving food and drink, where it's not always clear what our desires are, and where our immediate desires and long-term goals frequently conflict with one another. In looking at

---

3   Mill (1859/2003, pp. 80–81).
4   Mill (1859/2003, p. 158).

various philosophical defenses of the harm principle, we'll see that our view of the relationship between freedom and desire can significantly affect how we interpret the principle and its scope.

1.1 Deontological and Rights-Based Defenses of Liberalism

Rights theorists may argue that someone's right over their own body is absolute; interference with freedom is justified to protect someone else's rights, but when actions affect only oneself, even if they are harmful, there is no justification for interference. Traditionally, liberty is thought to be one of man's natural rights, and while rights theorists and contractarians acknowledge that in entering society, we necessarily give up some liberty to act on others, most agree that we retain the right to decide what happens to our bodies—which would seem to include what we put into them. But the relationship between freedom and desire is complicated, for reasons having to do with the concept of autonomy and how we interpret it.

Autonomy literally means, "self-rule." Kant claims that this capacity is essential to being a moral agent: it is only when we act in accordance with our rational nature, the one that determines its own ends or goals independently of external forces or inclinations, that we are truly free.[5] Kant tells us that the only thing with unconditional goodness is a truly free, rational will—a *good* will—that determines its own actions according to the moral law. Therefore, it is essential for the very possibility of morality that people be free to determine their own actions. But this doesn't mean people should be free to act according to their *desires*; Kant's conception of freedom is much narrower than Mill's. Unlike our rational volitions, our desires are outside forces—external compulsions that detract from, rather than contribute to, our free choices. When our emotions drive our behavior, we're being controlled by something external to the self: we're not autonomous, because the psychological influences shaping our decision don't properly belong to ourselves. Another instance of this is the phenomena of impulse or craving. We often talk of feeling powerless in the face of a craving or desire; in these cases, it's as though we are controlled by something from outside. An impulsive action doesn't originate from a reason or a decision, it simply happens to us.

Contractarians also endorse liberalism, though in extending the contractarian account from morality to politics, adjustments have to be made. Contractarianism applied to the political sphere must acknowledge the reality of moral disagreement. As we saw above, not everyone agrees that health is a matter for the government. But a government is only legitimate if it rules according to principles its citizens would reasonably assent to, despite their differing conceptions of the good. These principles

---

5   Kant (1785/1993, 4: 406).

for political cooperation will therefore remain silent on the question of which moral values to live by (Rawls uses the term "comprehensive doctrine" to refer to the set of beliefs that includes religion, morality, and a person's other values). Rawls claims that from behind the veil of ignorance, we would insist on retaining, "The maximum amount of liberty compatible with an equal amount of liberty for everyone else."[6] So contractarian accounts endorse liberalism as one of the foundations of a society that allows people with different moral values to coexist.

1.2 Consequentialist Defenses of Liberalism

As a utilitarian, Mill offers a consequentialist defense of the harm principle: allowing people to order their own lives creates the most happiness overall. My ends and plans are best for me because they are the ones I've chosen; acting freely contributes to my happiness. It's not just that people will choose the best actions, policies, or lives. Rather, we enjoy things more because we have chosen them. My life, my actions, and my possessions are meaningful to me because I have chosen them. If someone were to make those choices for me, I might enjoy them less or find them less meaningful. The utilitarian argument for liberalism is that autonomy is good for us because it is an important contributor to a happy life: as a matter of fact, we do enjoy having freedom and control over our lives; we feel bad when our choices are determined for us by others, or when we're not free to determine our own actions. Attempts at coercing others to act in certain ways for their own good tend to backfire, as Mill notes, "vigorous and independent characters ... will infallibly rebel against the yoke." The policy is also good for society as a whole, because society benefits from the existence of a diverse array of lifestyles. By allowing people to live as they choose, we avoid falling into a stifling conformity; by allowing various opinions and customs, we create opportunities for the best to flourish; where people make poor choices about how to conduct their lives, they'll suffer consequences, and we'll learn from their example. There are also the pitfalls of interference: "the strongest of all the arguments against the interference of the public with purely personal conduct is that when it does interfere, the odds are that it interferes wrongly, and in the wrong place."[7]

Mill's anti-paternalist argument is based on empirical assumptions about how people respond to having choices, and these assumptions may turn out to be false. As we will see below, people don't always (or even usually) make choices that improve their welfare. And the subjective experience of choosing may not always be pleasant—more choice isn't always better. Even if choice is generally beneficial, there's no guarantee that the benefits will be equally distributed—and there are reasons to think they won't be.

6   Rawls (1971, p. 266).
7   Mill (1859/2003, pp. 146–47).

2. LIBERTY: POSITIVE AND NEGATIVE CONCEPTIONS

Despite widespread agreement on the importance of liberty, there's disagreement about the implementation of liberalism and what it requires. This is partly because there are different interpretations of liberty itself.

Negative liberty can be understood as "freedom from": it means that one's actions are unconstrained by others. As the political philosopher Isaiah Berlin explained: "if I am prevented by others from doing what I want to do, I am to that degree unfree."[8] If I want to buy cigarettes but they are illegal and I am forbidden from buying them, I am not free to buy cigarettes. If I want to rappel down the Statue of Liberty, I am not free to do so. On the other hand, Berlin points out, the fact that I can't jump to the top of the Statue of Liberty doesn't imply any restriction of my freedom: I am simply unable to do it. On a negative conception of liberty, if one is neither constrained nor compelled, one is acting freely.

Positive liberty is a kind of "freedom to": one is free to the extent that one is able to determine one's own actions. This is freedom in the sense of autonomy discussed above; it is realized when we're able to act in ways that reflect our will, our choices, and our true desires and goals. This sort of freedom requires more than non-interference, it requires having the means to act according to our will. I am not free to sit in the first-class cabin, because while there's no law forbidding me from doing so, I lack the means to buy a ticket. There is room for disagreement about what, exactly, this conception of freedom requires. Is the freedom to develop my talents satisfied by providing me with the freedom to engage in them, or does it require I receive an education as well?

This is where things become more complicated, especially in the context of food choice. If we adopt a negative conception of liberty, being free to eat what we choose simply requires the absence of any laws prohibiting certain foods. But on a positive conception of liberty, lack of restrictions isn't enough. We also require the means to realize our dietary goals and desires. The point is not just about healthy food. Positive liberty with respect to eating also requires having access to foods that reflect one's choices, values, and identity. Since positive conceptions of liberty are closely tied to autonomy and the idea of *self*-rule, enjoying this kind of liberty requires that one's diet reflect one's own goals and values.

Because of its link to self-determination and the expression of one's choices and values, the positive conception of liberty is consistent with the arguments for liberalism discussed at the beginning of the chapter. Insofar as constraint is bad, negative liberty is a good thing, but it's in exercising positive liberty that we realize the value of choice and freedom. And the two conceptions are sometimes at odds: for example,

---

8   Berlin (1969).

if I wish to take a pill that will render me unable to make any further choices, simply out of curiosity (i.e., without any deep or good reason), should I be allowed to? If we value my ability to exercise positive liberty it seems we should say no, but preventing me from taking the pill curtails my negative liberty. We might also confront a choice between short-term and long-term freedom; many people find routines surrounding food to be comforting, and would happily relinquish their freedom to choose what they eat on a daily basis in order to achieve long-term goals or merely to relieve the mental burden of navigating their choices.

3. FOOD, FREEDOM, AND FAILURES OF WILL

We sometimes act in ways that appear to go against our considered ends or goals; we explain these actions in terms of a "lack of willpower." The very term "willpower" implies that making one's will effective requires effort. Partly, this is because we have long-term goals that may conflict with more immediate desires, and our immediate desires often win out. We want to eat less sugar, but there's a birthday party at work, and we're hungry and tired, and the cake is tempting, and it's right in front of us. Protecting us from this type of failure of willpower would require removing temptation altogether—a kind of "coercive paternalism" we'll discuss in Section 7 below. Effort is also necessary because it can be difficult to discern when an action furthers our goal, or how it will affect us in the long term. We want to eat less sugar, so skipping dessert seems like a good strategy—but only because we don't realize that the dressing, walnuts, and dried cranberries in our salad have as much sugar as a bar of chocolate.

This case suggests that the kinds of policies we usually think of as paternalistic may actually be compatible with and even conducive to the realization of liberal goals, if they help us better exercise will and willpower. And they can help in two ways: first, we're subject to cognitive biases, ignorance and irrationality, and failures of willpower. The way choices are presented affects the way we evaluate risks and gains. A label or menu icon indicating that the aforementioned salad is high in sugar can remedy ignorance and/or remind me of my goals. Having an office policy about the kinds of food served at social events removes opportunities for lapses of willpower (though some would argue it also removes one of the few consolations of office life). Second, we may lack the requisite resources and opportunities to act on our goals, ends, and desires. Policies ensuring that restaurants and shops offering affordable fresh food options are available in all neighborhoods, and that healthy snacks are available and affordable at school and at work, remove obstacles to exercising food choice. After looking at definitions of paternalism and some of the motivations for it, we'll examine the strongest version of the view—coercive paternalism—to see whether interventions can be justified even if they don't facilitate, but actively inhibit, our autonomy. We'll then look at some critiques that argue that framing the debate in terms of liberal versus paternalistic reinforces problematic assumptions about health and bodies.

4. PATERNALISM: WHAT AND WHY

Paternalism comes in a number of flavors, but all are committed to the claim that it is sometimes permissible to restrict someone's freedom for that same person's own good, even if their actions harm no one but themselves. As Gerald Dworkin writes, paternalism is, "interference with a person's liberty of action justified by reasons referring exclusively to the welfare, good, happiness, needs, interests, or values of the person being coerced."[9]

Understood this way, paternalism is the denial of the harm principle: we can restrict an individual's freedom for her own good, even if her actions don't harm anyone else. When exactly such interference is justified, and on what grounds, is something paternalists disagree about. Soft paternalists argue that interference with a person's actions is justified when those actions are uninformed or in some way involuntary: for example, if the person doesn't know the bridge they're about to cross is broken. Hard paternalists argue that we are justified in interfering even in cases where the action is free and informed. This is the strongest form of paternalism, since it supports restricting people's voluntarily chosen actions for their own good; it doesn't just act to help people realize their own goals and values, but rather says that some goals and values should be either imposed or forbidden to people, for their own sake. For this reason, some writers have argued that only hard paternalism really counts as paternalistic; soft paternalism (and libertarian paternalism, a view we'll discuss in a moment) is really just a way of helping people do what they already prefer.[10]

A related distinction concerns the permissible means of interference. Some paternalists advocate forbidding or requiring actions, using laws to punish people for engaging in or refraining from certain behaviors. This is the approach we take to illegal drugs, and in some states to euthanasia and seatbelts. But other paternalists advocate educating and informing people, rather than imposing legal penalties. For example, we allow people to smoke and drink alcohol, but we put warnings about these substances on their packages. As these examples illustrate, real-world paternalism takes many forms; we are soft paternalists about some behaviors (smoking, drinking) and hard paternalists about others (heroin, seatbelts).

Libertarian Paternalism is the view that rather than taking away freedom, we can shift the way we present options to influence people's choice without limiting

---

9   Dworkin (1972, p. 65).
10   See Conly (2013, pp. 42–43).

it—hence the "libertarian" part of the name.[11] In this case, no options are actually removed, but the person is benefited by being "nudged" towards a better choice, hence the "paternalism" part of the name. Critics have argued that the view is not really paternalistic, because it doesn't take choices away, it just tries to shift behavior away from them. This may be a legitimate complaint; alternatively, one might argue that the view is really just a variant on soft paternalism: by structuring choices in a way that makes it more difficult to choose certain options, we are just making sure people really do choose, and aren't just falling into the behavior by default. Regardless of the legitimacy of the name, libertarian paternalism has received much attention, perhaps because it makes use of an increasingly popular (though recently somewhat troubled) body of research in social psychology and behavioral economics that purports to show that we often act irrationally and are susceptible to quite subtle forms of manipulation. Since these studies have been influential in motivating and designing paternalistic interventions, it will be worth spending a little time talking about them and what they show before we return to our discussion of libertarian paternalism in Section 7 below.

5. COGNITIVE BIASES, WEAKNESS OF WILL, AND PATERNALISM

We have lots of evidence that people are bad at planning their lives. We continue to browse the Internet despite the looming deadline. We light a cigarette that we know is bad for us. We spend money we don't have, choosing immediate gratification and suppressing questions about how we'll pay the credit card bill. We fail to contribute to retirement accounts, even when this means we pass up free money in the form of matching employer contributions. Over the last several decades, psychologists and behavioral economists have amassed an impressive catalog of our irrationalities; thanks to research into cognitive biases, we now know that we often fail to properly evaluate the evidence relevant to our decision-making, or, when we do evaluate it correctly, we fail to be guided by it. Here are just a few examples:[12]

- *Temporal discounting*: we tend to discount how valuable (or costly) money or other goods will be to us in the future. Hence, we acquire debts now, not thinking about the larger amounts we will have to pay back later; we

---

11   See Thaler & Sunstein (2003), who coined the term "libertarian paternalism," and discuss its implications for policy.
12   For a comprehensive overview of cognitive biases and their effects on decision-making, see Thaler & Sunstein (2008), Chapter 1, and Kahneman (2011).

continue to smoke now despite knowing it will have bad effects at a future date. We place less weight on future effects than on present ones.[13]

- *Anchoring effects*: when assessing situations, making guesses, or estimating value, we're heavily influenced by first impressions or our initial information. For example, if we're told a pair of shoes costs $800, but is on sale for only $400, the latter number seems like a good value, even if we would have considered it outrageously expensive had it been the first price we saw. (This is an interesting bias to consider in the case of calorie counts and food labeling, especially as food companies increasingly tell us their products now have "20 per cent less sugar!")[14]
- *Projection bias*: we assume our views and feelings will be similar in the future, not taking into account how changes in our circumstances will affect us, and we don't plan for changes of feeling or desire.[15]
- *Status quo bias*: we tend to default to our current situation and habits, eating the same foods and buying the same brands over time.[16]
- *Framing effects*: we are risk averse and tend to evaluate information differently depending on whether it is presented to us in terms of gains or losses—even if the information itself is exactly the same. For example, people prefer a treatment with a two-thirds success rate to one with a one-third failure rate—despite the fact that this is the same rate in each case.[17]

What makes these effects so troubling isn't their strength, it's their ubiquity. This is part of the motivation for paternalists in the first place: in their paper coining the term "libertarian paternalism," Thaler and Sunstein give the example of food options in a cafeteria. The options have to be presented in one order or another—there's no "unframed" way of offering people food. Dessert is either placed before the fruit, or after the fruit, and which placement is chosen will affect how much dessert is consumed. Similarly, we gravitate towards eye-level items on a store shelf. Since something has to be on those shelves, why not make it a healthy option? If all our choices are framed in one way or another, then the more opportunities we have to exercise choice, the more we will find ourselves susceptible to such effects. Of course, once aware of them, we can be on alert, but this is exhausting, which is one reason we're sometimes advised to adopt rules or policies about what we eat. But these rules can only get us so far, because they're only effective when they're based on good evidence, and when we obey them. The considerations above show that we're susceptible to

---

13   Thaler (1981); Stevenson (1992); Suranovic, Goldfarb, & Leonard (1999).

14   Tversky & Kahneman (1974); Furnham & Boo (2011).

15   Loewenstein, O'Donoghue, & Rabin (2003).

16   Samuelson & Zeckhauser (1988).

17   Tversky & Kahneman (1981).

errors in evaluating evidence—a vulnerability that food marketers are aware of. This brings us to challenges involving our ability to exercise willpower.

Even when we know that a choice is unhealthy and doesn't further our goals, we (sometimes) still opt for it, despite judging that we ought not to succumb. The reason might seem obvious: if food wasn't pleasurable, and didn't taste good, we wouldn't be tempted by it! But the point isn't that we sometimes decide to indulge ourselves and give in to pleasure; the philosophically more interesting cases are ones in which we succumb to temptation despite deciding not to.

5.1 Akrasia and Weakness of Will

The Greek term "akrasia" is often translated as "weakness of will" or "incontinence." It refers to cases where an individual acts against her better judgment, or when self-control seems to fail. Some philosophers have been skeptics about the phenomenon: Plato writes, "it is not in human nature ... to wish to go after what one thinks to be evil in preference to the good; and when compelled to choose one of two evils, nobody will choose the greater when he may the lesser."[18] If someone does act in a way that runs counter to their goals, or brings them pain, Plato argues, it is because they are mistaken about the best course of action: the failure is one of knowledge, not of will. No one would knowingly choose what she judged to be the inferior option. I might judge that I should avoid ordering fries for health reasons; if I order them nonetheless, this doesn't show a failure of will but rather a decision that health reasons are outweighed by considerations of taste—my "all things considered" judgment is that the fries are the best choice. Aristotle is more sympathetic to the possibility of failures of willpower. He describes, "a sort of man who is carried away as a result of passion and contrary to right reason—a man whom passion masters so that he does not act according to right reason, but does not master to the extent of making him ready to believe that he ought to pursue such pleasures."[19] This "incontinent man" retains the judgment that he ought *not* pursue the pleasures in question, but he is overwhelmed by desire so that he pursues them anyway. Aristotle acknowledges that sometimes, I reach an all-things-considered judgment that I ought not order the fries—and yet, somehow, they end up in front of me, either because I am conflicted and desire wins out over reason, or because I simply act on impulse without considering my action.

Which of these accounts is correct? This depends in part on how we define the relationship between acting and choosing: Plato's view is that it's impossible to knowingly and willingly choose an action we think is bad or imprudent, because choosing implies a kind of endorsement. But it's also a question about the psychology

18   Plato (1997c, 358d).
19   Aristotle (1984a, 1151b).

and phenomenology of temptation and will, and here it is helpful to reflect on our experiences giving in to temptation. J.L. Austin points out that in many such cases, it doesn't *feel* like we're overwhelmed by emotion or desire—our behavior doesn't become unhinged:

> I am very partial to ice cream, and a bombe is served divided into segments corresponding one to one with the persons at High Table: I am tempted to help myself to two segments and do so, thus succumbing to temptation and even conceivably (but why necessarily?) going against my principles. But do I lose control of myself? Do I raven, do I snatch the morsels from the dish and wolf them down, impervious to the consternation of my colleagues? Not a bit of it. We often succumb to temptation with calm and even with finesse.[20]

This is a helpful example, but many people *do* find themselves "losing control" in the face of temptation, especially when it comes to food: we sometimes do wolf and raven (and here it is instructive to note Austin's choice of words—when reason succumbs to desire, we describe our actions in animal terms). We don't intend to finish the entire container, but somehow, without consciously choosing, we find ourselves holding an empty bag or box. Not all cases involve action, either: we fail to get off the couch, we fail to start the paper that's due tomorrow. Nor is health the only area of our lives that stands to benefit from a greater understanding of this phenomenon. Our moral judgments can fail to translate into action as well. Most of us judge that we ought to do more for the environment than we actually do, whether that's recycling, buying organic rather than conventional produce, not eating fast-food burgers, and so on. While the discussion in this chapter focuses on how we might use our knowledge of cognitive biases to influence health-related choices, it has implications for some of the issues discussed in previous chapters—assuming that we could agree on the content of our moral obligations, how might we best go about trying to influence people's behaviors to better realize moral goals? We won't have time to explore those issues in detail here, but I encourage the reader to think about ways in which the approaches discussed below might be applied to our moral behaviors, and whether they are any more or less justifiable in moral contexts.

5.2 Libertarian Paternalism and Weakness of Will

Given the number of choices we make about what to eat every day, it seems inevitable that we will at some point fall prey to cognitive bias and weakness of will. That's why libertarian paternalists propose enacting policies that will correct for some of these

---

20   Austin (1956, p. 198).

biases, making it easier to conform to our better judgments. The easier choices are to make, and the easier temptation is to resist, the less we need to rely on willpower to overcome desires or cravings. Even simple obstacles, the libertarian paternalist argues, can make a significant difference: placing healthy foods at eye-level but unhealthy foods high up or lower down on shelves; putting the healthy foods first on the cafeteria line, so customers walk past the salad bar before they encounter other options; making portion sizes smaller so that customers who want to consume more popcorn or soda must buy a second helping. Portion size has been an especially contentious topic, as we saw with Bloomberg's attempt to limit soda sizes, but in light of the anchoring bias, we can see why it might be significant: if the default size of a soda is 12 ounces, a 24-ounce soda will seem large. But if the default size is 24 ounces, or 32 ounces, a 40-ounce soda seems only a bit big, and a 12-ounce soda seems quite small indeed. Portion size limits don't necessarily try to control what we eat by limiting our choices. They also work by reframing our beliefs and attitudes about the choices available to us.

Because libertarian paternalism relies on the way options are presented to us in order to encourage good choices, its proponents argue that it is not unacceptably coercive. It doesn't actually prevent us from doing anything—all our choices remain open. One criticism is that since the view relies on gentle behavioral "nudges" and cognitive biases in order to be effective, it detracts from our capacity to make *rational* decisions, by appealing to our more intuitive, less reflective thought. Critics object that the view is manipulative and disrespectful because it allows and even encourages our cognitive biases to influence us. But of course, these biases operate with or without nudging—the only effect nudging has is to change the direction they incline us toward. And external factors are significant too, since they determine which choices we're presented with: if there's no fruit on the cafeteria line to begin with, or no low-calorie options on the menu, re-ordering the items, or posting calorie information, can only do so much to influence our health. In the next section, we'll look at the influence of environmental factors on food choice, before re-examining the justification for paternalism.

6. FOOD ENVIRONMENTS AND FREEDOM

The idea that we are truly autonomous with respect to food ignores the fact that we can only eat what's available, and in many parts of the developed world, that limits us to unhealthy and processed foods, because many communities lack access to fresh, healthy food. This isn't simply a matter of a lack of stores or sources; access also requires transportation to and from stores. Lastly, and perhaps more importantly, access requires affordability. This is why one popular approach to encouraging healthy eating involves a combination of education and government subsidies for healthy foods. For example, recipients of SNAP money who spend their SNAP dollars at farmers' markets may (in some communities) be eligible for additional or sometimes even matching funds. We will talk more about issues involving hunger, health, and access to healthy food in the next chapter.

One might object to subsidizing some foods over others, arguing that government should remain neutral in questions of what people eat and refrain from interfering in both personal choice and the operations of the markets. The problem with this objection is that the government already subsidizes certain foods, both directly and indirectly. It directly subsidizes corn and dairy production by guaranteeing farmers a minimum price for their products and buying back surpluses. Through "checkoff programs" the government also underwrites and oversees efforts to promote certain food products. Campaigns such as "got milk?" or "Beef: it's what's for dinner" are the result of these programs, which collect money from farmers and put it into an advertising and promotion fund, which is in turn overseen by the US Department of Agriculture. A recent report estimates that in 2011, revenues from these efforts totaled about $200 million.[21] These funds don't just pay for advertising; government scientists work in conjunction with companies such as Taco Bell, Pizza Hut, and McDonald's to develop foods that will make use of surpluses of cheese and dairy products. Yes, even the stuffed crust pizza! So, the government is already deeply involved in our food system, and its actions already affect the choices available to us.

7. PATERNALISM REVISITED

Thus far we've been focusing on interventions that encourage people to engage in certain behaviors and avoid others, either by providing education, financial incentives, or by altering the environment and the way choices are presented to us. These policies are relatively weak forms of paternalism, because they don't actually take any options *off* the table: they leave our options intact while trying to draw our attention or incline us to certain ones. But some people argue that policies like these don't go far enough. If we have such a hard time acting autonomously with respect to food, why not simply take certain options off the table altogether? There is something apparently paradoxical about taking choices away in the name of preserving choice, but the appearance is illusory, since the justification for such forms of "hard" paternalism can draw on the distinction between having options and being autonomous. Our short- and long-term goals sometimes diverge, so we may need to remove some short-term options to preserve long-term goals. The hard paternalist may not even care if their view diminishes autonomy, as long as the end result is that people are better off.

---

21   Simon (2014).

7.1 Coercive Paternalism

Hard paternalism can be justified in both utilitarian and contractarian terms. The utilitarian may justify paternalistic interventions if they produce more good than harm, and in many cases, this is a reasonable expectation: while addicts might be frustrated by a ban on cigarettes, in the long run, such a ban would prevent many painful deaths. Above we saw the contractarian argument for liberalism, namely, that under conditions of the original position, we would want to preserve the maximum amount of freedom possible. However, we might also want to agree in advance to certain interventions. If we know that we will be tempted by certain acts (say, experimenting with a highly addictive drug) that will in turn result in a loss of autonomy, we might agree in advance to rules that prevent us from undertaking those acts. The classic example is Odysseus who, faced with the prospect of sailing past the sirens—whose songs lure sailors towards a certain death and who sing in a meadow surrounded by the bones of their victims—instructs his crew to tie him to the mast so that he cannot give in to temptation.

Hard paternalism seems to have effectiveness and efficiency on its side. If smoking is bad enough that we are willing to devote millions and millions of dollars to discouraging people from doing it, why not simply ban it altogether? Hard paternalists also argue that they are able to respect people in a way that other, softer forms of paternalists do not. Rather than trying to manipulate people through nudging, the hard paternalist forthrightly prohibits certain actions altogether.

Conly defends a version of hard paternalism she refers to as *coercive paternalism*, which holds that "we may and are sometimes morally obligated to force people to refrain from certain actions and engage in others," because "we are trying to control people on the grounds that their own decision making is not to be trusted."[22] She argues that there are four conditions any coercive paternalist policy must meet:

1. The activity to be prevented on paternalistic grounds really is one that is opposed to our long-term ends.
2. Coercive measures have to actually be effective.
3. The benefits have to be greater than the costs.
4. The measure in question has to be the most efficient way to prevent the activity.[23]

Hard paternalist approaches to obesity that have been suggested include a ban on all-you-can-eat buffets, limits on the total number of calories in a dish or meal, or

---

22   Conly (2013, p. 32).
23   Conly (2013, pp. 151–52).

a ban on certain foods outright. For example, in 2007, New York City enacted a ban on so-called trans fats, used in many fried foods and fast foods. Trans fats are particularly unhealthy, raising "bad" cholesterol levels (LDL) and lowering "good" cholesterol (HDL); they're linked to a higher risk of stroke and heart attack.

Conly argues that New York City's ban on trans fats meets the criteria for justified uses of coercion, and that restrictions on portion sizes would also meet them. She is somewhat more skeptical about the prospects for soda taxes, arguing that they would disadvantage poor people more than the rich (this is why such taxes are sometimes referred to as "regressive"), and that people who enjoy soda would most likely be willing to pay a premium for it. She ultimately concludes, "soda is sufficiently important to people that in some form it should remain available."[24] This is a significant concession, because it allows that even hard and coercive paternalists must take into consideration what people themselves value, and one criticism of paternalistic policies (especially in the domain of food) is that they cannot do so. In the remainder of this chapter we'll consider this and other objections to paternalism and the issue of regulating food in the name of health.

7.2 Objection: Whose Values?

One critique of the approaches described above is that they emphasize health as a reason for food choice but fail to do justice to the variety of values that influence our food choices. Paternalism justifies limits on people's actions by appealing to their own good. In limiting people's food choices in order to make them healthier, we assume that people's primary goal or value is health, and so helping them make healthier choices makes them better off and helps them achieve their goals. But we eat for all kinds of reasons—conscious reasons. We prefer to eat the birthday cake because on that occasion, tradition and celebration is more important to us than health. We make our grandmother's baked ziti because it comforts us. These examples may seem unproblematic; it's not like the paternalist says we should never indulge, and only a pretty strict health advocate would rule out a piece of birthday cake a few times a year. But other examples are more difficult. What about someone who values the pleasure they get from drinking two liters of soda on a daily basis, or having a pizza for dinner every night? Someone who truly claims to value these choices may seem irrational to us, but it's not irrational in the way that, say, believing 2+2 = 5 is irrational. Can we justify interference with their actions if they truly don't seem to have any goals that would be furthered by such interference? Or should we say that it is the goals themselves that are problematic and unacceptable and which

---

24   Conly (2013, p. 162).

need alteration? Conly claims that having any goal whatsoever (other than death) in turn entails a goal of not dying (since achieving anything else depends on that), so someone cannot rationally choose to act in ways that seriously threaten their health. If someone does consistently act this way, it's evidence (according to Conly) that they're under the spell of addiction or some other distorting factor, in which case coercion can only help them.

One justification for intervening to change people's values is that they will be better off after the change (we can think of this as a "they'll thank us later" defense), but there are both practical and philosophical concerns about this. Philosophically speaking, we might question whether it makes sense to say that a change in values makes someone better off if, prior to the change, there is nothing in their subjective attitudes or motivations that resonates with those values. For example, it may be true that were I to be transformed so that I come to value collecting cookie jars, I would be quite happy with this new value, and every new jar I acquired would bring me great joy. But right now, there's nothing about me or my psychology that has any interest in cookie jars, so it doesn't seem to make sense to say I'm made better off by coming to value them—even if, after the change, I'm happier overall. One might object that this is unlike the case we're considering, because unlike cookie jars, health is something everyone *ought* to value, but that's a claim that requires substantive normative argument—if valuing health makes even someone who does not care about health at all better off, it must be either because there's something objectively valuable about health, or because deep down that person has some existing interest or desire that is met by coming to value health.

Practically speaking, coercive paternalism is a hard sell, because it doesn't resonate with the affected person's own concerns at the time of the intervention. After all, if people wanted to stop drinking soda, the intervention wouldn't be coercive. It also raises concerns about government overreach: it's one thing to allow the government to interfere in order to help us realize our values, but allowing it to interfere in the values themselves is a different matter altogether. As we saw Mill point out above, the government makes mistakes and interferes badly. A related concern has to do with the means by which we would even go about trying to change values. The psychologist Paul Rozin argues that, in the case of smoking, we have "moralized" the behavior: what used to be a matter of personal choice is now considered a moral issue, so that we don't just think people who smoke are making a poor choice, we think they're making a *bad* choice—morally bad. Likewise, a coercive paternalism that aims to change people's ends to bring them in line with our social attitudes about health and physical well-being would end up moralizing health. And since health itself is invisible, the concern is that we will inevitably end up stigmatizing certain types of bodies. Indeed, according to some critics, we already have.

8. STIGMATIZATION, MORAL PANIC, AND THE SOCIAL POLICING OF BODIES

We began this chapter by observing that rates of obesity and overweight are climbing rapidly, and that this is associated with increased adverse health effects. Proponents of regulations on food rely on these data as the justification and motivation for their policies, but not everyone agrees that we should be so credulous. Overweight and obesity are defined in terms of a person's BMI—body mass index—obtained by dividing weight by the square of height in meters. Set ranges of BMI determine whether someone is underweight, healthy weight, overweight, or obese. But critics point out that the US lowered the cutoff point for "overweight" in 1998, a fact that's rarely mentioned in articles touting the alarming rise in the number of overweight Americans. Furthermore, critics argue that studies linking obesity to poor health don't always account for fitness, which is a potential confound—it might be that obese people are less fit than non-obese people, so that obesity is correlated with poor health but doesn't cause it. Even if obesity is increasing, characterizing the rise in terms of an "obesity epidemic" belies a certain attitude towards overweight and obese bodies: it treats obesity as a disease, something to be cured, or controlled; it implies that the obese body is a kind of threat and is potentially contagious. While the language used in debates over food policy appears descriptive and scientific, critics argue that apparently neutral, descriptive concepts such as BMI actually become, over time, normative, so that the definition of obesity is not purely medical or scientific—it's itself a normative judgment. Kathleen Lebesco argues that our current attitudes towards obesity bear all the hallmarks of a "moral panic":

> *concern* about an imagined threat; *hostility* in the form of outrage towards the individuals and agencies responsible for the problem; *consensus* that something must be done about the serious threat; *disproportionality* in reports of harm; and *volatility* in terms of the eruption of panic.[25]

Lebesco goes on to suggest, "Fat panic appears to be partly borne out of moral injunctions against sloth and gluttony in Judeo-Christian culture,"[26] arguing that though we express our judgments about obesity in terms of medical concerns, this masks an underlying moral judgment and anxiety about bodies (and especially women's bodies) that leads us to attempt to exert social control over them: "The language of health and risk has become a repository for a new kind of moralism."[27]

Obesity discourse and the policies stemming from it also risks exacerbating the stigma surrounding overweight bodies. Critics of these policies argue that the singular

---

25 Lebesco (2010, p. 73).
26 Lebesco (2010, p. 75).
27 Lebesco (2010, p. 72).

emphasis on health, and the equation of health and fitness with thinness, means that certain types of bodies are viewed as pathological and problematic, and that because public health discourse emphasizes individual choices as the root of obesity (more on this in a moment), it therefore encourages us to make negative character judgments and moral evaluations of individuals based on their bodies. Emphasizing weight loss rather than health, as many policies do, reinforces the idea that overweight is bad, and thinness is good, which in turn leads to negative judgments about certain types of bodies.

Those looking for evidence of social monitoring of bodies, rather than a concern for health, need look no further than policies such as laws passed in Georgia and Arkansas requiring public schools to collect information on students' height and weight as a way of measuring fitness, or proposals that would ban restaurants from serving obese people. The latter refers to a bill introduced (but not passed) in Mississippi's state legislature in 2008; its author claimed that he wanted to draw attention to the state's obesity problem, and in that respect the bill succeeded—it received lots of media attention. In 2013, Mississippi did pass a law concerning portion sizes: it made it illegal for cities, towns, or counties to limit portion sizes of foods or drinks.

9. HEALTH AND FOOD: WHOSE RESPONSIBILITY?

A broader critique takes aim at the framing of this debate in terms of individual choice and freedom. By focusing on the debate between liberalism and paternalism, I've chosen to filter the discussion thus far through the lens of government restrictions on individual action. The policies discussed so far all aim to alter behavior at the individual level, and the media attention they receive focuses the public debate on individual choice, thus contributing to the perception that obesity is caused by individual decisions. I've approached the issue this way partly because this is how the dialectic is often presented in both mainstream media and in scholarly, legal, and policy debates, and partly because the debate over obesity provides a useful example with which to introduce some debates in political philosophy. But many critics argue that by framing the debate this way, we only reinforce problematic assumptions about the causes of and solutions to these sorts of health problems: namely, that they are due to individuals making poor dietary choices.

There is controversy about the role that food plays in obesity. Some critics have argued that environmental factors, specifically certain chemicals that might affect human hormones, could be causing the increased rates of obesity.[28] Others point out that the increasingly suburban landscape, with its lack of sidewalks and walking paths, has resulted in decreased physical activity. Claims about the causes of obesity are controversial, and it's unlikely that there's a single overriding cause. Since this is a book

---

28   See Guthman (2011).

about food, I'll proceed on the assumption that food is at least a significant cause of increasing rates of obesity and overweight, even if it's not the sole cause. The question then becomes, who or what is responsible for our food consumption? As we've seen in earlier chapters, the government plays an active role in food policy. And, of course, companies profit from hyperpalatable foods high in salt, sugar, and fat. Given the many complex causes of obesity, why, then, has the attention, blame, and responsibility for fixing it all been placed on the shoulders of individuals? This focus on individuals contributes to the stigmatization we just discussed: if individual choices can solve the problem, then individuals who remain obese must be doing so by choice—or because they lack willpower—and are personally to blame. This is not to say that we consciously endorse such beliefs; rather, the idea that individuals are responsible for obesity, overweight, or poor health is an implicit attitude that we hold without necessarily being aware of it. It manifests itself in negative judgments about overweight and obese people. Multiple studies have found evidence that obese people are subject to workplace discrimination, negative judgments about their character, and receive inferior medical treatment.[29] These findings have led one researcher to conclude that "stigmatization of overweight and obese people appears to be one of the last socially acceptable forms of discrimination."[30] Discrimination and stigma may in turn contribute further to health problems, by stopping people from receiving help with their health and by causing stress and depression, which are also linked to poor health. The individualistic approach to the obesity issue therefore further entrenches the problem, by justifying (even implicitly) stigmatization of the overweight.

The problem isn't just that the individualistic approach has negative social consequences or is unproductive. It also obscures and distracts us from the other causes of, and responsibility for, health problems caused by food. It's often pointed out that humans evolved to favor sweetness, since it signifies calories, and to put on weight in times of plenty because famine might be around the corner. These explanations in terms of evolutionary psychology go on to point out that in our current environment, these tendencies are a problem, because sweetness does not signify nutrition, and the famine we're saving for never arrives. Perhaps the problem is the persistence of these tendencies into the modern era—our body is stuck in the evolutionary past. But perhaps we should be looking at how our environment has changed, and why.

Food manufacturers spend enormous amounts of money on market research to determine how to make their foods as palatable as possible. Sight, smell, even the sound a chip makes when we bite into it: all are carefully calibrated to ensure that we desire the food and will want to keep eating it. As it so happens, this is best achieved when food contains lots of salt, sugar, and fat. This is why there's sugar even in food

---

29   See, for example, Phelan et al. (2015), Puhl & Brownell (2001), and Brownell, Wang, & Wadden (2004).

30   Vartanian & Smyth (2013, p. 49).

that's not supposed to be sweet, and salt in food that's not salty: these substances contribute to color, shelf life, and texture as well as taste. And our responses to food are responses to appearance, and, of course, marketing.

10. ADVERTISING, AUTONOMY, AND TRUST

If the ethics of advertising is a tricky subject, the relationship between the ethics and epistemology of advertising is trickier. In Chapter Two, we introduced the concept of *bullshit*, a statement or speech made with no regard for truth—not a lie, because a lie aims to deceive, but rather an attempt to persuade without any interest in whether or not the speech is the truth. Advertising is a prime example of bullshit. Some advertising is, arguably, deceptive, but as we saw, the deception is secondary; the primary aim is to sell food. We can criticize deceptive advertising on the same moral grounds we criticize deception more generally, but advertising that's not explicitly deceptive is a more difficult issue: what, if anything, is wrong with it?

Advertising adversely affects autonomy in at least two ways. First, it can create desires that we wouldn't have otherwise. The most obvious way it does this is by presenting us with products we wouldn't be aware of (or need) without advertisements; products are invented in order to create desires in us, and not vice-versa. For example, fast-food chains are constantly experimenting with new menu items; we can't possibly need more forms of taco and cheeseburger, but once the product exists, we're curious to try it. The experiential nature of food and eating is especially amenable to this effect of advertising, since part of what we value in our food is novelty—we enjoy experiencing new flavors and textures. So simply presenting us with a novel or bizarre food combination is likely to create some level of curiosity and interest, if not outright desire. Food is also highly sensory, so we're susceptible to visual presentations of a sweaty can of soda, a string of cheese being pulled away from a slice of pizza, or the sound effect of a crunchy chip. Arguably we would still desire some of these things, in general, even in the absence of ads, but not the specific products marketed to us. Furthermore, the combination of widespread food advertisements on highway billboards and bus stops and the ubiquity of drive-through outlets means that in the moment where a desire is created, we will soon be presented with an opportunity to act on it. This marks another difference with other sorts of ads: most of us can't, after seeing a car commercial, simply pull into the nearest dealership and drive off in a new car moments later. So, it's not just the creation of desire that's problematic, but the ubiquity of opportunities to satisfy it.

Advertising also leads us to form false beliefs about food by using images that misrepresent the origins and contents of that food: fresh fruit and vegetables, as well as phrases like "100 per cent real ingredients," "homestyle," and "all natural." Almost all advertising appeals to emotion in one way or another, but these ads appeal to our emotions and our moral values, insinuating that the product will satisfy both. In fact, as we saw in Chapter Two, these phrases are literally meaningless. They create a superficial impression of health and moral goodness but fail to back it up.

Health claims are a major source of bullshit about food. They may operate by pointing out one desirable aspect of a food while neglecting to mention other, less desirable ingredients; for example, fat-free foods often contain higher levels of sugar and salt, though those latter features are never mentioned on the label. Food manufacturers also make claims to the effect that they've lowered calorie or sugar levels in food, but they don't mention that they accomplish this by reducing serving sizes rather than changing ingredients.[31] Such claims are not technically lies (and when they are, they're subject to government sanctions and/or consumer lawsuits), but they're certainly bullshit, and if they lead us to form unjustified or false beliefs, they may be epistemically, as well as physically, unhealthy.

Food marketing to children has proved especially controversial and has been a frequent target of proposed regulations. Critics especially object to the use of cartoon characters, athletes, and other popular figures to market foods to children. These practices exploit children's trust, the argument goes; the characters attract them to the ads and therefore lead them to pay attention, and because they like the character, they'll transfer this liking to the product. I bring this up not to dispute that the practice is problematic, but because one thing that's often left out of these conversations is the fact that the exact same form of manipulation is used in marketing products to adults. I'm not referring to Tony the Tiger or to the KFC Colonel, but to the many institutes and associations that put their mark of approval on "heart healthy," "high fiber," or "whole grain" products. These endorsements and labels work just like cartoon characters: they engage our attention and create positive associations. We might think there are two significant differences, namely, that these labels actually convey information and that adults are better able to evaluate information than children. But the arguments discussed so far in this chapter should give us pause about this.

CONCLUSION

This brings us back to the debate over paternalism, liberalism, and government regulation of food. In evaluating the extent to which regulations limit our autonomy, it's important to recognize that there are already forces at work nudging us: marketing, pricing, and the geographic distribution of food stores and restaurants (more on this

---

31   In 2017, a writer for the *New York Times* reported that the sugar in a serving of Honey Nut Cheerios—which has nine times the amount of sugar as plain Cheerios—had shrunk from 11 to 9 grams in the past ten years—because a "serving size" also shrank, from one cup to three-quarters of a cup.

in the next chapter) all affect our choices, and none of these is decided by the consumer. Environmental approaches to obesity attempt to mitigate these influences on our choices. One could argue that in doing so they restore some of our autonomy. Or, one could argue that they don't make us any more autonomous, nor do they make us any less so, so they're harmless at worst. But these approaches to the problem *can* in fact be harmful. They can draw time and attention away from the underlying issues and causes of the problem, such as the socioeconomic forces that shape our food environments and how we might disrupt these forces. And because they imply that changing individuals' behavior would reduce obesity, solutions that focus solely on increasing access to healthy food (over)simplify the issue and reinforce the idea that individuals and their choices are to blame. There are also problems with "interventions" to reduce obesity, pointing to the fact that such interventions are usually designed and imposed by a well-off, privileged group on less well-off minority, poor, and disadvantaged populations. We will talk more about the extent to which racial and economic differences play a role in our food environments in the next chapter.

Chapter Eight

FOOD
JUSTICE

INTRODUCTION

The food justice movement arises out of demands for a fairer, more equitable food system, both nationally and internationally. While the precise meaning of the phrase "food justice" has evolved, it has always involved a commitment to ensuring fair access to healthy food. Food justice activists also work towards fair treatment and conditions for farmers and laborers. Described thus, the movement's goals seem almost *too* uncontroversial: who could object to the idea that individuals should have access to healthy food, and that it should be produced in conditions that don't involve injury, abuse, and exploitation? If the answer is, "no one," then is food justice really a philosophical debate, or is it a matter of engaging in activism until these goals are achieved? As Thompson writes,

> One *might* question whether there is really a philosophical problem at all.
> On the one hand, the exposure of these atrocious practices [mistreatment of migrant workers] is seldom met with any defense ... [and] there is thus a sense in which offering a philosophical analysis of injustice in the food system is simply pointless. Everybody already knows, and nothing that a philosopher can say will do anything to further illuminate the problem ... it is not at all clear that the injustices in the food system are *philosophical* problems, and thus it is unlikely that they would be improved or resolved by a philosopher focused on food ethics.[1]

---

1   Thompson (2015, p. 59).

One way to address Thompson's concerns is through an examination of the issues of global hunger and food policy. While philosophers, economists, politicians, and activists have long agreed that hunger is a moral problem (though there are dissenters, as we'll see), there is deep disagreement about how to diagnose the problem. This, in turn, leads to disagreement about how we ought to go about addressing it. If the problem is primarily a lack of food, then we should focus on redistributing resources. But if there are deeper systemic injustices at work in the food production and distribution systems, as many philosophers and activists believe, then redistribution is at best a temporary remedy; we must look deeper to diagnose and address the underlying causes.

This chapter will look at food justice in both local and global contexts. We'll begin by discussing the debate over hunger and food policy. I start by giving a brief overview of the various philosophical approaches to hunger and famine, and discussing critiques of each. This material will help us understand the basis for these critiques of traditional approaches to hunger that focus on aid and alleviating famine, but fail to consider the effects of international policy on local food systems.

In the second half of the chapter, we'll look at food justice issues that arise from the industrial food chain: the impacts of food production on the environment, workers, and farmers, and the obstacles to fair and equal food access in communities. Before examining these problems in detail, we'll discuss theoretical approaches to food justice issues and explore the ways in which traditional philosophical views fail to account for the sources of injustice in our food system. As we'll see, food justice is a social, economic, racial, and environmental issue; the challenges it presents us with are not easily solved. We won't end up with a solution—that would require a much longer book—but by the end of the chapter we will have a better understanding of the problems. In the next chapter, we'll conclude the book by looking at possible directions for the future of food and food movements.

I. GLOBAL HUNGER AND MALNUTRITION

Both hunger and malnutrition are serious problems around the world. In discussing these issues, and the issues in the next chapter, it's useful to distinguish two concepts: *malnourishment* is receiving insufficient or inappropriate amounts of various nutrients such as vitamins, proteins, or salt; *undernourishment* is not receiving enough to eat. One can be malnourished without being undernourished if one is eating enough calories, but not enough nutrients, so obesity and malnutrition are not mutually exclusive.

The United Nations estimates that one in nine people around the world are undernourished. Worldwide, one in five children suffer from stunted growth caused by malnutrition and undernourishment; in developing countries, this number is as high as one in three. This statistic is worth emphasizing, because malnutrition and undernutrition in early childhood have significant and lasting effects on physical and cognitive development: childhood anemia affects brain development, and malnutrition during childhood is linked to greater risk for heart disease and diabetes later in life.[2] This in turn further increases social inequality and healthcare costs in developing nations. The observation that hunger is a health issue might seem obvious; the point here is that it is a health issue with lasting, irreversible, chronic effects, both for individuals and societies.

It seems obvious, then, that hunger is an urgent problem calling for immediate action. But what form should such action take? This is where we find disagreement—not just among philosophers, but policy-makers, economists, activists, and governments. In the remainder of this section, we'll look at various views and arguments concerning the causes and correct solutions to the problem of global hunger.

2. THE UTILITARIAN ARGUMENT FOR AN OBLIGATION TO AID

In his influential 1972 article "Famine, Affluence, Morality," Peter Singer argues that we all have a moral obligation to donate money to famine relief. He asks us to consider the example of a man walking by a child drowning in a pond: if the man keeps walking, refusing to save the child because he didn't want to ruin his new suit, we think he has behaved wrongly—there is no moral justification for valuing a suit above the life of a child. By refusing to help, the man is *responsible* for the child's death, since he could have easily prevented it at a relatively trivial cost to himself. Singer goes on to argue that there is no morally relevant difference between the situation described in the example and the situation of affluent people (people like us) in developed countries: we could save the lives of children who are dying of hunger at a relatively insignificant cost to us, and yet we don't do it. Just as the man in the example is responsible for the child's death, we too are responsible for the deaths of children dying from hunger and malnutrition.

Singer's argument can be put more formally as follows:

1. If we can prevent something very bad from happening without sacrificing anything of significance, we ought to do so.
2. The suffering and death caused by famine and malnutrition are very bad.

---

2   Food and Agriculture Organization of the United Nations, International Fund for Agricultural Development, UNICEF, World Food Programme and World Health Organization (2017, p. 6); see also Kent (2005), Chapter 1.

3. We can prevent suffering and death from famine and malnutrition by donating an insignificant portion of our incomes (the cost of a daily coffee or newspaper).
4. Therefore, we ought to donate a portion of our income to famine relief efforts.

The argument is controversial, though the first two premises are not: few people would disagree that we should prevent bad things from happening when doing so requires little of us, and few people deny that suffering and death are bad (a point we discussed at the beginning of Chapter Four). The controversial premise is the third one: the claim that each of us relatively affluent readers is in a position to prevent suffering and death—that we are in the same position as the man with the new suit.

Objections to this premise usually take one of the following forms:

1. If we start making small sacrifices, where do we stop? Won't we be required to give up all non-necessary purchases? But what will this do to our quality of life and the economy as a whole? Will we just end up living in a kind of communist society?
2. There is so much hunger and suffering in the world that any difference an individual donation makes is insignificant.
3. We don't really know where donations go—how do I know that my donation is making any difference at all?

We can revise the argument to address the second and third objections by reformulating the premises in terms of *probabilities*: if there is a chance that one can prevent a great deal of suffering at a relatively small cost to oneself, one ought to act (recall our discussion about whether giving up meat will actually prevent animal suffering in Chapter Four). Given that there will always be some degree of uncertainty about the consequences of donations and aid (and, perhaps, consequences more generally—perhaps the drowning child will meet some other tragic fate, or go on to commit a terrible crime), the utilitarian can argue that we shouldn't let the mere possibility of failure deter us from acting. The utilitarian is also unlikely to be impressed by the second objection. The relevant measurement of success, for the utilitarian, is not the number of lives saved, but the amount of suffering alleviated, even if only for a short time.

OBJECTION 1: DEMANDINGNESS

The first objection raises a more direct challenge. For a utilitarian, relieving suffering is imperative, so until the point of marginal utility—the point where our giving would cause us as much suffering as it prevents in others—we should continue to make sacrifices and donate. But the relief of receiving food when one is starving must be immense (not to mention the relief of parents finally able to feed their starving child). The amount of sacrifice needed to outweigh this seems like it would likely be very great. This is especially so in light of studies showing that increases in income and material goods only result in relatively modest, and quite transient, increases in happiness.[3] Having more money and more stuff doesn't make us much happier. So, if the utilitarian logic is correct, more might be required of us than simply small or insignificant sacrifices; we might be required to make significant sacrifices in order to help others.

One might wonder, though, whether this is really an *objection* to the argument. Doesn't it just show that more is morally required of us than we want to admit? Even if we are unable to fully satisfy our moral obligation to help, this doesn't justify doing nothing. If we can't make all the sacrifices required to save the number of hungry people we could save, shouldn't we nonetheless make what modest sacrifices we can—ten dollars a week, suppose—to save at least some people? Surely relieving some suffering, even if not morally sufficient, is better than relieving none at all. A similar rejoinder can be made to the second and third objections above: even if we can't save everyone, or relieve all suffering, we ought to do *something*. Suppose the man in the example were walking by a pond full of drowning children. Does the fact that he can't save all of them give him a reason not to try to save any? Surely not. Likewise, while we might not be certain that our donation helps, if there is a chance of saving a life at a relatively low cost, we ought to donate.

OBJECTION 2: UNREALISTIC PSYCHOLOGICAL DEMANDS?

Singer's comparison between the man walking past the drowning child and the American who passes up the opportunity to donate to famine relief treats distance—geographic, social, and emotional—as morally irrelevant. Singer's point is that it makes no difference how far away suffering takes place as long as we can have a causal impact on it. Distance may *explain* why we don't judge people as harshly for not donating as we do for walking by a drowning child (in fact, we rarely if ever have the chance to judge the latter act; it almost never happens). Morality emerged, in the first instance, as a way of regulating our actions towards our fellow community-members. For most of our history we've only interacted with people near us: people we know, people who resemble us. This gives us good reason to think that our moral intuitions and motivations are maladapted to dealing with moral problems at a distance and to mistrust our moral intuitions about whether we're obligated to help in such cases. But while this is an explanation, it's no justification. Rationally, distance makes no difference, even if emotionally it feels different. We ought therefore to follow reason, not emotion, in such cases.

---

3   Diener & Diener (2002), Kahneman & Deaton (2010).

A related example concerns the type of appeal that moves us to act. Studies have shown that the figures like the ones cited at the beginning of this chapter—statistics about the staggering number of deaths caused by hunger, the childhood growth stunted by malnutrition—are less effective in moving people to donate money than a picture of a single hungry child.[4] On one hand, this is irrational: knowing that millions of people are affected by hunger should make us more, rather than less, likely to act. However, what studies like this reveal is that our moral decision-making is not always driven by reason. The emotion we feel when confronted with the image of a hungry child may be more effective in moving us to act than knowing statistics about the effects of hunger and malnutrition. Again, this is not a justification of the response. Rather, it's an illustration of the ways our moral intuitions fail us when confronted with overwhelming problems like hunger.

OBJECTION 3: A RIGHT NOT TO AID?

Another way of understanding the first objection is as saying that the argument requires us to sacrifice things to which we have a right: our earnings, our property. But this is surely too demanding. If Singer's argument were sound, according to this objection, we should also give up a kidney, or an eye, to help a stranger. But our kidneys, and our eyes, are things to which we are entitled. Absent some special relation, such as having made a promise, or the person in need being our child, we have no obligation to give up a kidney—or a significant portion of our income—to another. Instead, we should think of these as examples of *supererogatory* acts: acts that are morally laudable but not required. Strangers do not have a right to our aid; we do not have an obligation to aid them.

Another critique of Singer's argument as an approach to the moral problem of hunger is that it locates responsibility in the wrong place: it is not individuals but nations who ought to intervene to prevent and ameliorate famine and hunger. By arguing that individuals are obligated to donate to famine relief efforts, Singer's arguments make hunger seem like a problem to be solved by individual actions, and these will never be able to fully remedy the problem. The two approaches are not mutually exclusive, though: since governments are unlikely to eliminate hunger any time soon, our individual responsibility to act remains.

---

4   See Small, Lowenstein, & Slovic (2007).

3. THE LIFEBOAT OBJECTION—AN ARGUMENT AGAINST AID

Around the time Singer's article was published, a number of writers were arguing against famine relief on the grounds that such interventions only prolonged the inevitable: massive famine as a necessary curb on unsustainable population growth. According to these writers, the world simply could not produce enough food to feed its growing population. Garrett Hardin uses the analogy of a lifeboat:

> Approximately two-thirds of the world is desperately poor, and only one third is comparatively rich.... Metaphorically, each rich nation amounts to a lifeboat full of comparatively rich people. The poor of the world are in other, much more crowded lifeboats ... hoping to be admitted to a rich lifeboat, or in some other way to benefit from the "goodies" on board. What should the passengers on a rich lifeboat do? This is the central problem of "the ethics of a lifeboat."[5]

Hardin argues it would be "suicidal" for the lifeboat passengers to allow others in, because a lifeboat can only carry so many. Likewise, Paul Ehrlich argues that the earth is nearing its carrying capacity, and warns

> the underdeveloped countries of the world face an inevitable population-food crisis. Each year food production in these countries falls a bit further behind burgeoning population growth, and people go to bed a little bit hungrier. While there are temporary or local reversals of this trend, it now seems inevitable that it will continue to its logical conclusion: mass starvation.[6]

Ehrlich was prescient in many ways, but the catastrophic population boom he forecast has yet to come to pass; in a later essay Ehrlich admits that he overestimated the extent of the food supply challenge, partly because he underestimated the impact the green revolution would have on yields. Even if Ehrlich were right, this doesn't justify Hardin's claim that each nation is responsible exclusively for its own citizens. There are also questions about who determines the right level of population, and who is entitled to contribute to that level: if we must significantly curtail reproduction, who is entitled to reproduce? It's tempting to dismiss these questions and the debate over lifeboat ethics as historical artifacts of a pre-green revolution era, but this would be a mistake. In the face of climate change and increased challenges facing food

---

5   Hardin (1974, p. 561).
6   In Ehrlich's *The Population Bomb* (1968); for a similarly alarming title, see also Paddock & Paddock's *Famine—1975! America's Decision: Who Will Survive?* (1967).

production such as those discussed in the last chapter, the ethics of procreation has received increasing philosophical scrutiny.[7]

Singer's argument rests on the claim that we have an obligation to aid the hungry because it alleviates suffering; we might also argue for an obligation to act on the grounds that food is a basic *right*. Alternatively, one could argue that we have an obligation to act on the grounds that we are *responsible* for creating the situations that lead to hunger and famine, and that this responsibility generates an obligation for wealthier nations to help the less well off. I'll discuss each of these arguments in turn.

4. FOOD: A BASIC RIGHT?

In its 1948 Universal Declaration of Human Rights, the United Nations stated,

> Everyone has the right to a standard of living adequate for the health and well-being of himself and of his family, including food, clothing, housing and medical care and necessary social services, and the right to security in the event of unemployment, sickness, disability, widowhood, old age or other lack of livelihood in circumstances beyond his control.[8]

Why think that food is a right? One reason is that food is a necessity—without adequate food, we can't exercise any other rights. The right to an education, for example (article 26 in the UN declaration above) can't be taken advantage of if one doesn't have enough food to survive. In other words, having adequate food is a *precondition* for any other right we might want to claim.[9] This makes it a basic right: a right upon which all of our other rights depend.

Above we saw that Singer's view can be criticized on the grounds that, while it would be good to aid the hungry in developing nations, we are under no *obligation* to do so, because we don't stand in any relation that would generate a claim upon us, or a right of the hungry to receive assistance from us. In response to this type of criticism, some have pointed out that we in fact do have such obligations, because the wealth that developed nations enjoy was acquired through a historical pattern of injustice and exploitation of the very countries who now stand in need of aid. Indeed, our dependence is not only historical: our phones and computers are built using minerals mined in developing countries; our coffee and chocolate is grown there; our goods are manufactured there. Given this dependence, it seems wrong to say that we have

---

7   For an argument against procreation, see Benatar (2006); see also Conly (2015).

8   United Nations (1948).

9   See Shue (1980), Chapter 1, for discussion and elaboration of this point.

no relationship with these nations that would generate a right (on their part) to claim assistance from us.

One way this right could be understood is as the right that someone in a relationship has on the assistance of another: the sort of right that family members can claim upon one another. Because we are engaged in relationships with these countries, we have rights and obligations created by this relationship, and one of these is to assist where we can. Another explanation for our obligation would be that, when one has caused harm, one is obligated to rectify or ameliorate it when possible. Because many countries that suffer from hunger are countries affected by colonialism and slavery, we in the developed nations have harmed them in the past; thus, we have a responsibility to aid them now. But what form should this aid take?

5. HUNGER: BEYOND SCARCITY

Traditional ways of framing the debate over hunger, such as the ones described above, focus on the issue of aid—whose obligation is it, and what form should it take? Critics argue that these questions miss—or, worse, actively obscure—the point. The focus on aid treats the hungry as passive recipients of help, rather than active participants in markets and society; it also encourages us to view hunger as a kind of emergency, rather than an inevitable result of an unfair food system.

According to the "population bomb" objection, the problem is that we can't grow enough food for a growing population. But critics argue that this is a misleading explanation of the problems facing the current global food supply. For example, during the 1943 famine in West Bengal, which killed almost two million people, the Indian Raj continued to export food to feed the British as part of their war effort. We find a similar pattern when we look at Ireland's "potato famine": during its famine years of 1844–48 it exported over 100,000 tons of grain, even as one-eighth of the population died of starvation.[10] It is not the amount of food, but the way we distribute it that's the problem:

> In Africa ... recent starvation, mass-scale hunger, and hunger-related deaths have not been triggered by an absence of appropriate crops. The truth is more complicated. Hunger is the result of a cluster of factors, including armed conflict, resource shortages, blood diamonds, recovery from the Cold War, and the dismantling of existing social mechanisms (so-called "moral economies") designed to mitigate food emergencies.... In many of the countries where food aid has been sent ... sufficient food to feed the population has

---

10   See Sen (1981), Chapter 6, for detailed discussion of the Bengal example; also Keneally (2011), especially Chapter 6, for a discussion of the Irish famine.

been present. What have failed have been the channels of distribution. Does ... Monsanto propose to address these? They do not, for that is not what they sell.[11]

Critics like Raj Patel argue that corporations like Monsanto, which make their money selling seeds, pesticides, and fertilizers, benefit from framing the problem of hunger in terms of scarcity; they can then respond to environmentalists' objections to biotechnology by pointing to the need to feed a growing population (as we saw in Chapter Six, when we discussed arguments in favor of GM crops). Patel doesn't deny that the Green Revolution has increased crop yields, but it hasn't done anything to change the economic structures that prevent hungry people from benefiting from these increases. As he points out, in many communities, farmers can't sell their crops directly to the stores, because the stores buy their food from international distributors. This highlights a shortfall of the "population bomb" argument, and the complexity of the problem of hunger: it is not always, or even primarily, due to a scarcity of food. It is caused by changes in food production, prices, and distribution. Hunger is not a problem we can understand or address in isolation; it's rooted in the economic and political structures that govern national and international relations. Patel and other critics illustrate the need for a more nuanced conceptual scheme that can help us understand how hunger persists even in the face of adequate or surplus food supply.

5.1 Sen's Entitlements Theory

In the 1980s, economist and political theorist Amartya Sen introduced the "entitlement approach" to extend our understanding of the various causes of hunger and starvation beyond just scarcity. As Sen writes, "Starvation is the characteristic of some people not *having* enough food to eat. It is not the characteristic of there not *being* enough to eat."[12] Entitlement theory identifies a variety of relationships a person has to their food supply; hunger occurs when those relationships fail to enable the person to acquire enough food to eat. The term "entitlements" refers (in this context) to the food a person is able to acquire, using the resources available to her. (The term entitlement is purely descriptive and shouldn't be read as implying that a person has a *right* to these things, merely that they have the means of acquiring it.) Sen describes four types of food entitlements: *production-based* entitlements involve growing or producing one's own food; *trade- or income-based* entitlements involve buying or trading for food; *labor* entitlements are working for food; *transfer* entitlements involve being

---

11   Patel (2012, pp. 157–58).
12   Sen (1981, p. 1).

given food by others (for example, in the form of aid from an organization, or food stamps from one's government) or inheriting the means to produce food. Most people possess a combination of entitlements; we can use the term "exchange entitlement" to refer to the things they can obtain (in this case, food and related commodities) using their entitlements.

Entitlement theory demonstrates that thinking of policies as "alleviating" or "causing" hunger is too simple: policies affect groups differently depending on the form of their entitlements. Those with trade-based entitlements will suffer from hunger if the prices of food are too high, since their income may no longer be sufficient to buy food. But they might also suffer if the price of food drops too low, if the good they are trading, or the way they derive their income, is tied to the price of food. After all, even subsistence farmers are rarely *entirely* self-sufficient; most depend partly on selling some of what they produce to buy other goods. Those with production-based entitlement will suffer if crops fail (of course, crop failure could drive up prices, affecting the former group as well), but again, farmers might also suffer if they cannot sell some of what they produce. Those with labor-based entitlements are often affected by mechanization and industrialization of farming, since these tend to reduce the need for human labor. This approach allows us to take a more nuanced view of policies aimed at relieving hunger. Because there is no single entitlement held by everyone in the affected society, policies will have different effects on different groups: what relieves hunger in groups with income entitlements may actually make things worse for groups with production entitlements.

This brings us to what Thompson calls, "the fundamental problem in food ethics." Singer's argument aimed to convince us that people in developed nations were obligated to aid the hungry and, as it happened, the US had, at the time, a great deal of surplus grain. The obvious solution at the time was to send this grain overseas as food aid, which the US did. But, Thompson points out, this is not the win-win scenario it might initially seem to be: "When food aid shows up on the doorstep of an impoverished nation, it surely does benefit the people with income-based entitlements.... But simple economics suggests that it is also going to depress the price of food that was already there." This is a problem for people with production entitlements, since they rely on selling at least some of what they produce in order to buy other foods (very few farmers grow *everything* they eat, from grain to fruit to vegetable to cooking oil). Thompson goes on: "In short, the practice of extending charitable assistance to the urban poor (or supplementing their income-based entitlement with a gift or grant) actually undercuts the livelihoods of people with direct production food entitlements. And that *is* the fundamental problem in food ethics."[13]

---

13   Thompson (2015, p. 114).

5.2 When Enough Isn't Enough: Food Sovereignty Movements

Sen's entitlement view reveals that focusing on food supply alone is an overly narrow approach to famine. Thompson's critique of international aid programs demonstrates that food aid alone can do as much harm as good. When we view hunger as the result of international economic policies, it becomes clear that which solutions we offer affect nations' long-term prospects for reducing hunger and increasing self-sufficiency. For example, foreign aid and loans often come with inducements encouraging developing nations to grow crops for export, such as flowers, chocolate, and coffee.[14] This in turn leads to a greater reliance on imports of basic food crops, which makes those nations vulnerable to price fluctuations in the global market. But it is this same market, critics argue, that created the problems with the current system in the first place:

> For the activists, food is quite simply a right, and they categorically reject the idea that global market forces should determine how, in what quantities, of what type, and for what market farmers should produce their food. Instead, they usually insist that these market forces and mechanisms caused the crisis in the first place.[15]

This has led activists to argue for a shift in policy goals, from *food security* to *food sovereignty*. Whereas the goal of food security is to ensure that countries (and communities) have an adequate supply of food, the goal of food sovereignty is to enable countries to be both self-sufficient and self-determining with respect to their food supply. The contemporary food sovereignty movement originates with the peasant collective and activist group La Via Campesina, who introduced the concept at the 1996 World Food Forum in Rome:

> Food sovereignty is the right of peoples to healthy and culturally appropriate food produced through sustainable methods and their right to define their own food and agriculture systems. It develops a model of small scale sustainable production benefiting communities and their environment. Food sovereignty prioritizes local food production and consumption, giving a country the right to protect its local producers from cheap imports and to control its production.[16]

---

14   For a sustained critique of international food aid policy, see Rieff (2015), especially Chapters 5 and 7; also George (1977).

15   Rieff (2015, p. 71).

16   La Via Campesina (n.d.).

Food security is aimed at ensuring an adequate supply of appropriate food, but it is indifferent to how that food is produced and who supplies it. A nation can be "food secure" despite relying entirely on other countries for its food supply. As the quote from Thompson above illustrates, food security also fails to address the effects of food aid and policy on local economies and producers. Food sovereignty, by contrast, places an emphasis on food that will benefit local populations and economies, opposing large shipments of foreign food and grain as a solution to hunger. Food sovereignty also argues for the right of communities to define their own food systems. By insisting on a role for local farmers and communities in food policy, food sovereignty rejects the idea that international aid organizations and foreign assistance are the right means by which to address hunger.

6. FOOD ACCESS, FOOD PRODUCTION, AND DISTRIBUTIVE JUSTICE

So far, we've been focusing on hunger as an international issue. The remainder of this chapter will look at more localized food justice issues. These don't exist in isolation; one lesson from the discussion in the preceding sections is that food markets are global and far-reaching, so our food choices have far-reaching effects. But food activism is local, too, and in this section, we'll look at some of the issues that food justice activists have pursued at the community level. Specifically, the remaining sections of this chapter will focus on three problems: food deserts and food access, unfair and harmful labor practices, and the environmental costs of food production. We'll start by returning to the question of food justice and looking at the concept in more detail.

We began the chapter with Thompson's claim that we don't need a philosophical argument to help us recognize instances of food injustice. But as we've seen, different ways of conceptualizing the problem offer different diagnoses and treatments. Consider some definitions of food justice offered by activists and scholars working in the field:

- We characterize food justice as ensuring that the benefits and risks of where, what, and how food is grown and produced, transported and distributed, and accessed and eaten are shared fairly.[17]
- Essential to the food justice movement is an analysis that recognizes the food system itself as a racial project and problematizes the influence of race and class on production, distribution, and consumption of food....

---

17   Gottlieb & Joshi (2010, p. 6).

Through food justice activism, low-income communities and communities of color seek to create local food systems that meet their own food needs.[18]

- The food justice movement is the struggle against racism, exploitation, and oppression taking place within the food system that addresses inequality's root causes both within and beyond the food chain.[19]

- Food justice involves stakeholders being: (1) informed of the likely benefits and risks of decisions affecting their food system, (2) provided with sufficient information to be able to understand the implications of those risks and benefits, (3) adequately educated so that they are competent to make decisions, and (4) able to assent or dissent from decisions without coercion.[20]

These four definitions share a conviction that the food system is an important locus of social and economic justice, but offer three different diagnoses of where the injustice and the remedies lie: distributive issues, social and racial inequality, lack of community input into food policy. In the remainder of this section, we'll look at these three ways of framing the problem, and in the next section, we'll turn to some specific issues and see how these definitions can help us understand specific struggles in food justice activism.

6.1 Distributive Food Justice

The first definition above characterizes food justice as a distributive issue. On a distributive view, the task of justice is to find a fair way to allocate the costs and benefits—both material and immaterial—of living in society. For example, living in society means giving up some freedoms; which freedoms should be sacrificed, and by whom? Living in society also means access to certain services, but who should have access to them? Should they be free? How is the burden of taxation to be distributed? One approach is to adopt a strict egalitarianism, according to which everyone gets the same amount of goods as everyone else, and everyone bears the same costs. However, this does not take into account people's needs and abilities: some people may need more food, or healthcare, or assistance; other people may need less, or be able to contribute less. So, a strict egalitarianism, while apparently fair insofar as everyone receives exactly the same thing, is unfair in another sense, since some people's needs are met, while others' are not. Another approach to distribution comes from Rawls, whose contractarian view we discussed in Chapters Four and Seven above;

---

18   Alkon & Agyeman (2011, p. 5).
19   Rasheed Hislop, quoted in Alkon (2014, p. 29).
20   Loo (2014, p. 788).

here, rather than agreeing to principles of morality, we imagine citizens negotiating the principles of justice from behind a veil of ignorance. According to Rawls, this process will yield the following principles of justice:

1. Each person has an equal claim to a fully adequate scheme of equal basic rights and liberties, which scheme is compatible with the same scheme for all; and in this scheme the equal political liberties, and only those liberties, are to be guaranteed their fair value.

2. Social and economic inequalities are to satisfy two conditions: (a) They are to be attached to positions and offices open to all under conditions of fair equality of opportunity; and (b), they are to be to the greatest benefit of the least advantaged members of society.[21]

Why these two principles? Since we don't know where we'll be in the resultant society, we will want to protect the worst-off. By arranging inequality so that the worst off are better off than they will be in any other arrangement, we can justify the inequality as benefiting those in the most vulnerable position.

Injustice in the food system involves both distribution and lack of opportunity. It's not just that people don't have equal amounts of food, or equal access to food. The problem is that the inequalities disadvantage the most vulnerable members of society: those who already face social, economic, and other challenges. By denying these groups access to healthy food, or by making them travel further and thus spend more time to find that food—as we'll discuss in Section 7 below—the industrialized food system imposes further disadvantages on the worst-off.

While the distributive conception of justice is helpful in identifying the inequities in our food system, critics argue that it is less helpful in diagnosing their causes and remedies. Some critics charge that the distributive system places too much emphasis on distribution itself, rather than on social and political equality. By viewing the food system as a set of goods to be distributed, they argue, the distributive picture entrenches the very problems it should be addressing: it treats food like any other economic good; it focuses only on the distribution, and not on the underlying injustice and inequality that creates that distribution.

6.2 Food Justice as Social Justice: Critiques of the Distributive Paradigm

The second and third conceptions of food justice above demand that we ask not just whether a particular distribution is just or unjust, but why unjust distributions arise

---

21   Rawls (1971, p. 53).

and how they're maintained. Why do some neighborhoods have more fast-food restaurants than others? How do race and socioeconomic status influence access to healthy food? How do past political injustices influence the distribution of food aid today? Rawls' conception of justice can't tackle questions like these, precisely because Rawls views justice as a process that takes no account of factors like race, class, and gender. Since the distributive paradigm locates justice in a set of principles that are constructed under abstract conditions in which no one is aware of their race, gender, or class, it excludes these factors from explanations of the principles; nor can the principles be aimed at remedying injustices arising out of racism or socioeconomic inequalities. The principles are not discussed or formulated in a world where such problems exist. We might use our knowledge of current social problems to try to construct principles that would prevent future injustices from arising, but this ignores the fact that inequality and discrimination aren't just the result of starting from ill-formed principles, but from the application of those principles in our actual society and its institutions, by people with actual biases, desires, and shortcomings. The point is not that Rawls' theory of justice is unrealistic—Rawls does not intend to be describing an actual or even attainable situation. The point is that it's unable to explain and remedy injustice. The philosopher Iris Marion Young writes that Rawls' paradigm, "tends to focus thinking about social justice on the allocation of material goods ... [and] ignore[s] the social structure and institutional context that often help to determine distributive patterns." Furthermore, distributive views have trouble accounting for "nonmaterial social goods," such as power and cultural representation, because by treating them as things to be distributed, it "represents them as though they were static things, instead of a function of social relations and processes." In other words, we can come up with the fairest distribution we like from behind the veil of ignorance, but once the veil is removed, we begin a process of social exchange and interaction during which goods and opportunities are redistributed, and this is how injustice emerges. The problem is not the principles we begin with, but the processes that follow. Young suggests that we focus instead on the relationships within society that govern these processes: "the concepts of domination and oppression, rather than the concept of distribution, should be the starting point for a conception of social justice."[22]

6.3 Food Justice as Participatory Justice

The concept of food sovereignty was introduced in our discussion of international food aid in Section 5.2 above. But the concept is useful in understanding struggles for food justice in local communities as well. Both the second and fourth defini-

---

22   Young (1990, pp. 15–16).

tions of food justice above emphasize communities' right to determine their own food systems through education and participation in decision-making processes that affect the community. Because these definitions emphasize communities' right to self-determination, they often accompany the kind of critique described in the preceding section, viewing communities' exclusion from decision-making processes as a form of domination. As Young explains, "Domination consists in institutional conditions which inhibit or prevent people from participating in determining their actions or the conditions of their actions. Persons live within structures of domination if other persons or groups can determine without reciprocation the conditions of their actions, either directly or by virtue of the structural consequences of their actions."[23] We see domination at work in the factors that determine communities' access to food: "Communities of color and poor communities have time and time again been denied access to the means of food production, and, due to both price and store location, often cannot access the diet advocated by the food movement."[24] The conditions that prevent poor communities from accessing healthy or ethical food are not conditions that those communities determine, they're conditions that are determined by outside forces, and therefore represent a kind of domination. In the remaining sections of this chapter, we'll look at three contexts in which domination plays out: the environmental costs of food production, the treatment of workers in the food system, and the problem of so-called food deserts.

6.4 Food Justice and Environmental Costs

In earlier chapters, we observed that most forms of agriculture impose significant environmental cost, whether from the drift of airborne pesticides and herbicides, or the lagoons of animal waste produced by factory farms. These costs are not distributed fairly or equally. Farms and feedlots are concentrated in low-income and minority communities, where they affect the health of residents and depress property values (with the consequence that people cannot afford to sell their homes and move away).[25] The benefits of cheap meat are enjoyed widely, but the costs of producing it are borne locally. In discussing pesticide runoff in Chapter Five, we observed that it leads to depleted fish stocks even in oceans thousands of miles away, as when pesticides travel down the Mississippi river from Iowa and Illinois into the Gulf of Mexico. This depletion affects small fishermen the most, since they are less likely to have the means to travel further offshore to reach the remaining fish. This is yet

---

23   Young (1990, p. 38).

24   Alkon & Agyeman (2011, p. 5).

25   See, for example, Wing, Cole, & Grant (2000).

another example of the ways in which the costs and benefits of industrial agriculture are distributed inequitably: those who benefit from the practices don't bear the costs.

Doesn't everyone benefit from cheap food, though? It's tempting to think so. Americans spend a lower percentage of their income on food today than they did 50 years ago, leaving more remaining for education, housing, and other necessities. But farmers don't benefit, and neither do workers. The consolidation of food production and retail has meant increased power for a few companies, and less power for farmers and farm workers, as well as laborers in the meatpacking, food production, and food service industries. Ironically, it is these very same workers who often suffer from food insecurity: studies show that food workers are more than twice as likely to rely on food stamps (SNAP) as workers in other industries.[26] We'll look at this issue next.

6.5 Labor and Food Justice

Farm workers who harvest fruits and vegetables work long hours, often without access to bathrooms or shade. Many of these workers are illegal immigrants, which gives their employers a kind of leverage: because of their precarious status, the workers are unwilling or unable to complain about their treatment. In his book *Tomatoland*, Barry Estabrook described migrant workers subject to indentured servitude: locked in trucks, told that they owed their captors for meals, showers, and lodging, workers are beaten if they refuse to work. They are unable to leave; they are modern-day slaves. And while Estabrook's work galvanized activists in the US to improve working conditions by targeting fast-food chains and other buyers of tomatoes, some companies have shifted to buying produce grown in Mexico, where conditions may be even worse. Similar working conditions are rampant in the seafood industry: according to the US state department, shrimp workers in Thailand are often victims of human trafficking, kidnapped from neighboring countries and forced to work 18-hour days while surviving on a single bowl of rice.

Even where workers are legal and documented, conditions can be hazardous. Slaughterhouses and meat processing plants emphasize speed over all else: in the last century, the number of cattle slaughtered per hour has gone from about 50 to over 400 at some plants. This leads to high rates of injuries, both from accidents and repetitive stress injuries. In his book *Fast Food Nation*, Eric Schlosser described some of the dangers of slaughterhouse work:

> Lacerations are the most common injuries suffered by meatpackers, who
> often stab themselves or stab someone working nearby. Tendinitis and
> cumulative trauma disorders are also quite common. Meatpacking workers

---

26   See Jacobs, Perry, & MacGillvary (2015, April 13).

routinely develop back problems, shoulder problems, carpal tunnel syndrome, and "trigger finger" (a syndrome in which a finger becomes frozen in a curled position). Indeed, the rate of these cumulative trauma injuries in the meat-packing industry is far higher than the rate in any other American industry. It is almost thirty-five times higher than the national average in industry. Many slaughterhouse workers make a knife cut every two or three seconds, which adds up to about 10,000 cuts during an eight-hour shift. If the knife has become dull, additional pressure is placed on the worker's tendons, joints, and nerves. A dull knife can cause pain to extend from the cutting hand all the way down the spine.[27]

The workers who clean slaughterhouses also risk injury, often climbing into the processing machines to clean out blood and grease. In fact, meatpacking jobs have the highest rate of injury of any industry in the US. And while some of the workers are legal, many are not, a fact that complicates attempts to gain compensation for workplace injuries. Injured workers may be laid off, and the process of filing for compensation can be drawn out for months.

A lack of representation in determining working conditions isn't just a problem for workers in slaughterhouses and meatpacking plants. The farmers who raise pigs, cows, and poultry are also subject to unjust contract and bargaining conditions: they often go into significant debt to start their farms, and the price they receive for their product is determined by what processors or buyers are willing to pay. Because so few companies dominate the beef market, there is often only one processor to sell to in the area, so that a cattle farmer has no choice but to accept the price she's offered.

Chicken farmers are dependent on big companies like Tyson. These farmers are responsible for the cost of building their farms, but they don't technically own the birds—they're "contracted" by the company to raise birds that the company provides; the company also provides farmers with feed and instructions. At the end of a fixed period, the company buys the chickens for a price that is set using a so-called tournament system in which farmers are ranked against one another on the basis of their productivity, with the highest-ranked farmers receiving the highest prices (and the lowest-ranked farmers sometimes receiving nothing at all). Tyson's website explains the process this way:

> Poultry farmers are essentially paid for how well they take care of the chickens and how much weight the birds gain while they're on the farm. We use a performance-based incentive system that rewards poultry farmers who effectively convert the feed we provide into weight gain in the birds they raise. The payment formula includes such factors as the number of birds,

---

27 Schlosser (2001, p. 173).

the amount of feed used, the performance of their flock compared to those raised by other contract growers and the weight of the birds delivered to the processing plant.[28]

If a farmer feels they're being offered an unfair price, they have no recourse. Because most farmers are so far in debt (the contracting company can also require a farmer to take out loans to upgrade their buildings or equipment), he or she has no power with which to negotiate. Because the companies deliver chicks that they technically own, the farmer cannot sell the animals to another company. Farmers who protest the system have reported receiving unhealthy or smaller chicks as punishment, which forces them out of the system, since the company won't buy the chickens back from them at the end of the cycle. These farmers often end up losing their farms.[29]

Furthermore, companies will choose not to compete by focusing on different regions; as a result, there is often only one company who is paying chicken farmers in a given area. A similar situation holds for cattle: the companies that slaughter and process cattle typically don't compete with one another in the same geographic regions, so a farmer will often have only one option when it's time to sell his animals. Just four companies control 80 per cent of the beef market; similar situations apply in the chicken and pork industries. Because these companies are responsible for processing animals and distributing the products, if a farmer doesn't feel that they are receiving a fair price for their product, they may have nowhere else to go—federal regulations limit the places where an animal can be slaughtered and processed, and as retailers like Walmart come to dominate markets, smaller farmers rely on big processors and distributors to act as middlemen.

This hurts consumers, too, since the fact that so few companies control so much of the market makes it easy for these companies to drive up food prices by restricting supply. This might sound far-fetched, but in the 1970s, the government sued over collusion and price-fixing in the poultry industry. When the price of eggs or chicken drops, a company like Tyson (which, together with one other competitor, controls 40 per cent of the US chicken supply) can simply hold back some of its supply, driving prices back up. This is made possible by the fact that it's not the company who bears the cost of that held-back chicken, but the small contract farmer from whom Tyson is (no longer) buying back birds.

7. FOOD "DESERTS" AND FOOD ACCESS

Another source of injustice in the food system involves consumers' access to food. In the preceding chapters, we encountered arguments that, at the international level,

---

28   Tyson (2018).
29   See Leonard (2014), especially Chapter 1.

hunger is not an issue of supply, but of distribution. This is not just an issue internationally; even in the relatively affluent United States, there are a number of factors that prevent consumers from accessing fresh and healthy food. It has become common to use the term "food deserts" to refer to the phenomenon of geographic areas lacking access to food. Typically, a food desert is defined as an area that lacks a grocery store (or where consumers must travel long distances to reach a grocery store). These deserts are almost always in low-income neighborhoods or areas whose residents are primarily people of color. Scholars often focus on urban areas, but food deserts also occur in rural areas as well. As bigger stores such as Walmart have moved into rural communities, they've driven local chains out of business, putting more and more distance between stores. And if the Walmart then happens to go out of business, residents may have to drive an hour or more to buy fresh groceries.

The term "food desert" is misleading for a number of reasons. First, grocery stores are not the only place people buy food, and many urban areas dubbed food deserts actually contain a number of convenience stores and fast-food restaurants. The issue is not whether food is available, but what kinds of food. A related issue with the definition is that it measures deserts by looking at distance from stores, but distance alone is an inadequate measure of accessibility: a store that's a mile away but requires traveling on highways is less accessible to someone without a car or public transport than a store the same distance but located within a neighborhood with sidewalks and crosswalks. Whether one drives or walks to the store also affects how much one is able to buy at one time, which in turn affects both the price one pays for food (in terms of the price per item, it's cheaper to buy things like diapers and dry goods in bulk) and how often one must return to the store, which, depending on accessibility, can be a time-consuming chore.

These are practical objections to analyzing access to food using the concept of food deserts, but the activist Karen Washington has raised an objection to the connotations of the term itself: deserts are naturally occurring phenomena, but food deserts are not natural, they're formed by social, political, and economic factors.[30] Washington suggests we replace the term with the more accurate, "food apartheid," a term that evokes both the racial disparities in food access and the sociopolitical causes of those disparities. Retailers point to the cost of real estate and to concerns about profitability as reasons for avoiding urban areas, but this doesn't explain why even within cities, wealthy neighborhoods have anywhere from two to four times as many grocery stores as low-income neighborhoods. Moreover, research suggests that racial makeup, and not just income, correlates with the availability of groceries; stores are less likely to be located in low-income neighborhoods with predominantly black populations than similar neighborhoods with predominantly white or Latino populations, and stores in low-income neighborhoods are less likely to stock fresh fruits and vegetables, bread,

---

30   Brones (2018, May 7).

and milk.[31] This suggests that race, not just economics, plays a role in the location of supermarkets and other food stores.

Rural food deserts occur in part because retailers like Walmart can afford to sell their products for less than competitors, driving local stores out of business. This is partly because they pay their workers less, and partly because they pay suppliers less: because they control so much of the market, Walmart can contract directly with suppliers, eliminating the need for intermediate distribution. But this also means that farmers and other suppliers are often left with no one else to sell to, and therefore must accept whatever price Walmart offers them.

The issues discussed in this section, like so many of the issues facing our food system, are deeply interconnected. The use of pesticides, the conditions on factory farms and in slaughterhouses, and the asymmetries in bargaining power between large food processors and small farmers and workers, all have significant effects on the well-being of workers—who are also consumers. Migrant workers often receive low pay and have little access to healthy food, either because they lack transportation to grocery stores, or because they can't afford fresh food. The communities that produce or transport our food often bear the costs without receiving the benefits: Hunts Point in the Bronx houses the largest food hub in the state—almost all of New York City's produce passes through it. Yet the surrounding community has few grocery stores or fresh food vendors (though as of this writing, plans were in the works to create a "greenmarket hub" for residents). The residents of Hunts Point bear the costs of living near a "food hub"—pollution and noise from the trucks that travel to and from the market each day—but don't receive any of the benefits.

CONCLUSION

The challenge of food justice is partly the challenge of who pays the costs of food production. Globally, hunger and malnutrition can be exacerbated by aid that disrupts people's food entitlements and depresses prices for small farmers; attempts to create high-yield crops can end up creating dependency on expensive technology, driving farmers further into debt. Locally, farmers are often dependent on large companies in ways that preclude fair negotiation and exchange. From a consumer perspective, lack of participation in food justice means that access to fresh and healthy food is often inequitably distributed, in ways that replicate and reinforce other forms of social inequality. This shows that hunger and malnutrition are not natural phenomena, nor are they inevitable. They are wicked problems, with no easy solutions. Addressing them will require us to dramatically rethink our food system, and it's easy to feel pessimistic about the prospects for success in such a venture. In our concluding chapter,

---

31   Treuhaft & Karpyn (2010, pp. 13–15).

we'll discuss some possible directions such a re-examination might take, and look at food movements and possible directions for the future of food. My hope is that we will find some cause for optimism.

Conclusion

THE
FUTURE
OF
FOOD?

We've spent the last several chapters looking at problems in our food system: moral, environmental, social, and political. But we began the book by looking at the ways we interact with food: as a concept, food as an object of knowledge, as an aesthetic and even artistic experience. In this final chapter, we'll explore how these two subjects relate to one another: if our attitudes towards and interactions with food play such a significant role in shaping what food is and how it's consumed, how might we use this influence to approach the problems we've identified? It seems only appropriate to conclude our discussion by examining emerging food movements and alternative approaches to food: local food movements, urban agriculture, technological approaches to food production (and replacement), protein alternatives such as insects and synthetic meat. One theme uniting these disparate movements is that each highlights the environmental, social, and ethical costs of our current food supply and challenges us to reconsider our notions of what food is and where it comes from.

1. THE FUTURE OF MEAT: ANIMAL FREE?

A recurring theme throughout this book has been the high environmental cost of animal agriculture, and the toll it exacts on both animal and human welfare. These considerations are the main motivation for vegetarian and vegan diets. Because the food system is so complex, even those vegetarians and vegans who acknowledge that there may be cases where meat and animal products don't cause suffering and would therefore be permissible to eat might refrain from eating any meat whatsoever, because it's so difficult to know where one's food actually comes from. Meat eaters who tell themselves that they only purchase meat from "happy" animals, on the other hand, might wonder how they can be so certain of this. The moral complexities of eating meat and the epistemic complexities of navigating our food system are bound up in one another.

Concerns over the costs of animal agriculture are one reason that a number of companies are working to invent better, more realistic meat, shellfish, and dairy substitutes, ones that will appeal to meat-eaters and not just (or even) to vegetarians. The "Impossible Burger" currently on the menu of some New York and California restaurants touts its ability to convincingly "bleed" on the plate, just like a burger made from meat. These foods may not appeal to those who favor unprocessed foods, and their resemblance to meat may not appeal to vegetarians, but if they replace some of the factory-farmed meat in people's diets, their proponents argue that they can play an important role in reducing the environmental impact of our diets.

Other technological innovations go even further: why not grow real animal tissue, but without involving actual animals? Lab-grown, or "in vitro," meat doesn't come from a living animal; it's created from stem cells, which are placed into a culture where they grow into muscle fibers and tissue. The cells are either placed onto a kind of scaffolding, where they grow muscle fibers that are then "harvested" for consumption, or they are placed into a petri dish with a nutrient-containing culture where the cells then grow into muscle tissue. (From now on, I'll use the term "lab-grown meat" to refer to both of these processes, though some refer to the first as "in vitro" and the second as "lab-grown." Companies investing in the technology prefer the term "clean meat," which admittedly has better marketing potential.) The first technique can be used to make hamburger and other processed meats; the second technique results in actual muscle tissue, so it could be used to grow steaks, chops, and roasts. At the moment, such technology is extremely expensive, and questions remain about whether and when it will be cost-effective: the first lab-grown hamburger was served in London in 2013 with an estimated price tag of over $300,000. Another challenge is flavor: since the meat consists entirely of muscle, there is none of the fat that gives a hamburger its flavor. And finally, there is the question of whether people will accept lab-grown meat: will it be doomed by the yuck factor?

These are practical objections to lab-grown meat. There are also ethical objections. We might revisit the objection to GM animals based on animal integrity: does lab-grown meat violate animal integrity? The procedure does use animal stem cells, and one could argue that this violates animal integrity by removing part of the animal's body, thereby violating its wholeness. But if removing even a small number of cells violates wholeness, then animal integrity sets the bar very high indeed. A related objection might be that the act of eating animal flesh is disrespectful to animals, whether or not the flesh comes from an actual animal. An analogy might be to the practice of burning someone in effigy: though the actual person is not harmed, the willingness to destroy his or her image evinces a certain attitude of disrespect. Likewise, one might argue, even if no animal is actually harmed by the eating of a hamburger, the attitude it expresses towards animals is morally objectionable. This objection, like the integrity objection, only appeals to those who already believe eating meat is morally wrong. Is there any principled basis on which to eat some meat, but reject lab-grown meat?

One reason to think not is that lab-grown meat solves the two biggest ethical problems with eating meat: animal suffering and environmental effects. Because no animals need to be raised or killed for food, animal suffering and death are avoided. If lab-grown meat were to completely replace animals, billions of animal lives each year would be saved. That in turn would mean no runoff from factory farms, no grain or soy required to feed those animals, land that could be used for other purposes, and fewer antibiotics and other drugs used on animals. On the other hand, it would also mean no grass-fed beef or free-range chickens. If, as some have argued, these animals do live happy lives, might it be a bad thing to replace them with insentient lab-grown meat?

This is a hard question to answer, both philosophically and practically. There is some disagreement about what role in vitro meat will ultimately come to play in our food supply. Some foresee it replacing factory-farmed meat in fast food and processed foods, but predict that consumers who currently eat meat from small farms will continue to do so. Others argue those consumers will favor lab-grown meat, because it addresses their concerns about animal welfare and the environment. Obviously, if lab-grown meat does not supplant factory-farmed meat, it will not represent significant moral progress, instead being a kind of curiosity or luxury item. But most proponents and developers do think that, once it can be made cost-effective, lab-grown meat will play a significant role in our diet.

Will it gain acceptance? It's hard to say. Could a vegetarian or a vegan ever endorse lab-grown meat? Animal rights organizations like PETA already have, but endorsing something in theory is different from ingesting it in practice. In many ways, lab-grown meat would accord quite well with vegan and vegetarian ideals, since it has a relatively minimal environmental footprint and doesn't require any animals to suffer (which, as we'll recall from Chapter Five, isn't true of any traditional forms of agriculture).

We might go even further in the direction of synthetic food. Soylent, which we encountered in Chapter One, is a drink designed to meet all the body's nutritional needs; it can be consumed for every meal (its makers claim), eliminating the need for food. Fans cite its convenience, as well as the fact that it eliminates the need to make choices regarding food. It also requires less room to store, is easier to transport than fresh food, and has a long shelf life, eliminating a great deal of food waste. Could food substitutes like Soylent be the foods of the future?

Environmental arguments for lab-grown meat may feel strangely misplaced, since the value we place on environmentally friendly food is more traditionally associated with local food movements and the organic food movement. This might show that we're actually not motivated by environmental concern—or not solely motivated by those concerns. If so, is this just a form of hypocrisy, or is there another explanation of our food values that allows us to express concerns about the current food system while resisting radical reforms such as lab-grown meat?

We've already discussed the role that disgust plays in our judgments about food. One might hope that the moral considerations in favor of lab-grown meat will override any disgust we might feel at the thought of eating tissue grown in a petri dish. But alternatives to our current diet don't necessarily require advances in technology or food substitutes, they just require rethinking what we consider appropriate to eat. There are foods which we have good moral reason to pursue but which disgust prevents us from embracing: insects are an excellent source of protein, and require few resources to grow, making them environmentally friendly—they are much more efficient at converting feed to protein, and don't need much water. In fact, insects can convert food waste into food—certain species can feed off agricultural byproducts. They can also be grown pretty much anywhere—in former warehouse buildings in cities, or in smaller spaces—crickets don't need much space, and don't mind relatively crowded conditions. In fact, people can grow insects right on their kitchen counter. But few Americans do. This illustrates the power of emotion in food choice. Insects are, logically, an ideal food: they're environmentally friendly, healthy, humane, and hyper-local (it doesn't get more local than home-grown!). But many people view them with disgust, so they've been slow to catch on in America (traditional societies have recognized the value of entomophagy for millennia). Developers of insect-related food products have attempted to make insects more palatable by making cricket flour into cookies, coating insects in chocolate or flavoring powder, and incorporating them into protein bars or even burgers (which have recently gone on sale in supermarkets in Switzerland). But while this may make insects themselves more palatable, swallowing the idea of insects as food will take more work. The problem is not anything intrinsic to insects, but rather the ideas we have about them: that they are pests, dirty, unfit to be eaten. These ideas can change with time—lobster used to be considered a dirty food, and was fed to prisoners; there are reports of prisoners striking because they were fed lobster too often.[1] This illustrates the relative rapidity with which our ideas about what is appropriate or disgusting to eat can change. It also suggests that what we want from the norms governing our food choices isn't just a way of eating, or a set of moral principles, but a conception of ourselves and our relationship to, and role in, the community around us.

---

1   Wallace (2004, p. 55).

2. LOCAL FOOD MOVEMENTS AND ALTERNATIVE FOOD SYSTEMS

The so-called locavore movement emphasizes locally grown foods, often purchased from farmers' markets or through community-supported agriculture. As the name suggests, locavorism is often characterized as a geographic preference—adherents prefer to eat food that comes from nearby, some even adopting a 100-mile radius as the cutoff point—and critics argue that this preference is arbitrary and irrational, since "local" doesn't guarantee that a food is organic, or sustainable, or humanely produced. In light of these criticisms, locavorism might look like a kind of prejudice, but I'll argue that it is actually a kind of heuristic: a rule of thumb that, while not always a perfect guide, helps us track a set of values that would otherwise be complex and require prohibitive amounts of information or research to identify. The locavore is neither irrational nor ignorant; they're simply using the concept of local as an admittedly imperfect procedure for food choice.

One motivation for locavorism is environmental: if you eat food grown nearby, it doesn't have to travel far to get to you. This means your food requires fewer fossil fuels and creates less pollution. A second motive is that when people buy local foods, they are putting money back into the community. This is a good thing because it supports local business and workers, and stabilizes local communities. A related motivation is that farmers' markets and community supported agriculture (CSA) provide a social space in which communities come together, and allow people to get to know the people who produce their food.

Viewed in this light, it's clear that locavorism involves more than commitment to a place. The 100-mile radius rule might lead one to a diet that meets these ideals, or it might not, but understood as a heuristic, it's a kind of approximate guide to realizing the values of community and sustainability. Local food isn't always good for the environment: someone who buys meat produced at the factory farm down the road is consuming food with a heavy environmental footprint, perhaps more so than the person who buys an organic apple from New Zealand. The driving required to travel from farm to farm, or for the farmer to drive to different markets every day, is also an environmental consideration. Depending on where one lives, local food may also require more water than food from far away, or require the use of more fertilizer. These examples suggest that if one's goal is to keep the environmental costs of one's diet low, local food may sometimes be a step in the right direction, but is no guarantee.

Local food does also put money back into the community, but again, whether this is the goal we ought to pursue depends in part on who the local businesses are. Local is not synonymous with ethical: the farms that treat tomato- and strawberry-pickers to conditions that have been compared to slavery are local to someone. It is true that farmers' markets can become places for the community to gather, and that buying at these markets or through CSA allows people to get to know their local farmers and producers. And certainly, the money from these markets supports these farmers and producers. But this is not sufficient support; as the farmers' markets and the growing season come to an end, farmers must rely on other income or on savings. And small farmers who sell at these markets often have trouble competing with bigger grocery stores and getting their product to customers. They're more vulnerable to fluctuations in weather, pests, and other challenges that affect their harvests. This is not to say that people should not support local business by buying at markets and through CSA, but that this may not be sufficient to support local businesses.

On the other hand, some critics question why we should aim to support local business in the first place. Singer has written that "to adhere to a principle of 'buy locally,' irrespective of the consequences for others, is a kind of community-based selfishness,"[2] because those dollars could potentially make more of a difference if spent on products from a needier community. It's unclear whether anyone really thinks we should buy local regardless of the consequences for others, though. Furthermore, Singer is contrasting locavore purchases with purchases from farmers in developing nations, in particular, goods sold under the "fair-trade" designation. For most Americans and Europeans this is a false dichotomy. Fair-trade products tend to have tropical origins: chocolate, coffee, bananas. Few of us can buy these products locally. This is why all but the most stringent locavores embrace some imported products, while returning dollars to their community as well.

Another reason to buy from local businesses is that as people get to know local farmers and producers, they will become more aware of the processes by which food is produced, and the seasons in which foods are grown. This in turn will lead people to ask questions about industrial agriculture and processed foods: how is there asparagus in the grocery store in November, when asparagus is a spring crop? Because it comes to us all the way from Peru. This is the ideal put forth by authors like Michael Pollan, who argues for a return to return to "real" food, exhorting his readers to avoid unpronounceable ingredients and "anything your great-grandmother wouldn't recognize as food."[3] The suggestion that we return to eating locally grown, unprocessed foods is not necessarily wrong—doing so would indeed bring health and moral benefits. But it is not a route that's open to everyone: many people don't have access to farmers' markets and CSAs, either because of geography or finances. People may not have time to shop or cook for fresh food. Even Pollan's invocation of grandmothers is problematic. As one critic explains:

> He ignores the fact that "our" great-grandmothers come from a wide variety
> of social and economic contexts that may have informed their perceptions of
> food quite differently. Some were enslaved, transported across the ocean,

2   Singer & Mason (2006, p. 141).
3   Pollan (2008, p. 148).

and forced to subsist on the overflow from the master's table. Others were forcibly sent to state-mandated boarding schools, in which they were taught to despise, and even forget, any foods they would previously have recognized. And those who have emigrated from various parts of the global south in the past few generations may have great-grandmothers who saw the foods they recognized demeaned, or even forbidden, by those who claimed their lands.[4]

These critics acknowledge the important work that advocates of local food have done with their critique of industrial agriculture and the attention they've drawn to its costs. But, critics argue, the way the discourse has been conducted focuses largely on wealthier, white communities who have and can afford alternatives, while ignoring the issues that affect poorer and minority communities.

3. URBAN AGRICULTURE

For those who live in cities, local food might take the form of urban agriculture—farms located in parks or city lots, on rooftops or within city buildings themselves. There are a number of rooftop farms in New York City, some of which sell to restaurants and the community, others of which are located on top of stores and restaurants themselves. Rooftop farming is also becoming increasingly popular in Hong Kong, where corporations like Bank of America and Cathay Pacific have installed rooftop farms that give produce to company employees (who provide their labor) or donate it to food banks. Another urban food source is community gardens, which allocate plots to neighborhood residents, or where locals devote time each week in exchange for produce. Commercial urban farms promise the same sorts of environmental benefits as locavorism more generally, but perhaps even more so, since there are so many consumers in cities and they don't need to drive to markets or farms. However, it is unlikely that urban farms will be able to supply a significant portion of a city's food. Rooftop farms are limited by the size of rooftops themselves, which are rarely bigger than a few acres. In cities like Detroit, empty lots and factories have been converted to farming, but as neighborhoods become revitalized—often by the farms themselves—land becomes more expensive, and farms may be driven out. And some residents would prefer to see land developed into affordable housing or businesses that create jobs, instead of farms.

However, even if urban farms can't feed cities on their own, they have other potential benefits: they can bring fresh foods into neighborhoods where access is lacking, for example. By allocating plots to residents they can allow communities greater control over their food choices. Many have pointed to urban farming as exactly the sort

---

4   Alkon & Agyeman (2011, p. 3).

of practice the food sovereignty movement should aspire to. However, this only works if urban farms integrate themselves into communities and are truly community-run. Farms that sell exclusively to high-end restaurants, or which are located in neighborhoods that already have good access to fresh food, won't necessarily further goals of food access or social justice.

Another contribution urban farms can make is as vehicles for education: by placing agriculture into urban settings, students and community members can learn more about how to grow and prepare food. Many urban farms offer education programs to schoolchildren, and some offer apprenticeships and job training. This has two potential benefits: first, as mentioned above, it may raise awareness about agricultural and food-related issues; second, it may increase opportunities and teach students, not just how to grow and cook food, but also leadership and entrepreneurial skills, by helping them think about ways that urban farms and agriculture can solve community problems. Some critics object that involving students in urban farming businesses reinforces an individualistic and entrepreneurial approach to problems with the food system, implicitly affirming that communities themselves must take responsibility for their food supply, and entrenching the same values that have created our current food system, rather than demanding more sweeping changes.[5] However, the two goals are not mutually exclusive: urban farms can teach students to farm as well as to advocate for social change.

Rooftop and community farms aren't the only models for urban agriculture. So-called vertical farms, which use hydroponic or aeroponic technology to grow food without soil, are becoming increasingly popular in cities; these farms operate by growing plants in either water or air (in which case they're sprayed with mist), inside temperature- and light-controlled buildings. Unlike rooftop farming, vertical farming is, in theory, capable of producing enough food to feed a city, and pollution and soil contamination is not a concern, since these methods don't use soil at all. Vertical farms currently exist in cities around the world. Most grow salad greens, since these grow quickly and are highly profitable, but they could in principle grow any number of vegetables, as well as rice. Should insects ever become part of the mainstream diet, these, too, would be suitable for urban farming.

4. FOOD MOVEMENTS REVISITED: FOOD, IDENTITY, COMMUNITY

These food movements (including urban farming) are often criticized as unnecessarily restrictive—why set an arbitrary geographic restriction on what one eats? They're also critiqued for being unrealistic or as indulgences available only to upper-middle-

---

5   See, for example, Weissman (2015).

class consumers. But while these critiques are useful reminders of the limitations of these movements, they also fail to appreciate what the movements are really about: not a set of rules or principles to guide our eating, but a set of values through which we understand ourselves and our place in a set of aesthetic, epistemic, and political practices. To identify with the local food movement—or with the lab-grown meat movement, or with a Soylent-based lifestyle—is not to commit to eating only certain foods. It's to endorse a set of values that guide one through an otherwise overwhelming set of food choices. The local food system may, in this sense, be a misnomer; what we really want for ourselves is a holistic food system, one that comes not just with moral values but epistemic guidance and aesthetic pleasures. This doesn't have to mean a trip to the farmers' market; it might be the pleasure of knowing one's burger came from a shiny stainless-steel reactor staffed by scientists in lab coats. What matters is that one's food choices offer a way of navigating the world, and also a way of understanding one's place in it.

I mentioned early on in the book—when we discussed philosophers' distrust of pleasure—that the bodily functions involved in ingesting, digesting, and excreting food are somewhat anxiety-producing, potentially embarrassing, and often disgusting. One theory of disgust is that it is essentially tied to anxiety about the inevitable death and decay of our animal bodies; the many norms we invent to govern disgusting actions are a way of managing this anxiety.

In fact, disgust and food are similar this way: food reminds us that our bodies make demands on us that we can't ignore. At the very beginning of this book, I observed that food is arguably what creates human communities in the first place. It makes society (and, by extension, philosophy) possible. It should come as no surprise, then, that the act of deciding what to eat and the act of deciding how to navigate the social world are essentially the same. Our food choices tell us who we are, and they tell others who we are, too. They identify us with a culture and with a set of goals and values.

Pluralism has also been a recurring theme throughout this book, because of the many seemingly irreconcilable values at work in our food system. I don't just mean moral value. We also face the challenge of balancing competing goals like managing anxiety about risk, without exposing ourselves to danger; being adventurous and open to experiences, without being overwhelmed by choice or manipulated by misinformation; trusting others, but not being naïve; or helping others, without sacrificing meaning in one's own life. The ability to skillfully navigate competing demands and choices is part of what virtue consists in.

Virtue is a moral concept, but also a psychological one: it tells us about our social and familial obligations, the importance of ritual and habit, how to think about knowledge and intellectual skills, and how and when to find pleasure in our activities—in beauty, but also in everyday decisions and encounters.

One reason virtue as a concept sometimes seems unhelpful is precisely because it is so ambitious. It doesn't give us a set of rules or principles; it doesn't offer a procedure for ethical decisions. Rather, it tells us to think about what kind of people we want to be, and to shape our lives accordingly. I suggest that what we want from our diets is something similar. We want our diets to offer us a way of eating, in the most holistic sense: a system of knowledge, value, beauty, health, and justice. This is an awful lot to ask, so it's not surprising that none of our food movements is up to the task. But like food itself, food movements are an ongoing project, a social construction. As our beliefs change, so will the nature of food and food movements, but our beliefs must also be responsive to the nature of food and its production. Being aware of the ethical, political, personal, and social implications of our food choices is a crucial step in constructing a better food system, but being aware of our role in constructing it—and the role of our beliefs and values—is equally important. This is the optimistic note on which I want to end: if food is a social construction, we can continue to build on the system we're given.

REFERENCES

Adajian, T. (2005). On the prototype theory of concepts and the definition of art. *Journal of Aesthetics and Art Criticism, 63*(3), 231–36.

Adams, C. (1995). Caring about suffering: A feminist exploration. In J. Donovan & C. Adams (Eds.), *The Feminist Care Tradition in Animal Ethics: A Reader* (pp. 201–27). New York: Columbia University Press.

Alkon, A.H. (2014). Food justice and the challenge to neoliberalism. *Gastronomica: The Journal of Critical Food Studies, 14*(2), 27–40.

Alkon, A.H., & Agyeman, J. (2011). *Cultivating Food Justice: Race, Class, and Sustainability.* Cambridge, MA: MIT Press.

Anderson, E. (2005). Animal rights and the values of nonhuman life. In C.R. Sunstein & M.C. Nussbaum (Eds.), *Animal Rights: Current Debates and New Directions* (pp. 277–98). Oxford: Oxford University Press.

Aristotle. (1984a). Nicomachean ethics. In J. Barnes (Ed.), *The Complete Works of Aristotle: The Revised Oxford Translation* (Vol. 2, pp. 1729–1867). Princeton, NJ: Princeton University Press.

Aristotle. (1984b). Politics. In J. Barnes (Ed.), *The Complete Works of Aristotle: The Revised Oxford Translation* (Vol. 2, pp. 1986–2129). Princeton, NJ: Princeton University Press.

Austin, J.L. (1956). A plea for excuses. *Proceedings of the Aristotelian Society, 57*, 1–30.

Auvary, M., & Spence, C. (2008). The multidimensional perception of flavor. *Consciousness and Cognition, 17*(3), 1016–31.

Barry, B. (1978). Circumstances of justice and future generations. In R.I. Sikora & B.M. Barry (Eds.), *Obligations to Future Generations* (pp. 204–48). Winwick, England: White Horse Press.

Beamer, P. (2011). Pesticide exposure of farmworkers' children. In M. Stoytcheva (Ed.), *Pesticides in the Modern World—Effects of Pesticides Exposure* (pp. 79–100). Rijeka, Croatia: InTech Europe.

Beardsley, M.C. (2004). An aesthetic definition of art. In P. Lamarque and S.H. Olsen (Eds.), *Aesthetics and the Philosophy of Art: The Analytic Tradition* (pp. 55–62). Malden, MA: Blackwell.

Benatar, D. (2006). *Better Never to Have Been: The Harm of Coming into Existence.* Oxford: Oxford University Press.

Bentham, J. (1970). *An Introduction to the Principles of Moral and Legislation.* J.H. Burns & H.L.A. Hart (Eds.). Oxford: Oxford University Press. (Originally published 1780).

Berlin, I. (1969). Two concepts of liberty. In I. Berlin, *Four Essays on Liberty* (pp. 118–72). Oxford: Oxford University Press.

Bernstein, L. (2005). *Leonard Bernstein's Young People's Concerts.* Jack Gottleib, ed. New York: Amadeus Press. First published 1962.

Better dead than GM fed? GM crops in Africa. (2002, September 19). *The Economist.*

Bloom, J. (2011). *American Wasteland: How America Throws Away Nearly Half Its Food (and What We Can Do about It).* Cambridge, MA: Da Capo Lifelong Books.

Borlaug, N. (2001). Are we going mad? In G. Pence (Ed.), *The Ethics of Food: A Reader for the Twenty-First Century* (pp. 74–79). Lanham, MD: Rowman & Littlefield.

Brones, Anna. (2018, May 7). Karen Washington: It's not a food desert, it's food apartheid [Interview]. *Guernica.* Retrieved from https://www.guernicamag.com/karen-washington-its-not-a-food-desert-its-food-apartheid/.

Brownell, K.D., Wang, S.S., & Wadden, T.A. (2004). The influence of the stigma of obesity on overweight individuals. *International Journal of Obesity, 28,* 1333–37.

Carson, R. (2002). *Silent Spring (40th Anniversary Edition).* New York: Houghton Mifflin. (Originally published 1962).

Chen, M., Chang, C.H., Tao, L., & Lu, C. (2015). Residential exposure to pesticide during childhood and childhood cancers: A meta-analysis. *Pediatrics, 136*(4): 719–29.

Cohen, C. (1986). The case for the use of animals in biomedical research. *The New England Journal of Medicine, 315,* 865–70.

Collingwood, R.G. (1958). *The Principles of Art.* Oxford: Oxford University Press.

Conly, S. (2013). *Against Autonomy: Justifying Coercive Paternalism.* Cambridge: Cambridge University Press.

Danto, A. (1964). The artworld. *Journal of Philosophy, 61*(19), 571–84.

Dean, J. (2003). The nature of concepts and the definition of art. *The Journal of Aesthetics and Art Criticism, 61*(1), 29–35.

Diamond, C. (1978). Eating meat and eating people. *Philosophy, 53*(206), 465–79.

Dickie, G. (1974). *Art and the Aesthetic: An Institutional Analysis.* Ithaca: Cornell University Press.

Diener, E., & Diener, R.B. (2002). Will money increase subjective well-being? *Social Indicators Research, 57*(2), 119–69.

Dining on Roadkill. (2017, July 27). *The News Tribune.*

Dufresne, W., & Meehan, P. (2017). *WD~50: The Cookbook.* New York: HarperCollins.

Dworkin, G. (1972). Paternalism. *The Monist, 56*(1), 64–84.

Ehrlich, P.R. (1968). *The Population Bomb.* New York: Ballantine Books.

Engel, L.S. et al. (2005). Pesticide exposure and breast cancer risk among farmers' wives in the agricultural health study. *American Journal of Epidemiology, 161*(2), 121–35.

Engel, M. (2000). The immorality of eating meat. In L.P. Pojman (Ed.), *The Moral Life: An Introductory Reader in Ethics and Literature* (pp. 856–90). New York, Oxford: Oxford University Press.

Eschliman, D., & Ettlinger, S. (2015). *Ingredients: A Visual Exploration of 75 Additives & 25 Food Products.* New York: Regan Arts.

Escoffier, A. (1907). *A Guide to Modern Cookery.* London: William Heinemann.

Estabrook, B. (2011). *Tomatoland: From Harvest of Shame to Harvest of Hope.* Kansas City, MO: Andrews McMeel Publishing.

European Parliament, Council of the European Union. (2002, January 28). Regulation (EC) No 178/2002 of the European Parliament and of the Council of 28 January 2002 laying down the general principles and requirements of food law, establishing the European Food Safety Authority and laying down procedures in matters of food safety. OJ L 31, 1.2.2002. Retrieved from https://eur-lex.europa.eu/eli/reg/2002/178/oj.

Federal Food, Drug, and Cosmetic Act, 21 U.S.C. § 322f. (2018).

Food and Agriculture Organization of the United Nations, International Fund for Agricultural Development, UNICEF, World Food Programme and World Health Organization. (2017). *The State of Food Security and Nutrition in the World 2017: Building Resilience for Peace and Food Security.* Rome: Food and Agriculture Organization of the United Nations. Retrieved from: http://www.fao.org/3/a-I7695e.pdf.

Food. (n.d.). In *English Oxford Living Dictionaries.* Retrieved from https://en.oxforddictionaries.com/definition/food.

Frankfurt, H.G. (2005). *On Bullshit.* Princeton, NJ: Princeton University Press.

Fricker, M. (2007). *Epistemic Injustice: Power and the Ethics of Knowing.* Oxford: Oxford University Press.

Furnham, A., & Boo, H.C. (2011). A literature review of the anchoring effect. *The Journal of Socio-Economics, 40*(1), 35–42.

Gates, B. (2013, November 12). Here's my plan to improve our world: And how you can help. *Wired.* Retrieved from https://www.wired.com/2013/11/bill-gates-wired-essay/.

Gauthier, D. (1987). *Morals by Agreement*. Oxford: Oxford University Press.

George, S. (1977). *How the Other Half Dies: The Real Reasons for World Hunger*. Montclair, NJ: Allanheld, Osmun & Co.

Gettier, E. (1963). Is justified true belief knowledge? *Analysis, 23*(6), 121–23.

Godfrey-Smith, P. (2016). *Other Minds: The Octopus, The Sea, and Deep Origins of Consciousness*. New York: Farrar, Straus & Giroux.

Godoy, M., & Chow, K. (Hosts). (2016, March 22). When chefs become famous cooking other cultures' food. *The Salt: What's on Your Plate*. NPR. https://www.npr.org/sections/thesalt/2016/03/22/471309991/when-chefs-become-famous-cooking-other-cultures-food.

Goodman, N. (1968). *Languages of Art*. Indianapolis: Bobbs-Merrill.

Gottlieb, R., & Joshi, A. (2010). *Food Justice*. Cambridge, MA: MIT Press.

Gross, T. (Host). (2015, October 8). Sculptor Andy Goldsworthy turns rain, ice and trees into "ephemeral works." *Fresh Air* [Podcast]. NPR. Retrieved from https://www.npr.org/2015/10/08/446983201/sculptor-andy-goldsworthy-turns-rain-ice-and-trees-into-ephemeral-works.

Guthman, J. (2011). *Weighing In: Obesity, Food Justice, and the Limits of Capitalism*. Berkeley, CA: University of California Press.

Hakim, D. (2017, November 10). Are Honey Nut Cheerios healthy? *The New York Times*.

Hardin, G. (1974). Living on a lifeboat. *BioScience, 24*(10), 561–68.

Harris, L., & Tan, H.J. (2004). Selling meat and meat products. University of California Division of Agriculture and Natural Resources Publication 8146. Oakland, CA: University of California, Agriculture and Natural Resources. Retrieved from http://ucfoodsafety.ucdavis.edu/files/26481.pdf.

Heldke, L. (2001). "Let's eat Chinese!": Reflections on cultural food colonialism. *Gastronomica: The Journal of Critical Food Studies, 1*(2), 76–79.

Herzog, H. (2010). *Some We Love, Some We Hate, Some We Eat: Why It's So Hard to Think Straight about Animals*. New York: HarperCollins.

Hume, D. (1987). Of the standard of taste. In E. Miller (Ed.), Essays: Moral, Political, and Literary (pp. 226–49). Indianapolis: Liberty Classics. (Originally published 1777).

Hume, D. (1978). *A Treatise of Human Nature* (with L.A. Selby-Bigge and P.H. Nidditch) (2nd ed., revised). Oxford: Oxford University Press. (Originally published 1740).

Jackson, F. (1982). Epiphenomenal qualia. *The Philosophical Quarterly, 32*(127), 127–36.

Johnston, M. (1992). How to speak of the colors. *Philosophical Studies, 68*(3), 221–63.

Kahneman, D., & Deaton, A. (2010). High income improves evaluation of life but not emotional well-being. *Proceedings of the National Academy of Sciences*, *107*(38), 16489–93.

Kahneman, D. (2011). *Thinking: Fast and Slow*. New York: Farrar, Straus, and Giroux.

Kant, I. (1974). *Anthropology from a Pragmatic Point of View* (M.J. Gregor, Trans.). The Hague, The Netherlands: Martinus Nijhoff. (Originally published 1798).

Kant, I. (1993). *Grounding for the Metaphysics of Morals* (J.W. Ellington, Trans.) (3rd ed.). Indianapolis, IN & Cambridge, MA: Hackett. (Originally published 1785).

Kant, I. (2000). *Critique of the Power of Judgment* (E. Matthews, Trans., P. Guyer, Ed.). Cambridge: Cambridge University Press. (Originally published 1790).

Keneally, T. (2011). *Three Famines: Starvation and Politics*. New York: PublicAffairs.

Kent, G. (2005). *Freedom from Want: The Human Right to Adequate Food*. Washington, DC: Georgetown University Press.

Kittay, E.F. (2005). At the margins of moral personhood. *Ethics: An International Journal of Social, Political, and Legal Philosophy*, *116*(1), 100–31.

Kivy, P. (1983). Platonism in music: A kind of defense. *Grazer Philosophische Studien*, *19*(1), 109–29.

Korsmeyer, C. (2002). *Making Sense of Taste: Food and Philosophy*. Ithaca, NY: Cornell University Press.

Kripke, S. (1972). *Naming and Necessity*. Cambridge, MA: Harvard University Press.

La Via Campesina. (n.d.). The international peasant's voice. *La Via Campesina International Peasant's Movement*. Retrieved from https://viacampesina.org/en/international-peasants-voice/.

Lebesco, K. (2010). Fat panic and the new morality. In J. Metzl & A. Kirkland (Eds.), *Against Health: How Health Became the New Morality* (pp. 72–82). New York: NYU Press.

Leonard, C. (2014). *The Meat Racket: The Secret Takeover of America's Food Business*. New York: Simon & Schuster.

Leopold, A. (1949). *A Sand County Almanac and Sketches Here and There*. New York: Oxford University Press.

Levenstein, H. (2012). *Fear of Food: A History of Why We Worry about What We Eat*. Chicago, IL: The University of Chicago Press.

Levinson, J. (1980). What a musical work is. *Journal of Philosophy*, *77*(1), 5–28.

Locke, J. (1975). *An Essay Concerning Human Understanding* (P.H. Nidditch, Ed.). Oxford: Oxford University Press. (Originally published 1689).

Loewenstein, G., O'Donoghue, T., & Rabin, M. (2003). Projection bias in predicting future utility. *The Quarterly Journal of Economics*, *118*(4), 1209–48.

Logue, A. (2015). *The Psychology of Eating and Drinking*. New York: Routledge.

Loo, C. (2014). Towards a more participative definition of food justice. *Journal of Agricultural and Environmental Ethics, 27*(5), 787–809.

Marinetti, F.T. (1989). *The Futurist Cookbook* (S. Brill, Trans.). New York: Penguin. (Originally published 1932).

Masterpiece Cake Shop, Ltd. v. Colorado Civil Rights Commission, 584 US (2018). Retrieved from https://www.law.cornell.edu/supremecourt/text/16-111.

Matthes, E. (2016). Cultural Appropriation without Cultural Essentialism? *Social Theory and Practice, 42*(2), 343–66.

Meigs, A. (1984). *Food, Sex, and Pollution: A New Guinea Religion*. New Brunswick, NJ: Rutgers University Press.

Meskin, A.R., & Robson, J. (2015). Taste and acquaintance. *Journal of Aesthetics and Art Criticism, 73*(2), 127–39.

Midgley, M. (2000). Biotechnology and monstrosity: Why we should pay attention to the "yuk factor." *Hastings Center Report, 30*(5), 7–15.

Mill, J.S. (2003). *On Liberty* (D. Bromwich & G. Kateb, Eds.). New Haven and London: Yale University Press. (Originally published 1859).

Mill, J.S. (2009). *Utilitarianism*. Portland, OR: The Floating Press. (Originally published in 1879).

Mintz, S., & DuBois, C. (2002). The anthropology of food and eating. *Annual Review of Anthropology, 31*, 99–117.

Naylor, R., et al. (2000). Effect of aquaculture on world fish populations. *Nature, 405*, 1017–24.

Neufeldt, V., & Guralnik, D. (Eds.) (1997). *Webster's New World College Dictionary*. (Third edition). New York: MacMillan.

Norcross, A. (2004). Puppies, pigs, and people: Eating meat and marginal cases. *Philosophical Perspectives, 18*(1), 229–45.

Norris, M. (Host). (2005, August 1). The shelf life of a vintage Twinkie. *All Things Considered* [Radio Episode]. NPR. Retrieved from https://www.npr.org/templates/story/story.php?storyId=4780900?storyId=4780900.

Parfit, D. (1986). *Reasons and Persons*. Oxford: Oxford University Press.

Patel, R. (2012). *Stuffed and Starved: The Hidden Battle for the World Food System*. Brooklyn, NY: Melville House.

Pence, G. (Ed.). (2001). *The Ethics of Food: A Reader for the Twenty-First Century*. Lanham, MD: Rowman & Littlefield.

Peterson, M., & Sandin, P. (2013). The last man argument revisited. *Journal of Value Inquiry, 47*(1–2), 121–33.

Phelan, S.M., et al. (2015). Impact of weight bias and stigma on quality of care and outcomes for patients with obesity. *Obesity Reviews, 16*(4), 319–26.

Plato. (1997a). Gorgias (D.J. Zeyl, Trans.). In J.M. Cooper & D.S. Hutchinson (Eds.) *Plato: Complete Works* (pp. 791–869). Indianapolis, IN: Hackett.

Plato. (1997b). Phaedo (G.M.A. Grube, Trans.). In J.M. Cooper & D.S. Hutchinson (Eds.) *Plato: Complete Works* (pp. 49–100). Indianapolis, IN: Hackett.

Plato. (1997c). Protagoras (S. Lombardo and K. Bell, Trans.). In J.M. Cooper & D.S. Hutchinson (Eds.) *Plato: Complete Works* (pp. 746–90). Indianapolis, IN: Hackett.

Plumwood, V. (1986). Ecofeminism: An overview and discussion of positions and arguments. *Australasian Journal of Philosophy, 64*(S1), 120–38.

Pollan, M. (2006). *The Omnivore's Dilemma: A Natural History of Four Meals.* New York: Penguin Press.

Puhl R., & Brownell, K.D. (2001). Bias, discrimination, and obesity. *Obesity Research, 9*(12), 788–805.

Putnam, H. (1975). The meaning of "meaning." *Minnesota Studies in the Philosophy of Science, 7*, 131–93.

Rawls, J. (1971). *A Theory of Justice.* Boston, MA: Harvard University Press.

Ray, K. (2016). *The Ethnic Restaurateur.* London: Bloomsbury Academic.

Regan, T. (1985). The case for animal rights. In Peter Singer (Ed.), *In Defence of Animals* (pp. 13–26). Oxford: Blackwell.

Rieff, D. (2015). *The Reproach of Hunger.* New York: Simon & Schuster.

Roberts, P. (2008). *The End of Food.* Boston, MA: Houghton Mifflin Harcourt.

Rose, J.D., et. al. (2012). Can fish really feel pain? *Fish and Fisheries, 15*, 97–133.

Rousseau, S. (2012). *Food and Social Media: You Are What You Tweet.* Lanham, MD: AltaMira Press.

Routley, R. (1973). Is there a need for a new, an environmental, ethic? *Proceedings of the XVth World Congress of Philosophy, 1*, 205–10.

Rowlands, M. (1997). Contractarianism and animal rights. *Journal of Applied Philosophy, 14*(3), 235–47.

Ruhlman, M. (2009). *The Making of a Chef: Mastering Heat at the Culinary Institute of America.* New York: St. Martin's Press.

Running, C.A., Craig, B.A., & Mattes, R.D. (2015). Oleogustus: The unique taste of fat. *Chemical Senses, 40*(7), 507–16.

Rutgers, B., & Heeger, R. (1999). Inherent worth and respect for animal integrity. In Dol, M., et al. (Eds.), *Recognizing the Intrinsic Value of Animals: Beyond Animal Welfare* (pp. 41–51). Assen, The Netherlands: Van Gorcum & Comp.

Ryder, R. (2009). Painism versus utilitarianism. *Think, 8*(21), 85–89.

Ryle, G. (1949). *The Concept of Mind.* London: Penguin Books.

Samuelson, W., & Zeckhauser, R.J. (1988). Status quo bias in decision making. *Journal of Risk and Uncertainty, 1*, 7–59.

Schatzker, M. (2016). *The Dorito Effect: The Surprising New Truth about Food and Flavor.* New York: Simon and Schuster.

Scheffler, S. (2016). *Death and the Afterlife.* New York: Oxford University Press.

Schlosser, E. (2001). *Fast Food Nation: The Dark Side of the All-American Meal.* New York: Houghton Mifflin.

Science and Environmental Health Network. (1998). The Wingspread Consensus Statement on the Precautionary Principle. *Visionary Science, Ethics, Law and Action in the Public Interest.* Retrieved from http://sehn.org/wingspread-conference-on-the-precautionary-principle/.

Searle, J. (1997). *The Construction of Social Reality.* New York: The Free Press.

Secretariat of the Convention on Biological Diversity (2000). Cartagena protocol on biosafety to the convention on biological diversity: text and annexes. Montreal: Secretariat of the Convention on Biological Diversity.

Sen, A. (1981). *Poverty and Famines: An Essay on Entitlement and Deprivation.* Oxford: Clarendon Press.

Sherman, J.D. (1924, June 14). Muscle shoals. *Cambridge Sentinel, XX*(20).

Shriver, A. (2009). Knocking out pain in livestock: Can technology succeed where morality has stalled? *Neuroethics, 2*(3), 115–24.

Shue, H. (1980). *Basic Rights: Subsistence, Affluence, and U.S. Foreign Policy.* Princeton, NJ: Princeton University Press.

Sikora, R.I., & Barry, B.M. (Eds.) (1978). *Obligations to Future Generations.* Winwick, England: White Horse Press.

Simon, M. (2014, June 11). Whitewashed: How industry and government promote dairy junk foods. *Eat Drink Politics: Countering Industry Harm to Improve Public Health* (pp. 1–32). Retrieved from: http://www.eatdrinkpolitics. com/2014/06/11/whitewashed-how-industry-and-government-promote-dairy-junk-foods/.

Singer, P. (1972). Famine, affluence, and morality. *Philosophy and Public Affairs, 1*(3), 229–43.

Singer, P. (1989). All animals are equal. In T. Regan & P. Singer (Eds.), *Animal Rights and Human Obligations* (pp. 215–26). Oxford: Oxford University Press.

Singer, P., & Mason, J. (2006). *The Ethics of What We Eat: Why Our Food Choices Matter.* New York: Rodale.

Small, D.A., Loewenstein, G., & Slovic, P. (2007). Sympathy and callousness: The impact of deliberative thought on donations to identifiable and statistical victims. *Organizational Behavior and Human Decision Processes, 102*(2), 143–53.

Sneddon, L. (2003). The evidence for pain in fish: The use of morphine as an analgesic. *Applied Animal Behaviour Science, 83*(2), 153–62.

Stanley, J., & Williamson, T. (2001). Knowing how. *The Journal of Philosophy, 98*(8), 411–44.

Stevenson, M. (1992). The impact of temporal context and risk on the judged value of future outcomes. *Organizational Behavior & Human Decision Processes, 52*(3), 455–91.

Suranovic, S., Goldfarb, R., & Leonard, T. (1999). An economic theory of cigarette addiction. *Journal of Health Economics, 18*(1), 1–29.

Taylor, P.W. (1981). The ethics of respect for nature. *Environmental Ethics, 3*(3), 197–218.

Telfer, E. (1996). *Food for Thought: Philosophy and Food.* Oxford: Routledge.

Thaler, R. (1981). Some empirical evidence on dynamic inconsistency. *Economic Letters, 8*, 201–07.

Thaler, R., & Sunstein, C. (2003). Libertarian paternalism. *The American Economic Review, 93*(2), 175–79.

Thaler, R., & Sunstein, C. (2008). *Nudge: Improving Decisions about Health, Wealth, and Happiness.* New York: Penguin Books.

Thompson, P.B. (1994). *The Spirit of the Soil: Agriculture and Environmental Ethics.* Oxford: Routledge.

Thompson, P.B. (1997). Ethics and the genetic engineering of food animals. *Journal of Agricultural and Environmental Ethics, 10*(1), 1–23.

Thompson, P.B. (2012). Nature politics and the philosophy of agriculture. In D.M. Kaplan (Ed.), *The Philosophy of Food* (pp. 214–33). Berkeley, CA: University of California Press.

Thompson, P.B. (2015). *From Field to Fork: Food Ethics for Everyone.* Oxford: Oxford University Press.

Tolstoy, L. (1996). What is art? (A. Maude, Trans.). https://books.google.ca/ books?id=PNVaWI-Cev8C&lpg=PA51&ots=w6EEbIdZyH&dq=a%20 human%20activity%20consisting%20in%20this%2C%20that%20one%20 man%20consciously%2C%20by%20means%20of%20certain%20external%20 signs%2C%20hands%20on%20to%20others%20feelings%20he%20has%20 lived%20through%2C%20and%20that%20other%20people%20are%20inf- ected%20by%20these%20feelings%20and%20also%20experience%20them.&p g=PA51#v=onepage&q&f=false.

Treuhaft, S., & Karpyn, A. (2010). *The Grocery Gap: Who Has Access to Healthy Food and Why It Matters.* Oakland, CA: Policy Link; Philadelphia, PA: The Food Trust. Retrieved from http://thefoodtrust.org/uploads/media_items/ grocerygap.original.pdf.

Tversky, A., & Kahneman, D. (1974). Judgment under Uncertainty: Heuristics and Biases. *Science, 185*, 1124–31.

Tversky, A., & Kahneman, D. (1981). The framing of decisions and the psychology of choice. *Science, 211*, 453–58.

Tyson. (2018). How are the farmers for broiler chickens paid? Contract poultry farming. Retrieved from https://www.tysonfoods.com/who-we-are/our- partners/farmers/contract-poultry-farming.

Unger, P. (1996). *Living High and Letting Die: Our Illusion of Innocence.* Oxford: Oxford University Press.

United Nations. (1948). *Universal Declaration of Human Rights*. Geneva, Switzerland. Retrieved from: http://www.un.org/en/universal-declaration-human-rights/index.html.

United Nations Conference on Environment and Development. (1992). *Agenda 21, Rio Declaration, Forest Principles*. New York: United Nations. Retrieved from http://www.unesco.org/education/pdf/RIO_E.PDF.

United States Copyright Office. (2012). Recipes (FL-122). *Copyright.gov*. Retrieved from https://www.copyright.gov/fls/fl122.html.

United States Department of Agriculture. (2014, September). *2012 Census of Agriculture Highlights: Farms and Farmland, Numbers, Acreage, Ownership, and Use*. ACH12–13. Washington, DC. Retrieved from https://www.agcensus.usda.gov/Publications/2012/Online_Resources/Highlights/Farms_and_Farmland/Highlights_Farms_and_Farmland.pdf.

United States Department of Agriculture. (2016a). Livestock slaughter summary report. Washington, DC.

United States Department of Agriculture. (2016b). Poultry slaughter annual summary. National Agricultural Statistics Service. Washington, DC.

United States Department of Agriculture, Economic Research Service. (2018, July 19). Irrigation and water use. Retrieved from https://www.ers.usda.gov/topics/farm-practices-management/irrigation-water-use/.

van Huis, A., et al. (2013). *Edible Insects: Future Prospects for Food and Feed Security*. FAO Forestry Paper 171. Rome: Food and Agriculture Organization of the United Nations. Retrieved from http://www.fao.org/docrep/018/i3253e/i3253e.pdf.

Vartanian, L.R., & Smyth, J.M. (2013). Primum non nocere: Obesity stigma and public health. *Journal of Bioethical Inquiry, 10*, 49–57.

von Frisch, K. (1973). Decoding the language of the bee [Nobel Prize Lecture, delivered December 12, 1973]. Retrieved from https://assets.nobelprize.org/uploads/2018/06/frisch-lecture.pdf.

Vorstenbosch, J.M.G. (1993). The concept of integrity. Its significance for the ethical discussion on biotechnology and animals. *Livestock Production Science, 36*(1), 109–12.

Wall, R.J., et al. (2005). Genetically modified cows resist intramammary Staphylococcus aureus infection. *Nature Biotechnology, 23*(4), 445–51.

Wallace, D. (2004, August). Consider the lobster. *Gourmet*, 50–64.

Weissman, E. (2015). Entrepreneurial endeavors: (Re)producing neoliberalization through urban agriculture youth programming in Brooklyn, New York. *Environmental Education Research, 21*(3), 351–64.

Wells, P. (2006). The new era of the recipe burglar. *Food and Wine, Nov 1*. Retrieved from https://www.foodandwine.com/articles/new-era-of-the-recipe-burglar.

Wing, S., Cole, D., & Grant, G. (2000). Environmental injustice in North Carolina's hog industry. *Environmental Health Perspectives, 108*(3), 225–31.

Wittgenstein, L. (2001). *Philosophical Investigations.* Oxford: Basil Blackwell. (Originally published in 1953).

World Health Organization. (2018). Fact sheet: Obesity and overweight. Retrieved from http://www.who.int/news-room/fact-sheets/detail/obesity-and-overweight.

Wrangham, R. (2009). *Catching Fire: How Cooking Made Us Human.* New York: Basic Books.

Young, I.M. (1990). *Justice and the Politics of Difference.* Princeton, NJ: Princeton University Press.

Young, J.O. (2005). Profound offense and cultural appropriation. *Journal of Aesthetics and Art Criticism, 63*(2), 135–46.

Young, J.O. (2010). *Cultural Appropriation and the Arts.* Chichester, England: John Wiley & Sons.

Zagzebski, L. (1996). *Virtues of the Mind: An Inquiry into the Nature of Virtue and the Ethical Foundations of Knowledge.* Cambridge: Cambridge University Press.

Zimmerman, M. (1995). The threat of ecofascism. *Social Theory and Practice, 21*(2), 207–38.

INDEX